the
new
office

the new office

FRANCIS DUFFY

With contributions from
Kenneth Powell

conran
OCTOPUS

First published in 1997 by
Conran Octopus Limited
37 Shelton Street
London WC2H 9HN

Half title page **Breaking through into the limitless world of the new office. ORMS's conversion for Greenalls Brewery, Warrington (see page 76).**

Title page **The atrium of Norman Foster's mould-breaking building for the Hong Kong and Shanghai Bank, Hong Kong (see page 72).**

Below **Looking down into the reception of Mario Bellini's office, converted for his own practice from a factory in Milan (see page 100).**

Commissioning Editor: Denny Hemming
Senior Art Editor: Tony Seddon
Picture Researchers: Rachel Davies and Ally Ireson
Production Controller: Mano Mylvaganam

Opposite from top **The office reinvented as a club (see page 45). Intense teamwork made possible by intelligent use of the right space (see page 64). An operable roof demonstrating a new concern for the environment (see page 69).**

British Library Cataloguing-in-Publication Data
A catalogue record for this book is available from the British Library

ISBN 1 85029 891 2

Printed in China

Contents

the potential of office

design

The difference between the old office and the new: the skyline of Dallas, real estate that isn't that real any more, contrasted with the mobile and highly personal reality of virtual work being carried out at a café table.

James Joyce had a word for moments of insight when we see right through convention and suddenly appreciate how things really are. He called such moments 'epiphanies'. Such a flash of insight happened to me three or four years ago in Texas. I had been explaining to the senior partners of a very large international client how they could use their office space far more effectively. Since these partners were rightly concerned with driving down occupancy costs, including rent, property taxes, service charges, and energy costs, throughout all their operations everywhere, my proposals were very acceptable. Immediately after this minor consultancy triumph – how nice to be able to make a universally popular, cost-saving proposal — I glanced out of the window of the presentation room and saw before me the whole of downtown Dallas, glistening under the pale, dusty blue November sky. Four unpalatable truths came to mind. First, half the shiny office buildings I was looking at were less than ten years old; second, half were half-empty because of enthusiastic over-building in that highly volatile city in the late 1980s; third, I had just been explaining how, quite practically, my clients could reduce the amount of office space that they would normally have expected to use by one-third or even half; and finally, I was almost certain that about half of the partners I had been speaking to had some portion of their pensions invested in funds that owned such buildings as the ones I was staring at.

Right *Even the greyest office buildings of the 1960s can be brought up-to-date to satisfy the emerging demands of new kinds of government work. The new glazed portico and entrance to the conference centre at the Department of Trade and Industry offices, London. Architect: DEGW.*

Suddenly real estate didn't seem so real any more. I realized just how rapidly ways of working in the office were changing, and how radically these changes would affect the conventions upon which office design and real estate practice have been based for decades. But I saw that what was more important was that everyone will be affected by the changes because they are irreversible. The future of the economies of all advanced countries, as well as of the shape and the quality of life in our cities, depends upon architects and people in business not only anticipating, but taking full advantage of, all the changes that are taking place.

These changing ways of working are being generated by an unprecedented combination of global economic pressure and extraordinary advances in information technology. While intense, international competition is forcing businesses to examine and rethink their organizational structures, modern technology is making it possible to use time, as well as space, in the office in new and creative ways. No longer is it necessary for an individual to occupy a particular place from nine to five, five days a week. Equipped with the mobile telephone,

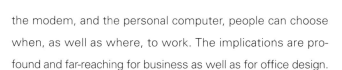

business life in a variety of ways because the pathology of poor office design is so extensive: space that costs too much to run; leases that cannot be escaped from in times of recession; square footage that suddenly becomes too abundant or too scarce; cranky building forms that make face-to-face internal communication difficult; parcels of space that are fragmented and exacerbate internal divisions; design features that insidiously overvalue status; inadequate physical apparatus such as clogged ducting that can cripple an electronic network; and environments that poison and pollute. Above all, and often perilously underestimated, is the

Below **A break area in the building for British Telecom, Stockley Park, London, where informal meeting spaces are critically important to office staff who are free to choose when as well as where they wish to work. Architect: DEGW**

the modem, and the personal computer, people can choose when, as well as where, to work. The implications are profound and far-reaching for business as well as for office design.

Just as a business must flex and change to survive, so the most vital function of an office building is to facilitate and accommodate change. The wrong one in the wrong place, fitted out in the wrong way, can quickly snuff out organizational initiative. Many people do not realize the crucial effect that buildings can have on business. Bad architecture can sap

Above **This converted warehouse has three key ingredients of the new office: few physical constraints, robust cabling, and unremitting teamwork. Wired's offices, San Francisco, USA.**

Right **An heroic factory of the 1930s Modern Movement has been brought back to life as an office. Boots the Chemist, Nottingham, UK. Architect: In-house Amec team.**

importance of the messages that are broadcast by architectural imagery about the values of the organizations and of the people who work in them.

Designed well, however, office buildings can play a pivotal role in business success. The right fit-out, for example, might call for greater initial capital investment, but is easily justified when spectacular reductions are made in revenue wasted on space per year. But more than this, good buildings can become the means by which the achievement of commercial objectives is accelerated. Properly used and professionally managed, they can be instrumental in driving forward change. And in an increasingly fluid business environment, the relationship between success and the design and use of office space is critical. This is why systematic measures of a building's performance – such as the telltale comparison between the cost of accommodating a person per year and the income generated by that person over that period of time — are becoming so important. Such indices inform top management of how well office space is serving business; and

push architecture, space planning, and interior design from being nothing but a nuisance, or simply decoration, into the cut-and-thrust world of strategic management.

This book could not have been written five years ago. It would have been hard to find enough convincing examples of innovative, new offices. It would not have been possible, as it is today, to show how closely office design relates to business success. Nor could the changing relationship between design and organizational structure have been described so clearly. Now we can see the potential that office design has as an instrument of change management. The opportunities must not be lost. Managing change must involve simultaneously rethinking the use of human resources, reinventing the ways in which information technology should be used, and redesigning the working environment. And it must be recognized that the ways in which office buildings are procured and managed are as important in determining the quality of the working environment as the physical structures and their interiors.

The heart of the book is a series of international case studies that describe some of the most innovative solutions to introducing new ways of working. Each one demonstrates

the book to explain, as systematically as possible, where offices have come from, why they look like they do today, how office organizations are changing, the technological and business reasons for these changes, and above all, the consequences that the changes are likely to have for office design at every scale from furniture to the landscapes of whole cities. This is very much a personal vision, and the opinions expressed throughout the book are, of course, my own.

The book ends with advice for clients and architects on how best to conduct the briefing process so that office buildings can be used in more practical ways to enhance organizational performance. There is also advice for readers, especially users of office buildings and those whose job it is to procure, construct, or manage office space, on how to find further sources of information. Ways of measuring how well office space can be made to perform in relation to business criteria are also described – without such ongoing feedback, the new office will make as little sense as the old.

This is not a book just for architects. Nor is it written only for business people. Its overriding aim is to question conventional solutions and help both designers and clients to work together to create their own versions of the new office.

organizational initiative and design invention. Some of the cases describe huge, new, custom-built office buildings. Others are modest fit-outs in off-the-peg speculative office spaces. Most are somewhere in between. However, what they all have in common is an ambitious client and a responsive designer who worked together in an open-ended way to achieve business success through design.

The case studies, however, only really make sense within the context of the attempt that has been made throughout

two
traditions

The difference between the North American and the northern European traditions of office building is typified by these two interiors. In that for S.C. Johnson, in Racine, Wisconsin, which looks remarkably the same today as when it was designed in the 1930s, architecture is used to express the importance of corporate discipline. By contrast, the headquarters of SAS, in Stockholm, was designed in the 1980s to enhance interaction among staff through being built round the idea of a street, and to promote individual self respect through giving all employees enclosed, equally well-furnished offices.

The office building is one of the great icons of the twentieth century. Office towers dominate the skylines of cities in every continent. The most visible index of economic activity, of social, technological, and financial progress, they have come to symbolize much of what this century has been about. What is extraordinary is not so much that the office has been such a success over the last one hundred years but that this success is so rarely acknowledged, and that the received image of the office is grey, not golden. Office work and office culture rarely feature in literature, in art, or in the theatre and, when they do, the picture tends to be grim. For Kafka the office was a nightmare – the physical manifestation of life-destroying bureaucracy. For the American painter Edward Hopper, the landscape of the office-bound city was the setting for a bitter commentary on the emptiness and melancholy of modern life. In the novels of Sinclair Lewis, Arnold Bennett, and H.G. Wells – not to mention the more colourful comic-book pages of Batman and Robin – office work provides the drab, diurnal backdrop against which a parallel, alternative world of fantasy and imagination is all the more entrancing. Film, that quintessentially twentieth-century medium, often presents the office in a more glamorous light but even in the movies offices are not usually the favourite environment of heroes.

And even though so many people in present-day North America, northern Europe, and Japan work in offices – at least 50 per cent of the working population, as opposed to a mere 5 per cent at the beginning of the century – fundamental anti-office attitudes seem to persist. It is easy to believe that the negative views expressed by certain artists and writers are shared by many office workers.

One particularly deep-seated reason may be that the values embedded in office architecture rank as one of the least attractive features of our times. Until the last decade of the nineteenth century 'real' work was done on the farm, in the mine, on the high seas; the dreary office, with its complement of compliant clerks, was peripheral – certainly not worth giving

Opposite **In Nine to Five, the 1980 story of three women office workers' revenge against the tyranny of their boss, Hollywood's idea of the office was surprisingly accurate: humdrum, hierarchical, and a long way from home.**

serious thought to or spending serious money on. The office, in its present form, exists directly as a consequence of the managerial changes that occurred in the western world at the end of the nineteenth century when it became both possible and necessary to exercise control over manufacturing and distribution through accumulating and manipulating large amounts of information. More and more people became necessary to carry out what were inherently very dull and repetitive tasks, largely paper-based. (It is easy to forget that the very term 'computer' referred originally not to machines but to the people who laboriously performed the arithmetical calculations that are carried out today, automatically and practically instantaneously, by electronic devices.) The top-down style of management associated with organizing such routine tasks was never associated with sensitivity or imagination.

Another reason for the general negative perception of the office – acknowledged as a common theme of mid-century sociology – is that even as their numbers grew, the status of the majority of office workers continued to decline during the first half of the twentieth century; more and more of these workers were women, with a tendency to underestimate their contribution to modern enterprise. By the 1960s the office began to be populated by wave after wave of new specialists – programmers, systems analysts, paralegals, marketing managers, consultants, designers. But they seem to have had little sense of their place in history (and generally even less of an interest in their working environment). Instead, they tended toward an overwhelming and exclusive interest in whatever they were doing at the time. The consequence was that very few office workers realized how numerous, different and diverse they were becoming. More importantly, they failed collectively to notice that their familiar office environment was very rapidly becoming the dominant factor in shaping the urban and social landscapes

of the twentieth century. So, although the status of office workers began to improve from the 1960s onwards, it seems that collectively they continued to be as unassertive as their less qualified predecessors and, in doing so, they failed to make much positive impact on the image of the office.

But perhaps the most fundamental reason why the importance of the office to twentieth-century society has always been underestimated is that much of what it generates is, to all intents and purposes, invisible – certainly to the outside world. Information cannot be seen. In a materialist century, if you expect something to be noticed and talked about, immateriality is, not surprisingly, a grave disadvantage. Yet today, more than ever before, offices are essentially all about knowledge, the highest form of information, and the most precious commodity we have. Its rapidly growing importance in modern society, and the prediction that the management of knowledge will be one of the chief features of twenty-first-century life, confirm the centrality of the office in modern society and make a serious re-evaluation of our attitudes imperative.

Below **The bleakness of American corporate office life was often captured in Edward Hopper's contemporary work. An example is this painting, Office in a Small City, 1951.**

Taylor's century

The dominant office culture of the twentieth century can be traced back to the work of Frederick Taylor, 1856–1915. He made his great contribution to the study of working methods at the Bethlehem Steel Mills at the end of the nineteenth century, revolutionizing, through careful observation and ruthless control, the way in which physical tasks were done.

Taylor's methods made possible Henry Ford's subsequent development of mass production. His great contribution to management thinking was called 'scientific management'. What it meant was treating people as if they were simply so many units of production. 'Taylorism', as it is also called, led to the dehumanization of work, first in the factory and then, a little later, in the office. People at work were observed and calibrated, literally with a stop watch, through carefully designed 'time and motion studies', conducted by men in white coats whose job it was to find the most efficient ways of using labour. It was not, however, the idea of measurement that was repugnant about Taylorism – measurement remains crucial to business and is one of the most important themes of this book – but the attitude that lay behind it: that people are managed best if they are treated as unthinking automatons. Taylor's unfeeling abuse of reason in the cause of productivity engendered the same denial of sentiment that made the horrors of the First World War possible. It is not surprising that among his greatest fans were Stalin and Hitler.

Textbooks on how to run the office in the Taylorist way began to appear in North America in the first decade of this century. The influence they exerted spread to Europe, but there the ideas were taken up with less wholehearted energy and more inhibitions from the past. What mattered most on both sides of the Atlantic were the impersonal bureaucratic virtues of order, regularity, and thrift. Intelligence and inventiveness were not expected from ordinary workers. Punctuality and synchrony certainly were, because with the only information technology of the time – the typewriter and the telephone – it was absolutely essential for all the clerks to be assembled together in one place at one time in order to get the work done. Supervision was another key feature of the office run on Taylorist principles. It was thought that people on their own could not be trusted, that without the

Above **Most early twentieth-century offices were based on industrial procedures and their layout and imagery reflect industrial values. With only primitive and limited technology – the telephone and the typewriter – available, most office work was clerical data-processing.**

presence of a constant watchful eye, they may revert to non-machine-like behaviour. Accepted norms in dress and behaviour naturally followed.

Implicit in Taylor's thinking was hierarchy. Everyone had their place; everyone knew their place. Male clerks were expected to stay in the same job for life. Honesty and commitment were rewarded with job security. With chronometer-like precision, career progress was marked by the gradual unfolding of rewards, often in what became the universal currency of space standards: a larger desk, more space around the desk and, best of all, your very own office. It is hardly surprising, given these values, that the typical early-twentieth-century office building became nothing more than what the American sociologist C. Wright Mills described as an 'enormous file'.

No one today takes Taylorism seriously – it has long since been superseded by far more sophisticated and humane ideas and practices in management thinking. Yet the kinds of office interiors, buildings, and cities that Taylor indirectly created are still being replicated. Until recently, it was only in the social democratic climate of certain northern European countries, particularly Scandinavia and Germany, in the years following the Second World War, that Taylorist office environments were seriously questioned and rethought. The Taylorist office may never have been much loved but it has certainly proved itself to be most remarkably persistent elsewhere. The reasons for this need serious analysis because Taylor's influence on the physical office environment is today hindering the adoption of new ways of working and is in danger of suffocating new management initiatives.

What happened was this: Taylorism was the dominant management philosophy when the office as a building type was created, so the particular values that Taylor emphasized – order, hierarchy, supervision, depersonalization – became an integral part of the architecture of those initial, pioneering, turn-of-the-century North American buildings. The creation of these buildings involved not just accommodating what were then the most up-to-date and perfect ideas in office organization, but also required equally bold inventions in construction, in building services, and in real estate practice. This mélange of innovations was so successful that, once established, the pattern of the office building immediately crystallized, and in that process of crystallization the transient values of the pioneers of office organization found their way into short-term interiors and long-term architectural forms. The consequence of so much success has been extraordinarily self-sustaining and resistant to change, particularly in the USA.

Meanwhile, management ideas moved on, in different ways in different parts of the world. From America streamed a series of inventive theories, including, in the 1960s, the notion of the office as cybernetic system – a kind of computer that connected people and machines. But until the 1990s, when managerial innovation gathered more momentum, stimulated by developments in

Below **A tiny minority of offices, once seen never forgotten, are used to express, without apology, explanation or reserve, the exercise of untrammelled power over people, information, money, and time. Fritz Lang, in his visionary 1927 film Metropolis, accurately predicted the moghul office of the future.**

Now, however, there is evidence of change. New kinds of office environment are appearing. In some organizations, for example, the office is turning into a kind of club. The traditional (usually gentlemen's) club allows an élite group, often of ambitious, successful, intellectual people with many common interests, to share what is, in effect, a kind of palace, a rich and diverse environment that provides a level of comfort and service that each member could not afford separately. Moreover by frequenting the same club, members are able to take calculated advantage of the probabilities of more or less accidental, more or less intended, personal encounters. Some businesses today are trying to emulate this in order to promote interaction among their staff, to give them access to richer resources, to accommodate more types of activity, and to save money at the same time. The conventional office is an exercise in simultaneity – it can only work when everyone is at their place. From this simple premise come the nine-to-five working day, the sharp separation of home and work, the dormitory suburb, and the vast apparatus of commuting which characterizes the cities of the twentieth century. The club-like office relies on a very different sort of timetable, one for networkers who don't have to be told what to do or where to be at a certain time but nevertheless need a place to meet, exchange ideas, and share resources. This approach has only been made feasible thanks to advances in communication and information technology.

Of course, rethinking the office as a club won't suit everyone, nor is this the only way forward either in organizational terms or in office design. Club-type offices happen to suit particular kinds of business. Other ways of rethinking the office are just as valid for other types of business where patterns of occupancy are less intermittent and activity is more intense. The case studies in Chapter 4 have been selected because they show a wide range of innovation in office design across many business sectors and in several different national cultures. They include some of the most striking initiatives. But in terms of overall numbers of all offices world-wide, this tiny trawl of innovation is still very far from being statistically significant. A more representative sample of the thousands of office buildings recently erected in the USA and on the Pacific Rim demonstrate how boring and repetitive the once-great North American tradition of office design has become.

information technology, these ideas had surprisingly little effect on the ways that designers thought about the physical office environment. Today, somewhat as it was in the North America of a hundred years ago, there is a revolution happening in the office work place. New ideas about organization are being actively explored. Old habits are being questioned and abandoned. The conventions that govern the relationship between home and office life are being renegotiated. As a result the discrepancy between the limited vocabulary of standard office layouts and increasingly novel forms of organization is becoming much more apparent. Until very recently, what little innovation there has been in office design has tended to lag behind, rather than anticipate, organizational initiatives.

Above **Temporary access to a quiet space equipped with low table, overstuffed armchair, and handy sockets for power and data signals the rejection of the conventional office. Offices for Chiat/Day, California, USA. Architect: Frank Gehry.**

The North American tradition

The office building, in its dominant twentieth-century form, was created in the context of the tremendous explosion of economic activity in North America, particularly in Chicago and New York, in the last two decades of the nineteenth century. The story of achievement in construction is well known – the rapid exploitation of the potential of the steel frame and the elevator to build tall – as is that of the development – rather more gradual – of such services as electric lighting and air conditioning to make these new buildings comfortable and attractive to work in. Less well known are the parallel advances in real estate practice and in city planning. Building tall meant multiplying the value of land, but to finance the construction of such huge edifices, and to make sure that they were profitably let and efficiently managed, required innovation in investment practice. Building tall meant that there was a constant struggle between developers responding to the roller coaster of the notoriously cyclical property market and those responsible in City Hall for environmental safety and civic quality.

Even less well studied is how the office technology of that period was taken up and put to work in organizations, many of which must have been quite modest even though they occupied huge and conspicuous skyscrapers. This failure to record the ordinary working lives of ordinary office workers, this collective amnesia about what such people actually did all day and how they set about their tasks, is a great pity. Clerks in myriad office enterprises, large and small, exploited developments in what we now call organization theory and information technology. This aggregation of enterprise is the underlying commercial reality that stoked the real estate market and attracted developers to risk employing geniuses, like the architects Louis Sullivan and Frank Lloyd Wright. These architects and their successors created the office buildings that shaped the twentieth-century city and became one of the most potent images of the twentieth century.

Left **The Chrysler Building, designed by William Van Alen, is, with the Empire State Building, one of the best known skyscrapers in New York. Buildings like this were the characteristic creation of the North American tradition of office design: on the one hand they were magnificent technological achievements; on the other, brilliant devices to achieve higher densities and thus to multiply the value of land.**

The Larkin Building, Buffalo, New York, 1904

Architect: Frank Lloyd Wright

Right **Now demolished, the Larkin Building's grand exterior was as much an expression of corporate self-sufficiency as of technical innovation in air conditioning – four heroic ducts mark the corners of this magnificent structure.**

most advanced office of its time with, perhaps, the most perfect relationship between architectural invention and organizational innovation

The history of one famous building (now sadly torn down) is unusually well documented and illuminates the changing relationship between new organizational ideas and design at the turn of the century. This is Frank Lloyd Wright's early commercial masterpiece, the purpose-built offices that housed the headquarters of the Larkin company. The story of how the Larkin Building was designed to accommodate a particular business and to reflect the values of its owners is especially interesting.

The Larkin brothers more or less invented the business of mail order. They devised a way to make money by delivering goods by mail to homes throughout the United States. To help them do this efficiently, they had to recruit a large, disciplined, and educated labour force of clerks – who turned out to be largely female – to handle the millions of pieces of paper that were being generated by so many tiny transactions. To get the most out of their employees, they had to install the latest office technology and to put in place the latest management ideas. They created the perfect model of enlightened Taylorism – ranks of busy clerks working within the ordered structure of a paternalistic enterprise.

The freshness of Frank Lloyd Wright's response to this management vision is evident in the photographs taken in the early years of the life of the building. It was probably the

that has ever been achieved. In the messages expressed to employees – through its overpoweringly disciplined architectural form, in the paternalistic homilies carved into the spandrel panels of the galleries, in the centrally controlled environmental services, and in the hierarchically ordered layout – it reinforced the managerial culture of its time. The Larkin Building set the standard by which the office architecture of the twentieth century is judged.

Opposite and above **White-collared men and white-bloused women, arrayed in immaculate corporate order, sat at architect-designed desks which expressed the limited freedom allowed to employees – the seats were cantilevered out and integral with the desks.**

Below **The first-floor plan shows how rationality, order and rigidity governed the environment thought to be appropriate for clerks, who were regarded as so many units of production.**

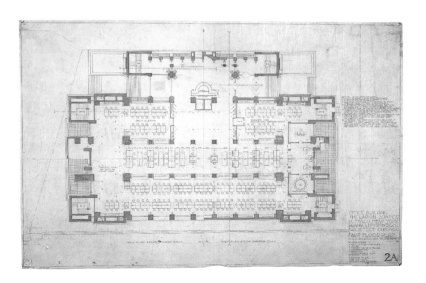

The Empire State Building, 1930–31

Architect: Shreve, Lamb & Harman

The Chrysler Building, 1928–30

Architect: William Van Alen

The mainstream of North American, commercial, inner-city office development between the two world wars is well represented by these buildings. Both are astonishing feats of construction. Both are tremendous endorsements of the benefits of a mature infrastructure of subways and railways, built to attract millions of commuters from a great hinterland. Both demonstrate the advances in environmental control that had made such huge buildings habitable and safe.

Opposite **Vast in every dimension, not just its record-breaking height of 102 storeys (85 of them office floors), which remained unchallenged for four decades, the Empire State Building in New York was built in an astonishingly brief 18 months. Hardly surprisingly, in those recessionary times it took far longer than the time of construction to fill the mighty floors with tenants.**

Discipline in construction and discipline in real estate shaped these buildings. The city-planning context was designed to make such skyscrapers a commercial success. Nothing was wasted, as much as possible was standardized. Constructional and servicing grids were ruthlessly aligned, with the simplest and most pragmatic assumptions about the ways in which the buildings would be let and sublet. Concern for what ordinary office workers might wish to choose in deter-mining their working environments was low on both the landlords' and the developers' lists of priorities. Despite the grace of the Chrysler Building in particular, what would now be called 'value engineering' ensured that real money was spent lavishly only in a few places – where a relatively small amount of visible opulence would have most impact upon the largest number of potential tenants.

Right **The three floor plans of the Empire State Building say more about how real estate worked in New York – and perhaps even more about how construction was organized – than they do about the kinds of businesses that were carried on within these rational floors in the late 1920s and early 1930s. Stepping back, storey after storey, the big floor-plates all follow the same planning logic: a disciplined, highly serviced central core, with neatly interlocking ducts, lavatories and banks of elevators, surrounded by a continuous 'race track' of subdivisable, easily rentable space.**

Form Follows Finance is an apt title for the fine study by Carol Willis of the legal and economic background which made such huge investments possible in Chicago and New York. Money drove everything. Before the financial crash of the mid-1930s, skyscrapers were often syndicated investments in which a developer would persuade many small investors to risk their savings – the perfect expression of the 'supply', as opposed to the 'demand', market forces that shaped these buildings. In this context, few questions were likely to be raised about the Taylorist assumptions that underpinned these magnificent architectural achievements.

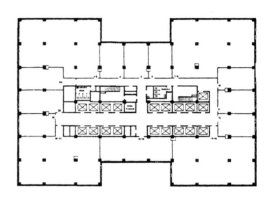

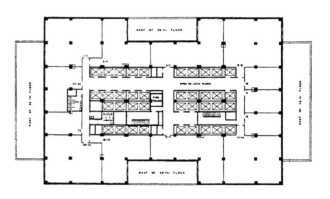

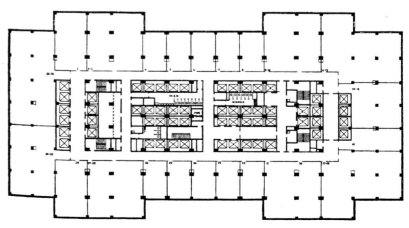

Johnson's Wax Buildings, Racine, Wisconsin, 1936–39

Architect: Frank Lloyd Wright

Above **Built as the administrative and technical centre of a big manufacturing company, the Johnson campus is a beautifully integrated mixture of high and low buildings.**

Right **Architecturally speaking, the interior, a top-lit hall, is inventive and spacious. But the people working there seem to have as little control over their environment as their predecessors, the first occupants of the building.**

Thirty-five years after the Larkin project Frank Lloyd Wright designed another low-rise, custom-built office within the North American tradition of corporate office design, this time for S. C. Johnson (Johnson's Wax). What had changed managerially since he designed the Larkin Building was that Taylorism had been softened by the superficially more humane values of the so-called 'human relations' school of thought, which emphasized the importance of the manner, if not the fundamental content, in which management dealt with office workers. The photographs of the interiors of the Johnson's Wax Buildings show a more informal but equally unassertive clerical work force. The architecture demonstrates that corporate imagery is still very important, but what

seems to have become even more important is the personal vision of the architect. It is possible that Wright, as an autonomous artistic phenomenon, had become more remote from management without addressing what ordinary office workers really wanted.

What conceivable managerial argument could Wright have used to justify his use of mushroom columns and clerestories of curved tubular glass? On what business basis could he justify so many open-plan workplaces without any external view? There is more architectural impetus here than organizational invention or social sensitivity. Even the workplace furniture, elegant as it is, seems more concerned with style than with the overtly Taylorist principles reflected in the Larkin furniture.

The imagery of the office as the palace of the patron has superseded the idea of the office as the brave new world of 'scientific management'. Office architects, even Frank Lloyd

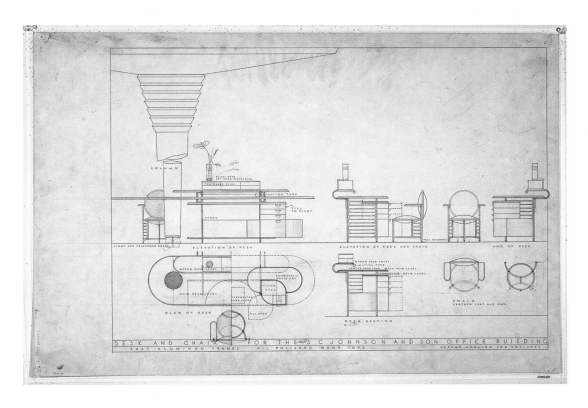

Left **Frank Lloyd Wright was convinced that his artistic mission would not be complete unless he designed every detail of the interior – including the steel desks and chairs that are still being produced by Steelcase for use in offices today.**

Below **Architectural style had developed since the beginning of the century, as the designer-styled furniture, tightly laid out in a noble space, shows; but the technology and rhythm of office work remained more or less the same. Bosses occupied offices at the perimeter, staff worked in disciplined rows within.**

Wright, have all too often tended to overrate patronage because it is simpler to deal with a single patron than with the complexities and contradictions of decision-making in large companies. As office organizations in the late 1930s showed the first tendencies towards becoming slightly more responsive to end-users, and as management issues were becoming more complex, Frank Lloyd Wright, like the majority of office architects before and since, obviously found it easier to retreat into stylistic and technical matters than to address the design consequences of organizational change.

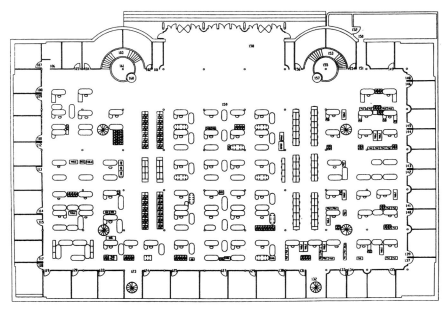

The Seagram Building, New York, 1954–58

Architect: Mies van der Rohe and Philip Johnson

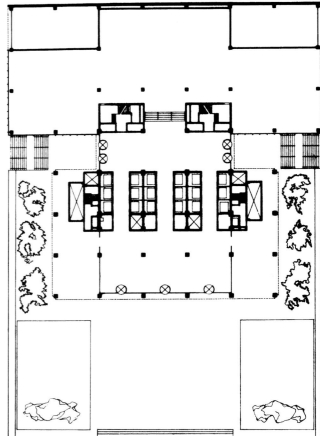

Above, left and above, right **In its minimalist cladding, and in the simple way it sits on its brilliantly exploited site, the late-1950s Seagram Building seems externally far more sophisticated than the skyscrapers of the 1920s and 1930s. The ground-level plan shows how nothing is allowed to detract from the clarity, the order, and the directness of the entrance.**

The Seagram Building is perhaps the most perfect realization of the North American, high-rise, city-centre, developer's office building. Its form is ultimately derived from prototypes like Sullivan's Guaranty Building, constructed in the same year and in the same city as the Larkin Building. The Guaranty is a speculative office building that addressed, through the discipline of an overriding architectural order, the design problem created by the multiplication of endless, more or less anonymous office cells.

While Sullivan's solution stretched the relationship between external architectural form and the realities of internal occupation, on the bland and immaculate exterior of the Seagram building there is no recognition of the complex pattern of occupancy within. This reflects what had happened to North American office design – once structure, floor-plates, and services had became standardized, the only scope for architectural initiative lay in the design of the external cladding. The skin became everything, and in the Seagram Building found its most elegant and understated expression. The iconography of the skin, at that time, was often expressed as an orthogonal grid to emphasize the only things that most North American office building owners were interested in – first, simplicity (and hence cheapness of construction) and, second, easy divisibility into separate and ever-changing rentable units.

Mies van der Rohe, while practising as an architect in Berlin in the 1920s, had already paid homage to the North American office tradition with his glass skyscraper designs, the fluency and grace of which were only possible in project form; they were fundamentally impractical and unbuildable.

Left **From the very beginning the architects' disciplined approach to interior design was (and continues to be) often contradicted by the exuberance and variety of the fit-outs in many separate tenancies on independently rented floors. By the late 1960s, very few of the Seagram building interiors were as chaste as this.**

In exile in Chicago, Mies learned exactly what real American developers wanted from office architecture. He quickly transmuted their demands into his own ideal of 'universal space' and succeeded as a commercial architect. What Mies van der Rohe appears never to have shown at any stage in this process was a sense of curiosity about the gradually increasing diversity, in the 1960s, of the requirements of the developers' potential tenants. For Mies, it was a virtue for all office space to be the same: all office users were presumed to have the same needs.

The marked tendency in the North American office tradition to separate inside from outside has been reinforced by the way in which relations between landlord and tenant have developed in the United States. Landlords and their architects are responsible for the long-term office-building shell; tenants and their interior designers or space planners (as they began to be called in the 1960s) are responsible for the short-term interior, designed to last only the length of the lease. The designers of the interior scenery and the architects of the external shell have learned to operate completely independently.

This explains my surprise when I first explored the Seagram Building, floor by floor, in the late 1960s: the differences, even then, in the style and layout of the interiors, expressing the tastes, budgets, and operational necessities of many different tenants, were completely denied by the classical restraint of the exterior. The Seagram Building says it all: in New York, at least, the worlds of real estate and of building use had completely diverged.

Below **This is the perfect expression of North American taste in corporate executive offices at the time, in the mid-1950s, when New York was the world's cultural as well as its economic capital.**

CIGNA Buildings, Bloomfield, Connecticut, 1954–57

Architect: Skidmore, Owings & Merrill

Interiors by Gordon Bunshaft and Florence Knoll

This office campus represents the high point in American 1950s economic confidence – a capitalist palace in a great park built for the Connecticut General Life Insurance company and as impressive in its way as Hampton Court near London or even Versailles near Paris. The magnificent buildings demonstrate how the hard-won and highly disciplined experience gained from constructing a million speculative office towers could successfully be put to work for a corporate client. They became the prototype of the rural, low-rise corporate office, replicated subsequently all over the Western world.

Right **This building complex can only be fully appreciated within the context of its vast park. Architecture and landscaping – buildings, trees, water and lawns – are combined to provide the perfectly controlled setting for the exercise of unquestioned corporate power.**

This complex expresses not just tremendous architectural sophistication but also impressive practicality. Everything is in its place; and everything works. It reflects the kind of military precision that could be achieved by the best architectural and engineering skills of a well-organized and wealthy nation at the height of its economic imperialism. The chief difference between this and the contemporary

Below **The same mixture of exquisite taste and total control is evident in the series of internal courtyards – landscaped by Isamu Noguchi – which everyone admires and no one enters.**

Seagram Building in New York is that here no conflict is tolerated between interior and exterior. Inside and out, the same aesthetic rules, and the same values of precision, order, and control apply. The external grid that expressed rational, constructional order as well as real estate flexibility in the Seagram Building is extended here to broadcast, without any hesitation or the slightest ambiguity, the message that corporate order resides within.

What is initially astonishing is that the interiors as well as the exteriors still seem as precise and orderly as they ever were. Rarely has such care been given to the integrated detailing of all components of the office interior – gridded ceilings, modular lighting, panelled partitions, beautifully proportioned, ceiling-height doors, and the very finest quality furniture available at the time. Only on reflection does it become clear that all this controlled perfection originally depended upon, and continues to reinforce, an equally rigid attitude to business. The insurance industry has continued to rely chiefly on a large, cheap, disciplined workforce and on the type of managerial conditions that created the Taylorist office.

Today, however, Connecticut General no longer exists, having been taken over by the far larger CIGNA Corporation. More significantly, the insurance business is now undergoing such spectacular organizational and technological changes that there seems little chance that the top-down, coherent, and orderly balance that was achieved in the 1950s will be preserved for very much longer.

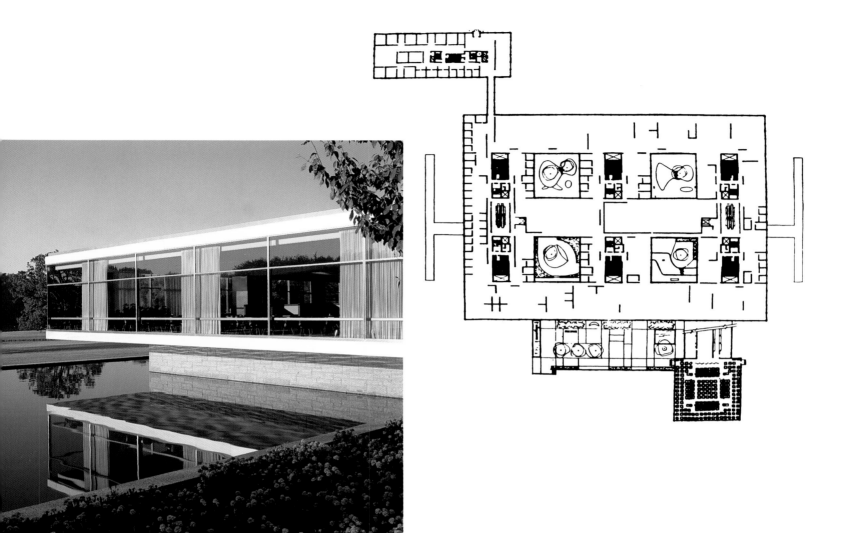

Above **The vast scale of the predominantly open-plan Wilde Building, the original and principal building on the site, is shown in this plan. The main block has four courtyards and six cores; one of the two outriding pavilions is an enormous staff restaurant overlooking the park.**

Left **The controlled interior persuades one to admire, if not to like, the business culture that such fine architecture certainly flatters. Perhaps because of their inherent quality, these interiors – designed by Gordon Bunshaft and Florence Knoll – are still almost perfectly preserved after 40 years of use.**

Ford Foundation Offices, New York, 1966–67

Architect: Kevin Roche, of Roche/Dinkerloo & Associates

The Ford Foundation Offices are remarkable for one main reason: the revival, after many years, of the atrium as a feature of office design. Atria, or internal covered courts, were relatively common devices for introducing light into the centre of the building in the early days of office construction – the Larkin Building being only one example. Kevin Roche's achievement in the Ford Foundation Offices not only brings extra daylight into a very dense urban environment, but has two further advantages. The first is that the atrium makes the whole building, and hence the whole organization, visible to everyone working within it. The second is that the same atrium links the building with its urban environment. Thus it is a rare example of an office that simultaneously contributes to improving the quality of the surrounding streetscape and, through the same highly visible atrium, to providing a softer and more humane internal office environment than is usual in downtown areas.

Right **Not only does the atrium symbolically unite the company by making the whole organization visible to itself, but it also links a great office interior with the surrounding urban fabric.**

Below **In plan, the building is a series of L-shaped office floors overlooking the atrium.**

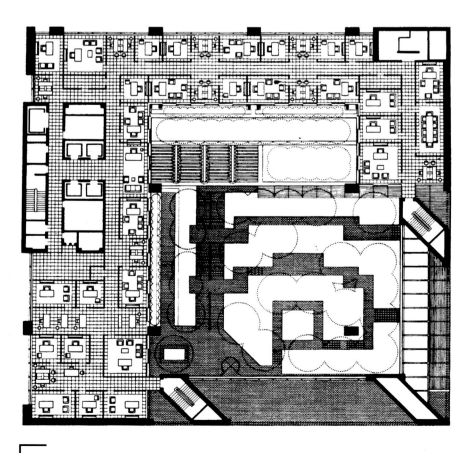

To appreciate fully Kevin Roche's originality, it must be realized that it was made possible by an enormously wealthy client prepared to flout the 1960s pressures of conventional real estate. Any deviation from the norms of the standard central-core office building, such as the classic Chrysler and Empire State Buildings, was becoming more and more difficult. Standardization of office design, shaped by the narrow rules of investment and by the tacit conventions of old-fashioned corporate Taylorism, had become dominant. Innovation was no longer a virtue in real estate circles, making the initiative of this client and architect all the more remarkable.

Above **Landscaped by Dan Kiley, the atrium, overlooked by sealed offices, is vast. One of its functions is to bring daylight deep into the building. Lush planting provides a complete contrast to the hard concrete and steel of its surroundings, and brings life and greenery not only into the building but also, because it can be seen by passers-by, into the city itself.**

Lloyd's of London, 1986

Architect: Richard Rogers Partnership

Above and opposite **Lloyd's of London deliberately displays its many ducts and elevators. The exterior complexity is not arbitrary; it is the direct consequence of a dazzling design move that achieved big, continuous, well-serviced office floors on the New York model. Instead of being wrapped round a dark internal core, these are brilliantly lit by a huge, soaring atrium.**

Right **The so-called '86 Building' provides a kind of covered market for the insurance industry, bringing buyers and sellers of risk and cover together. The Lutine bell, traditionally rung when a disaster occurs, symbolizes a way of working that goes back three centuries.**

This building is not located in North America, of course, nor is it, strictly speaking, entirely an office building since its principal function is to house a great insurance market. Nevertheless, like many features of contemporary British life, Richard Rogers' building for Lloyd's is a variant on a fundamentally North American theme. It is interesting because architecturally it is so novel and so ingenious. At one stroke Rogers turned the convention of the central-core, high-rise office building inside out and, at the same time, gave a new importance to the accessibility of services, especially cabling.

Although by no means tall by North American standards, Lloyd's is big, with a floor-plate equivalent in size to those of the larger office buildings in Manhattan or within the Loop in

Chicago. Rogers achieved all the virtues of the simple, rational, easily planned North American office floor by stripping out all the elements of the core – lifts, toilets, ducts – and distributing them round the perimeter, exploiting the irregular shape of the site. In so doing he created a soaring central, day-lit internal hall. At the same time, he anticipated the needs for new levels of servicing and for a permeable structure for cabling that were being created in the mid-1980s by the extraordinary proliferation of information technology. Although organizational innovation was not on Lloyd's main agenda, it was implicit in the prominence given by the client to the new technology.

By 1986 the originality, daring, and inventiveness that Rogers demonstrated so amply at Lloyd's was no longer, in practice, attainable in North America, given what had become an increasingly rigid, introspective, and cost-cutting real estate regime. The North American tradition of office design that had begun, one hundred years earlier, by solving so many new problems with such éclat was clearly faltering.

The northern European tradition

In northern Europe – in Germany, the Netherlands, and Scandinavia, rather than in the UK or France – the office building has developed in an entirely different way. The reasons are complex. Northern European cities are mostly old. They were settled, and achieved their identities, centuries before the modern office was invented. Hence tall new office buildings, although of huge and growing importance to the economies of these cities, still by no means dominate their skylines in the way that they routinely dominate the centres of North American and Pacific Rim cities. Office buildings have never been given such a prestigious place in the economy of European cities, which is perhaps another of the reasons that many European organizations were, until the 1960s, prepared to tolerate smaller and poorer quality offices than their North American competitors.

Below and opposite **The skyward aspirations of the North American city are nowhere more apparent than in Chicago, whereas northern European cities like Stockholm still prefer to hug the ground. Not only are these European cities older and more complex than their American counterparts, but also the building stock is smaller and more intricate, and the mixture of uses is traditionally richer.**

Developers, whose speculative ventures and practices have shaped North American cities, have played a far less central and influential role in northern Europe. In Germany, for example, businesses still tend to borrow money directly from the bank (which is likely already to be a shareholder) to to build new offices. Often they rely on competitions to choose the architects to design buildings for their own exclusive use, and also tend to spend far more management time than do their North American counterparts in planning to make sure that the building fits them, rather than assuming that they should fit it. The result is buildings which, because they are tailor-made for a particular business, vary far more in style and configuration than the North American stock, but are often, by North American and even British standards, inefficient in space-planning terms. Another critical factor which has strongly shaped the office stock is the social democratic climate of northern Europe. This has led to the development of elaborate statutory procedures through which the quality of working life is negotiated. Among the many factors that Workers' Councils in Germany, the Netherlands, and Scandinavia have the right to negotiate with employers is the quality of the working environment. As a result, office design reflects user preferences and demands in a variety of ways: buildings are usually extremely narrow to allow staff direct access to external views; highly cellular because of demand for enclosed office rooms; and very environmentally 'correct' because of concern for employees' health and safety.

Such historical and political influences have made northern European office buildings different in almost every respect from those in North America: they tend to be low- rather than high-rise, suburban rather than city centre, narrow rather than deep, rambling rather than efficient, naturally ventilated rather than air-conditioned, and influenced by the wishes of ordinary office workers rather than corporate in style. While the northern European experience has been far less influential on the world stage than the North American one, it presents a dramatically different view of what office design could and should be like, and has created the highest quality of office environment in the world.

The big, open-plan, landscaped offices of the 1960s were the direct result of an attempt to rethink the design of the office building from first principles, through a fundamental understanding of office communications and processes. An unusual set of circumstances led to this ambitious programme being embarked upon in Germany at that time: the reviving strength of the German economy, the relative weakness of German office developers, a fresh democratic spirit in industry, the first stirrings of a desire to create a less austere working life, and an influx of exciting new managerial ideas from North America. These ideas had made negligible impact on architectural form in America, but were a potent source of inspiration for a country in which there was an urgent need to rebuild its offices and its confidence after the damage inflicted in the Second World War.

The Schnelle brothers, office-furniture manufacturers with an interest in office design, had the genius to weave all these ideas and challenges into an attractive design and management consultancy package that could, they proposed, at one stroke, eliminate status and improve communications. What became known as *bürolandschaft* or 'office landscaping' involved open-plan layouts, with wall-to-wall carpets, decorative plants, and break areas, in deep-plan office buildings. Among the most successful and most attractive outcomes of the Schnelle brothers' vision was a small office building for Ninoflax, a textile company on the

German–Dutch border. This particular office came close to the Schnelles' dream of achieving managerial reform by decree through humane and sensitive design.

The dream turned out to be no more than a dream. The claims that landscaped offices delivered better communications and eliminated status turned out to be unfounded. Nor, more importantly, did such buildings match up to what the German labour force were beginning to realize that they actually wanted. The very deep, air-conditioned, and more or less completely open-plan offices of the 1960s would not be tolerated in Germany today because there the Workers' Councils have done their job of enforcing user-preferences so well. And in the Netherlands, where no one is allowed to sit further than 5 metres/16 feet from a window, they would be illegal. True industrial democracy, rather than that imposed – even by well-meaning idealists – from above, has meant that meeting the demands by office workers for enclosed individual offices, for views out, and for fresh air, have completely changed the shape of typical new northern European office buildings.

Left **The Ninoflax building in Nordhorn (architect N. Zobel, 1962) was one of the most likeable manifestations of the fashion for 'office landscaping', a form of planning that upturned traditional design by stripping away both status distinctions and dividing walls in a brave effort to improve communications between people, and to thrust the office into the age of cybernetics – linking people and information. As the floor plan shows, the conventional North American, orthogonal office grid was rejected in favour of what was felt to be a more complex, more dynamic, more organic geometry.**

Centraal Beheer offices, Apeldoorn, The Netherlands, 1970–72

Architect: Herman Hertzberger

This project was perhaps the last, and certainly one of the best, of the great northern European open-plan offices of the 1960s and 1970s. This was the turning point at which the attempt to create industrial democracy through the open-plan office was finally abandoned.

Herman Hertzberger's office building – for a successful and liberal cooperative insurance company – is unusual in that it is not only very beautiful, but is also based upon an elaborate intellectual structure. Ideas are everywhere. Chief among these was the architect's proposition that architecture should be both prescriptive – in the sense of establishing a strong overall sense of order, and liberating – in the sense of allowing all the end-users to create their own preferred kinds of environment within a structure. This collaborative view of the relation between office shell and office scenery is totally different from the pattern of indifference and non-communication

Below **Within a robust framework of voids (which are really top-lit mini atria), walls and columns, is an interlocking grid of four-person spaces. Within these, people are allowed a free hand to arrange their furniture in their own way, to paint the walls the colour of their choice, stick up posters, and import plants, pets, and goldfish.**

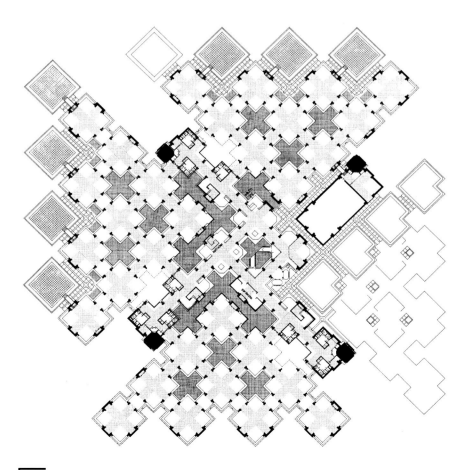

accepted as normal between the design teams of landlord and tenant in the North American system. In Centraal Beheer the zany, inventive, and continually changing introductions of the occupants of the building – furniture brought from home, murals, pets in cages, indoor horticulture – only served to respect and reinforce, by contrast, the overall architectural framework of strong columns and big spaces, devised by Hertzberger to accommodate individual choice.

Above and left **At its best, with the sun shining down through the top-lit voids and a busy hum of activity in the work spaces and main 'streets', Centraal Beheer seems more like a Mediterranean village than a conventional office.**

To have made this attempt to humanize the office environment, and allow the people working in it to create their own worlds within a world, was not only brave but successful. Centraal Beheer became nationally and internationally famous. The building still works well today. But, given the changes in the social democracy of northern European workplace design described earlier, the experiment was never repeated.

SAS headquarters, Stockholm, Sweden, 1988

Architect: Niels Torp

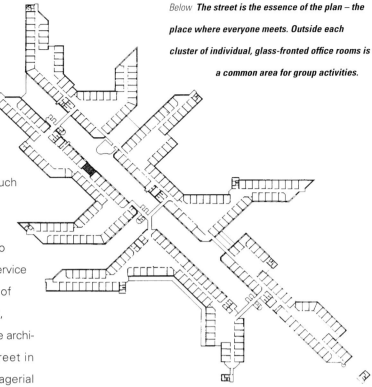

Below **The street is the essence of the plan – the place where everyone meets. Outside each cluster of individual, glass-fronted office rooms is a common area for group activities.**

Arguably the most brilliant example of the modern northern European tradition of 'street' office buildings, the SAS (Scandinavian Airlines) headquarters is a superb example of the use of architecture to create an interactive environment. Jan Carlzon, then chief executive of SAS, was, in a sense, almost as much the architect as the Norwegian Niels Torp. It was Carlzon's idea to use fine architecture to attract the calibre of young people that he needed in order to create what would be the prototype of the advanced service organization of the last decade of the twentieth century. As client, he placed very high priority on the architectural idea of the internal street in order to create a powerful managerial device for bringing the whole of his organization together. Circulation, a dry architectural term, is almost always minimized for economic reasons in North American office buildings. At SAS it is expanded and exploited. Systems analysts, for example, cannot help running into their colleagues from the marketing and service delivery departments every day. Serendipity aided by visibility and some very strategically placed bridges unites the company.

Below **Everyone enjoys a standard individual office with doors that shut, windows that open, and furniture that can be moved around at will.**

The building is a delight to enter and to walk through. Off the 'street' are training rooms, restaurants, sports facilities, and shops. SAS is also a fine example of the northern European notion that assumes that each employee has the right to an individual room – almost all of these are precisely the same size and identically equipped, but in such a way that the furniture and lighting can be arranged exactly as the occupant wishes.

The SAS headquarters, in retrospect, was perhaps too lavish, too well

equipped to house efficiently the number of people who were to occupy it. It was conceived at a time when competition in the airline business was less severe, and before it could benefit from the developments in information technology that are permitting more intensive space use. Contemporary business criteria would conclude that the building could, without losing any of its quality, be used more productively.

Left **The main board room is projected out above the street like a large lantern, in order to express a work culture of openness and transparency. Above it is one of the building's many break areas.**

Above **People spill out of meetings and training areas directly into the busy street which is always full of light and air. They meet each other on their way to restaurants and shops.**

ING headquarters, Amsterdam, The Netherlands, 1987

Architect: Ton Alberts

The headquarters in Amsterdam of ING, the largest bank in the Netherlands, is built – like SAS in Stockholm – around the organizationally integrating idea of the internal street. ING exhibits all the characteristics that make northern European office buildings so different from their North American contemporaries – horizontal rather than vertical circulation, relaxed attitudes to space-planning efficiency, extremely narrow space that is a response to user pressure for views and natural light rather than to real estate economics, tendencies to eccentric architectural forms rather than respect for the orthogonal grid. The bank clearly wanted its building to respect its own particular cultural values rather than generalized real estate criteria.

Another special characteristic of ING is the emphasis given in so many aspects of the design to the environment, to features that work in harmony with nature and promote harmonious relationships between employees. Each of the mini office towers, which follow the line of the street and give the ING building its basic form, has been designed as a self-sufficient environmental system with an ecological approach – solar collectors, natural ventilation, convection – to the conservation of energy. The vertical circulation in the towers is strongly biased toward

Below **The plan of the complex is like a necklace. All the towers – each with office space never deeper than two work stations – are linked by space that is the physical manifestation of interaction and mutual support.**

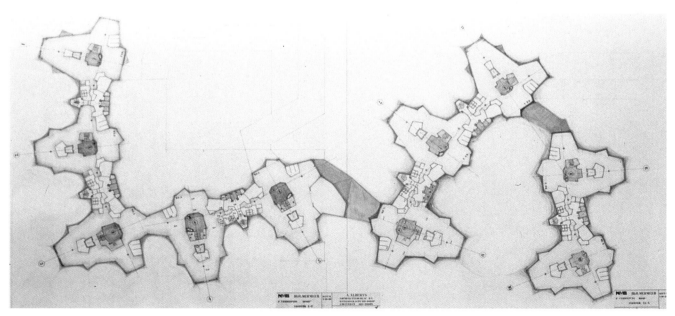

Left **Designed on organic design principles derived from the early twentieth-century mystic Rudolf Steiner, who drew them in turn from Goethe, the building avoids any such mechanistic shortcuts as parallel lines.**

Below **The street, designed in detail by the late Theo Crosby of Pentagram, is not just functional; it is a work of art. None of the usual pressures to minimize circulation in order to provide maximum rentable space has been applied here.**

staircases and the visible movement of staff. Elevators are there, but hidden away from the main routes because it is thought that as much movement as possible from department to department, from floor to floor, should be public and visible rather than private and secretive.

Partly pragmatic, partly idealistic, the architecturally idiosyncratic ING headquarters could not be conceived, let alone built, in the real estate and corporate culture of contemporary North America. And yet this Dutch bank continues to make money. The question for managers at ING is whether it is possible to be more productive – to make more money – through achieving an even better balance between design features that stimulate high morale and design economies that drive down occupancy costs.

The turning point

By the mid-1980s economic pressure, technological advances, and management thinking were, in different ways, making new demands which neither the North American nor the northern European office traditions could meet. A radical new approach was needed.

As always, necessity was the mother of invention. Paradoxically, it was in the conservative City of London that there was the first inkling of how office design of the future might develop. The British financial services industry had been deregulated in the early 1980s to head off competition from Frankfurt and Paris for the prize of remaining the dominant financial centre in Europe and being the chief competitor of Tokyo and New York. Simultaneously information technology, newly networked and ubiquitous, was making true globalization possible in financial services. The City of London responded by rebuilding and refurbishing approximately one-third of its stock of space to meet new needs. One project, in particular, succeeded in setting the highest international standards for accommodating the emerging needs of the financial services industry – Broadgate.

Broadgate, the City of London, 1985–90

Architects: Arup Associates and Skidmore, Owings & Merrill

Broadgate was the first speculative office development to be based upon serious market research. Driven by the forward-looking developers, Stuart Lipton and Godfrey Bradman, its design was the outcome of systematic, international user-studies of practices and trends. It shows what can be done when a developer's desire to produce innovative office design runs in parallel with client's enthusiasm to re-engineer and re-energize office work.

Two features that lay behind the development of Broadgate help to explain its instant and continuing success, and distinguish it from almost all contemporary office developments in North America, Britain, and the Pacific Rim: first, the importance given by the developers to market and user research and, second, their understanding of how information technology was, and is, changing the quality and pattern of demand for office space.

The market research, carried out as the project was being designed from 1985 to 1990, was sectoral and international because the objective was to determine which building features were most in demand by the newly globalized financial services industry. Focus groups were one of the most important means of establishing user priorities. Time and again one of the most important priorities turned out to be the need to accommodate change, often expressed in demands for big, simple, regular floor-plates designed for large numbers of highly paid and highly mobile professionals working in teams. Security was stressed as well as the necessity for environmental services that could cope with high concentrations of heat-producing and vulnerable electronic equipment.

Broadgate not only brought a proportion of the City of London stock of offices up to the same efficient space-planning standards taken for granted in New York, Chicago, Los Angeles, and, to some extent, Tokyo, but also took several crucial steps forward. Broadgate was innovative in that it demonstrated that relatively low-rise buildings could accommodate the most advanced financial services organizations. It also made a significant urban contribution to the City. Two other innovations, by international standards, were first, that big, simple, continuous floor-plates were achieved without excessively deep space by using atria to bring daylight into them and, second, that the level of environmental specification provided was substantially higher than contemporary North American standards.

Both innovative and user-led, Broadgate is a huge success. Stimulated by an urgent need for a new type of office space, the response was a development that marked a real advance in space planning. But while Broadgate represents the turning point, it is only the beginning. The changes that we are about to experience will not be confined to one city or to one sector. Change will affect all offices. With far higher stakes at risk, neither conventional North American nor northern European office buildings will be adequate to meet the number and complexity of the demands being made on office space. The North American tradition is too inhuman, too fundamentally unpopular with users; the northern European too particular to one kind of office culture and, more tellingly, too expensive to be competitive. By improving its office stock in the nick of time in the 1980s, the City of London has remained competitive. But an entirely new approach to office design, on a far bigger scale, is now needed everywhere in order to support re-engineered, re-invented, redesigned work processes.

Opposite **Broadgate totals 400,000 sq. m/more than 4 million sq. ft, and is ambitiously arranged round a series of three new urban squares. The ultimate 'groundscraper', it has a special place in the history of office development for three reasons. First, the plans and specification were based on extensive user research, unparalleled before or since, into the emerging demands of the various sectors of prospective tenants. Second, construction was managed at a ferocious pace to keep up with the exploding demands of the financial services industry after the City of London's early 1980s 'big bang'. Third, the development made a serious contribution to urban design, comparable in scale and ambition to that masterpiece of the 1930s, the Rockefeller Center in New York.**

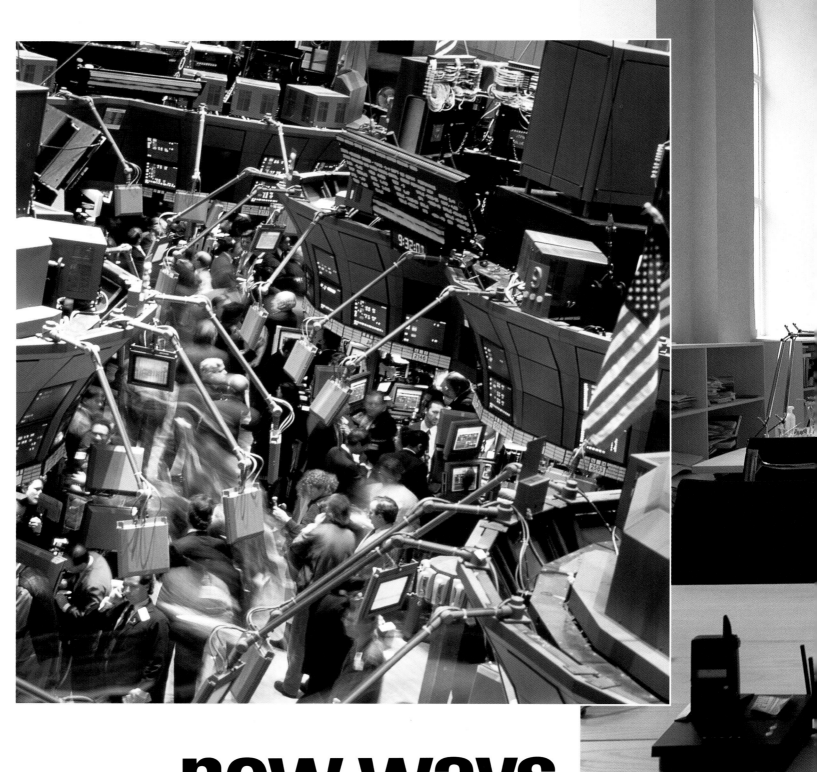

new ways
of working

The New York Stock Exchange exemplifies the wilder end of the widening spectrum of office activity. Technology and emotion are brought together in an environment where continuous competitive stimulus is everything. At the opposite end of the scale is the cool, calm space for an advertising agency in Stockholm, designed for a very different work force. Here itinerant staff, equipped with mobile telephones and each operating at his or her own pace, are given an environment that is as reflective and supportive as possible. Offices for Alm & Co. Architect: Love Arbén (with Claesson, Koivisto and Rune).

Ways of working are changing radically. Information technology is seeing to that. Based on very new and very different assumptions about the use of time and space, new ways of working are emerging fast. They are inherently more interactive than old office routines and give people far more control over the timing, the content, the tools, and the place of work. Office work itself is gradually becoming more varied and creative. Many straightforward procedures are being automated or exported to economies where they can be carried out far more cheaply. Much office work can now be done in ways that are mobile, peripatetic, even nomadic. What kinds of environment will be needed to accommodate and support these challenging new working patterns?

It is already very clear to many business leaders, especially in the USA and the UK, that hide-bound conventional office buildings and office interiors are getting in the way of more dynamic and profitable ways of doing business. This is because most existing office buildings are briefed, designed, built, serviced, and occupied with little regard for the emerging demands of new kinds of organization. The inertia of the Taylorist legacy, described in Chapter 1, has determined and shaped twentieth-century office design so fundamentally that there has been little possibility, until very recently, of any intelligent dialogue between those who are hammering out new theories, in order to try and make office organizations more efficient and effective, and the architects and designers, developers and builders, furniture manufacturers and environmental engineers who are literally being paid to preserve the past. The best professional rewards still tend to come from not asking the users too many questions and designing and delivering office buildings as cheaply as possible in their most conventional forms. However, stiffening competition, often international, means that many organizations are being forced to re-examine every way in which they can improve their performance – not least in finding the most intelligent ways of using the expensive resources of buildings, space, and facilities.

Efficiency and effectiveness

There are fundamentally two dimensions of improvement in the use of office space for business purposes that are open

*Below **The environment of efficiency: here there is engineered rationality where inputs are calculated and outcomes are predictable. Everyone sits together in preordained ways within a transparent, open, and visibly stable organizational structure. Offices for London Underground, Canary Wharf, London. Architect: Pringle Brandon.***

to management – gaining more efficiency and winning more effectiveness. The distinction between them, as Peter Drucker, who is perhaps the most influential of all the American management gurus, has pointed out, is that efficiency means 'doing something right' while effectiveness means something rather more fundamental – 'doing the right thing'. Doing things right and doing the right thing are essential for both business and buildings.

In an office environment, gaining more **efficiency** means driving down occupancy costs. Occupancy costs are what it takes to accommodate the business: the rent, property taxes, heating, cooling and lighting, the amortized costs of fitting-out, and the annual costs of managing office space and keeping it secure. In many administrative and service organizations these costs come second only to the cost of labour,

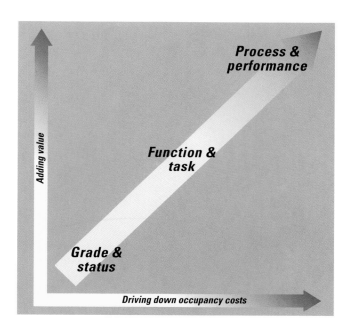

well ahead of the costs of information technology. Those who are most aware of occupancy costs are the real estate (i.e. property) managers, the project managers who look after new construction, and the facilities managers whose job it is to relate office space to changing business needs. It must be said that none of these three has the reputation of thinking strategically. All are notorious cost-cutters. The pressure to comply with their wishes means in practice, as architects very well know, eliminating every design feature that can be accused of being in the slightest way inessential.

Winning more **effectiveness** in the office means using the space in ways that improve the quality of the work being

done there or, in other words, adding value to business performance. Effectiveness is at least as important as efficiency to an organization because it affects directly a totally different set of people – the work force, the users of the office space. Sometimes efficiency can be the enemy of effectiveness, for example, when zealous, over-thrifty cutting down on circulation produces what appears on paper to be a commendably high proportion of rentable space, but at the cost to the user of the clarity, spaciousness, and generosity that can make an office floor or building a more interactive, hospitable, and stimulating place to work in.

The North Americans – and the British – have always tended to overestimate efficiency and glorify cost minimization. And in Japan, particularly in Tokyo

Above **The environment of effectiveness: here individuality is everything and day can turn into night without anyone bothering to notice as long as the bright software ideas keep flowing. Microsoft, Redmond, Seattle. Architect: Team Architecture.**

Left **The diagram represents the two fundamental imperatives that govern all office design: to drive down occupancy costs in order to use space as efficiently as possible; and to add value, i.e. to use the space in ways that improve performance. The vector that reconciles these two laws defines the trajectory of likely developments in office design – from allocating space in the old-fashioned way by grade and status to radically rethinking both office work processes and human performance.**

and Osaka where there is tremendous pressure on real estate, the drive to cut occupancy costs has been taken to extreme limits, resulting in what seem to outsiders to be somewhat bleak, overcrowded office environments. The northern Europeans, on the other hand, particularly in Germany, the Netherlands, and Scandinavia, have generally preferred effectiveness to efficiency and, operating within a social democratic climate, have tended to put far more emphasis on using office space to support staff morale and thus to add value to organizational performance. Both traditions are profitable in different ways but hitting the right balance between the two is obviously the most profitable route of all.

Above **Generous circulation space and lush staff amenities are characteristic of many northern European offices. Colonia, near Köln, Germany. Architect: Thomas Beucher.**

Below **The best offices in the North American tradition, wherever they are found, tend to be spacious and orderly. Offices for John Menzies, Edinburgh, UK. Architect: Bennetts Associates.**

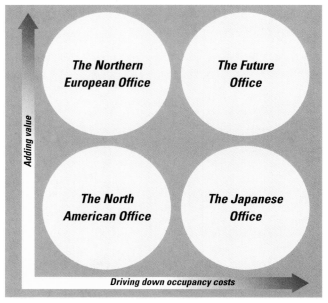

Adding value

The Northern European Office

The Future Office

The North American Office

The Japanese Office

Driving down occupancy costs

An environment of innovation: the theorists

Organization theory has been especially rich and inventive in the 1990s, particularly in North America. Why should this be so today, especially since theory used to have such a very bad name in pragmatic business circles? In a time of rapid technological change and unprecedented global competition, North American enterprises, especially in such advanced and highly vulnerable sectors as electronics, telecommunications and consultancy, have been forced to rethink every aspect of the way in which they do business. All the American corporate chiefs one meets are more than ready to debate what they call their 'corporate culture'. By way of contrast, innovation in office planning has fallen far behind. Colossal cost reductions have led to colossal inertia. The result is a widening gap between open-ended, fertile managerial aspirations and the closed, sterile physical reality of conventional offices.

Many new management theorists have focused on how organizational structures and work processes will have to change to enable businesses to become more responsive to customers, and thus more internationally competitive. Michael Hammer, a former computer science professor at Massachusetts Institute of Technology, has become famous, even notorious, for inventing the term 're-engineering' to advocate the radical redesign of office and other work processes. He feels that no conventional work practice should be left untouched, and that none of the conventions that have determined the sequence and the procedures for carrying out office work can be left

Left **The only way to cut costs and at the same time enjoy better environmental amenities is to redesign both work processes and the use of time in and out of the office – a development that new, mobile information technology is making both possible and attractive.**

Opposite **The diagram shows how differential pressures to cut occupancy costs and to add value have caused the office to develop differently in different cultures. North American offices, where space has been cheap and top-down corporate discipline strong, are often awash with space but lacking in environmental stimulus. Japanese offices have generally been both spatially tight and also dull. Northern European offices have tended to concentrate on stimulus without seeming to care too much about cutting costs. The future office everywhere will be shaped by increasing pressures to add value to the environment while at the same time taking the knife to all avoidable expenditure.**

Left **Rational but very tight use of space is a common characteristic of Japanese office design – not surprising in an economy where office rents are among the highest in the world. The Tokyo Stock Exchange.**

unquestioned. By implication, office design, shaped, as it generally is, by inherited and outmoded assumptions, must also be re-engineered. This means that there should be more diversity in the office workplace as well as a greater emphasis on ways of changing office layouts more rapidly and completely. George Stalk, a vice president of the well-known consultancy Boston Consulting, has coined 'time-based competition' to explain why companies must redesign work processes to minimize the cycle times for developing new products. Driving out wasted time in the office, he maintains, is even more important than recovering wasted space. The implication is that office space will be used more intensively, with less emphasis on traditional long-term 'ownership' of individual work places and more emphasis on more flexible and shorter-term 'ownership' of office space by ever-changing groups. David Nadler, founder of Delta Consulting, employs the metaphor 'organizational architecture' to describe a new form of organizational structure that has evolved around 'autonomous work teams' within 'high performance

work systems'. Again in the office context, the emphasis is on plural rather than individual ownership of resources such as space. The notion is that rapid business responses are made all the more achievable if the boundaries between individual discretion and the constraints – and opportunities – of long-term informational infrastructures are made more explicit. In terms of office space, this idea would certainly flourish in, and be supported by, an environment very similar to that advocated by the Dutch architect Herman Hertzberger, described in Chapter 1, in which striking, long-term office architecture permits and, more importantly, stimulates individual choice

Right **Charles Handy, the British leader in thinking about new ways of working and new kinds of organizational structure, has, not surprisingly, created for himself a very attractive working environment in his home in Norfolk, UK.**

and invention on environmental – as well on many other – matters at each workplace. Peter Senge, director of MIT's Systems Thinking and Organizational Learning Program, emphasizes the growing importance of knowledge rather than data in business organizations when he talks about 'the learning organization'. He argues that a business must become more of an intellectual entity if it hopes to continue to make money and survive. In terms of the design of the office environment, Senge's arguments mean that space must be organized to promote discourse and maximize learning through providing the opportunities for much more face-to-face interaction.

Charles Handy, the British philosopher and futurist, maintains that 'discontinuous change' is an inevitable feature of modern life. This means totally new approaches to the design of work, organizations, and indeed the entire landscape of our working lives. He argues that change – which 'isn't what it used to be' – is affecting the lives of practically everyone in modern society, at home as well as at work. The sanctity of the continuous 40-year career within a secure organization is as outmoded as the certainties of conventional office architecture. In this scenario, the traditional incremental rewards of status or longevity — a larger desk, more individual space, more carpet, more enclosure – have no place or meaning. Instead, offices in which the users have more control must be designed to permit rapid change. Even more importantly, new timetables, new patterns of location, new boundaries between work and home are inevitable. The logic of the old city-centre business district, in which everyone obediently took their long-term place, no longer applies.

John Kotter, the Harvard Business School's expert on leadership, believes that most US companies are over-managed and under-led. For him, organizations need to combine strong leadership (defined, interestingly enough, as the ability to create a changing environment) and strong management to cope with complexity. The demands this makes on office architecture are plain – offices that accommodate strong managers coordinating diverse tactical choices within a changing business world, while continuing to insist upon an overall strategic direction of corporate achievement, are unlikely to be homogeneous or stereotypical. They are also unlikely to be static or dull for very long.

Edward Lawler, of the University of Southern California, dislikes the commonly used management term 'empowerment', but is an advocate of what he calls 'high-performance involvement'. Lawler advises companies to break themselves down into small units, and give employees much more say in what they do and how they do it so that they can enjoy the satisfaction of ownership and responsibility. The implication is that office design and office location will be prompted by highly opinionated, intelligent, dispersed, and changing users, leading to an increasing demand for smaller and less centralized offices. C. K. Prahalad and Gary Hamel, of the University of Michigan and the London Graduate Business School respectively, urge firms to focus their strategy around what they do best – the core competencies upon which their success depends – and to build on these and only on these. In this vision of the future the inevitable out-sourcing of non-core services such as real estate departments will lead to

less centralization and thus inevitably to greater consumer choice and hence diversity in office design. Gerald Ross, a change management consultant and founder of Change Lab International, maintains that the 'new molecular organization' will be built around markets rather than products or functions. The implication for the office planner is, once again, that there will be a need to find dynamic new ways to accommodate ever-changing organizations that continually have to respond to an increasingly unstable and unpredictable business environment. Old-fashioned, hierarchical, stable ways of laying out offices cannot easily cope with change let alone help with its management.

Shoshana Zuboff, author of *In the Age of the Smart Machine*, speaks of the need not to 'automate' but to 'informate', which means using smart machines to interact with smart people. She is currently studying how 'model companies' can use technology to revolutionize the nature of work. She feels that because everyone who is at all familiar with information technology knows how rapidly it erodes every convention it touches, there is absolutely no reason to have any confidence in the long-term stability of traditional patterns of office work or indeed, by implication, office accommodation. Everything office workers have taken for granted for decades about their working lives and their working environments is certain to be challenged, and almost certain to be changed. The conventions that determine office layout, pre-dating the punch card, have little relevance in a world of work that is now totally dependent upon information technology. Even less relevant are old-fashioned assumptions about office location, and the relationship between work and home.

There is nothing at all abstract in what these organizational ideas mean for the office. Each one, if taken literally in the very physical way in which architects are trained to think, has its own direct consequences for the redesign of the physical environment of work. The inevitable conclusion is that offices will become more saturated by information technology, more obviously places for meeting and interaction, less hierarchical, more diverse in style and structure and able to be changed more rapidly; they will tend to become smaller and be in less centralized, less predictable and more dispersed locations; above all, they will come under the increasing control of, and be more responsive to, ever-changing teams of intelligent and demanding end-users.

Information technology as the agent of change

Information technology is the principal agent of change in office work and in office design. Without distributed intelligence none of the changes in organizational theory described in the previous pages would make any sense. None of the seismic shifts that are taking place in organizational structure would have started. It was only fifteen years ago at the beginning of the 1980s, with the invention and popularization of the personal computer, that computers escaped from their own rooms into the general office. A decade later and they were everywhere, dragging their cables behind them. With mobile phones, cordless laptops, and modems, it has now become possible to say with total conviction that the office really is where you are. There is continuing acceleration in the rate of take-up of all aspects of information technology practically everywhere, and the strategic importance of information networks in the global economy has become very apparent.

The ORBIT (Office Buildings and Information Technology) studies, perhaps space-planners DEGW's most important contribution to office design, were carried out in the UK and the USA in the early 1980s. They were the first serious attempt to explore the ways in which the new technology would be likely to affect the design of office buildings, environmental services, and interiors. The initial priority seemed to be to cut through the chaos that the first wave of distributed intelligence had caused in the office – undisciplined cabling, concentrations of heat-producing machines straining air-conditioning systems not designed to cope with hot spots, electronic devices susceptible to glare and dust, problems with controlling the security of information within the office and between offices, unanticipated ergonomic crises caused by the prolonged use of keyboards and screens. Rules were quickly established for designing buildings with

Below **In the 1960s, when vast computer rooms were given the status of shrines, the man–machine interface was dominated by the equipment rather than by the people.**

sufficient permeability – both vertically and horizontally – to cope with cabling and cooling problems, with finely zoned air conditioning that could isolate and absorb the heat problems, with space-planning concepts that dealt with environmental and security problems in the parts of office floors where heavier machine use could be anticipated, and with interiors that would be safe and comfortable for workers using the new equipment. All the better British office buildings of the late 1980s were profoundly influenced by the ORBIT specifications, especially those specifically designed for the information-based industries clustered around Heathrow Airport and in the Thames Valley, and for the newly deregulated, international financial services in the City of London.

However, the ORBIT studies had another, more fundamental theme. It was recognized, even as early as 1982, that information technology would have more far-reaching implications: in the need to accommodate the expanding aspirations of new kinds of office workers – more highly paid and more demanding – not just for a better quality of life in the office, but for more personal control over their own environments.

This is a sociological issue. Information was obviously going to change people's working lives. The jobs of highly disciplined clerical cadres would be increasingly automated. New kinds of office worker would emerge. The demography of the office would change from the old hierarchical pyramids in which a handful of self-important managers controlled a vast subservient labour force, to more complex organizational structures weighted, if anything, toward a preponderance of

Above **The direct effects of information technology – cables, hot spots, and ergonomic and environmental problems – were highlighted in the 1980s in the ORBIT studies.**

Above **Information technology is helping to humanize the office by breaking down the barriers between formal and informal working. The mobile laptop and the mobile telephone are increasingly as much at home in a break area as the cup of coffee. Barclays Bank, Birmingham, UK. Architect: Sevil Peach Gence Associates**

Right **Increasing mobility and laptop technology can break all conventional office boundaries.**

many organizations would exploit the possibilities inherent in information technology to allow staff to enjoy a new freedom in relating home, work, and leisure, while at the same time being able to cut occupancy costs through time-sharing offices. Nor did many people expect wireless communications to become a practical alternative to cabling in some applications – with obvious additional space-planning advantages in breaking the tyranny of the one-to-one ratio between fixed telephones or power points and fixed workstations.

One of the most significant trends affecting office design in this period has been the tendency for companies to define, and concentrate on, their core business. Many large corporations have begun to dismantle peripheral service functions such as property and facilities management. The result, as Prahalad and Hamel predicted, has been, in both the UK and the USA, a drastic reduction of these services in-house and

professional and senior managerial staff. The ORBIT studies foresaw all this and anticipated changes not only in the design of the new environment in order to cope with the physical consequences of these changes, but also in the way that office buildings would be procured and managed.

What the ORBIT studies did not anticipate, however, was the extraordinary increase, from the mid-1990s, in the so-called virtuality in the office. Not many observers in the early 1980s foresaw, for example, the rapid way in which

the parallel growth of powerful out-sources capable of managing, among many other things, office property and facilities on an international scale. The existence of such companies and the need for their services to be professionally procured and managed by their corporate clients have caused a huge improvement in the management of office accommodation – particularly evident in the way that occupancy costs are measured and related to business performance.

This kind of innovation in the provision of service functions is one example of the revolution in office culture that is now taking place. Stimulated by the opportunities and challenges offered by information technology, all aspects of organizational operations are under scrutiny. In the quest for maximum efficiency and maximum effectiveness, a new office culture is emerging.

Left **Mobility within the office is becoming almost as important as mobility outside it. In the Sol offices in Helsinki, Finland, no one has an assigned workplace – each person picks up their mobile internal phone when they come into work, allowing them to choose the work setting that best suits their current needs.**

Below **Within the 'hot desking' system in IBM's offices in New York State, each desk is time-shared by ten mobile workers who use it by reservation. Mobile laptops can be plugged in and used in parallel with a more powerful, hard-wired system with a larger screen.**

Old and new office cultures

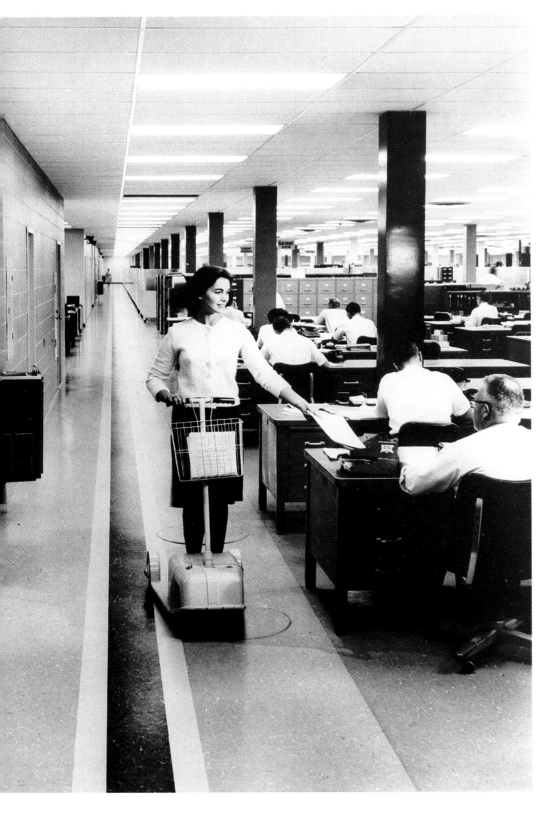

Above **In the old office, following the logic of the assembly line, work in the form of paper was delivered and collected by whatever devices came to hand.**

The physical differences between the old work culture and the new are striking. The physical features of the former tell us very clearly how work was assumed to be done, the level of technology, who was important and who was not, and, most importantly, the cultural values in the management of human resources that determined what was appropriate to make the work force, despite the low level of expectations, carry out such routine and often mindless tasks.

Conventional offices:

■ assume that clerical tasks are the staple of office work;

■ offer limited settings because the work is homogenous and undifferentiated;

■ accommodate one person per workstation, and then only from nine to five;

■ are excellent at expressing boundaries through physical barriers designed to keep functions and people apart;

■ are even better at reinforcing hierarchy through an apparatus of physical signs that indicate precisely how important – or unimportant – everyone is;

■ suit big groups – departments, businesses – rather than small;

■ say nothing about teamwork because little individual, let alone collective, initiative is necessary and very few resources are shared;

■ are unconvinced by the logic or potential of advanced forms of information technology.

The physical features and appearance of the new office will depend upon, and be stimulated by, powerful, integrated, interconnected, and ubiquitous information technology. The new office will express:

■ much greater attention to the economic importance of better use of time, taking advantage, for example, of office work as a parallel and serial, rather than a linear, process, leading to moves towards intensifying the use of space;

■ impatience with boundaries, because advanced organizations want more communication between departments and between specialisms in order to solve more complex problems more quickly;

■ little love of hierarchies, and even less of status, because, more often than not, what you can do is more important than who you are;

■ a tendency towards smaller, more rapidly changing organizational units, the result of stripping organizations back to

the core by 'out-sourcing' whatever activities are non-central and ruthlessly weeding out anything that is redundant;

■ the importance of group activity, reflected in the provision of work settings that are the focus for, and encourage, interactive, complex, open-ended teamwork – these are expected to be mostly open-plan and only partially cellular but with much more specialized support, often in the form of several different kinds of meeting and project areas;

■ the obsolescence of clerks and clerical ways because routine clerical tasks have been automated or exported off-site, away from the creative teams and decision-makers;

■ total confidence in the creative use of information technology;

■ a new flexibility, with an ever-wider range of work settings in response to choices in the timing of work and in the ways in which it is carried out.

Above **While much conventional office work is being challenged and changed by information technology, traditional clerical patterns of working still persist and must be properly accommodated. Kirin Brewery offices, Tokyo. Architect: Shin Takamatsu.**

Opposite ***A critical feature of the new office is teamwork – people are working together more intensely in order to tackle more complex problems with more powerful and open-ended technology. As the environment of the office becomes less solitary and more plural, so the balance between space given over to individual workstations and to group activities is shifting rapidly. A project group working around a table in the Chiat/Day offices in Venice, California. Architect: Frank Gehry.***

Many office organizations are already working in unconventional and very different ways. Some, just by doing what seems to them in their new circumstances to be sensible, are already far ahead of many designers in their thinking about what the new kind of office should be like. They are developing different and higher expectations involving employees' control of time and place, and the quality of their working environments and lifestyles.

The chart below summarizes the ways in which such organizations are changing how and where they work, how they use information technology, how they are using space over time in new ways, and what the implications are for the design of office layouts.

A variety of office layouts – as well as ways of owning or sharing space – is implied by these fundamental shifts in the shape and patterns of work. It would be a grave mistake to assume that the conventional office, which fails not least because it is attempting to solve all organizational problems with a single solution, should be replaced by a similarly singular stereotype. To anyone who recognizes the size and complexity of the emerging world of work it is clear that not all organizations are likely to use space in the same way. The reverse is more likely to be true. Nor is the rate of take-up of new forms of space-use likely to be modelled on the past.

Right ***The contrast between the assumptions that underpinned the conventional office and the expectations that are creating new office environments is very marked.***

	Conventional office assumptions	**New ways of working**
Patterns of work	Routine processes Individual tasks Isolated work	Creative knowledge work Groups, teams, projects Interactive work
Patterns of occupancy of space over time	Central office locations in which staff are assumed to occupy individually 'owned' workstations on a full-time basis, typically over the course of the 9–5 day. The office assumes one desk per person; provides a hierarchy (planned or enclosed); and is occupied typically at levels at least 30% below full capacity.	Distributed set of work locations (which may be nomadic, mobile, in the office or at home) linked by networks of communication in which autonomous individuals work in project teams. Daily timetable is extended and irregular. Multifunctional work settings are occupied on an as-needed basis. Daily occupancy of space near to capacity.
Type of space layout, furniture systems, and use of space and buildings	Hierarchy of space and furniture related to status. Individual allocation of space predominates over interactive meeting spaces.	Multiple shared group work and individual task-based settings. Setting, layout and furniture of the office geared to work process and its tasks.
Use of information technology	Technology used for routine data-processing, terminals in fixed positions served by mainframes.	Focus on mobility of IT equipment used in a wide variety of settings. Technology used to support creative knowledge work, both individual and group. File servers serve a variety of IT tools, including PCs and laptops, and shared specialized equipment.

Some companies, or parts of companies, will rush to innovate; others will have legitimate reasons to move more slowly towards adopting new ways of working and new ways of accommodating themselves. Timing, as in all aspects of management, is everything.

Left **Mobility and flexibility within the office is becoming more important. Circulation used to be minimized to save rent. Now the value of places where people can come into contact, more or less serendipitously, is being realized. It is also being recognized that providing pleasant, convenient surroundings, equipped so that part-time or more itinerant workers can temporarily touch down and plug in with ease, can be more important than allocating each person a particular workstation. Offices for Tinderbox, a post-production film company in London, where the work force come and go at all hours. Architect: Orange.**

The design logic of the new office

The new kinds of offices are likely to be perceived by management to be closely related to increasing the potential for organizational survival. The diagram displayed opposite explains why. It demonstrates the direct and dynamic relationship between client priorities and broad types of office layout. It explains why contemporary managerial thinking should be leading not only to richer and more diverse office layouts, but also to a particular sequence in which new kinds of layout are likely to be adopted.

Interaction and autonomy

The diagram opposite is based upon two organizational variables: interaction and autonomy. Taken together, these throw light on the ways in which office layouts are likely to differ and to change, and also explain the dynamics of change in office design. Since most companies differ within themselves the diagram can also be used as a means of measuring the state of all the parts of any complex organization at any given moment – and also of predicting how the proportions of different kinds of office-use are likely to change over time.

Interaction is the personal, face-to-face contact that is necessary to carry out office tasks. As the amount of interaction increases, there is more pressure to accommodate and support such encounters. Even more pressure is exerted as the quality – the intellectual content and the significance – of interaction increases. Forms of interaction vary as the complexity, urgency, and importance of the tasks being carried out increase, so settings for interaction can range from the most informal to the most formal meetings and from the most casual to the most structured encounters. Interactions that are not face-to-face, i.e. are via the computer, telephone, or other virtual media, are not directly significant, although they are likely to supplement, or become a substitute for, face-to-face interaction both now and in the future.

Interaction outside the organization is also relevant because it has a direct impact on occupancy: heavy interaction with clients and colleagues outside the office is often connected with intermittent space occupancy.

Autonomy is the degree of control, responsibility, and discretion each office worker has over the content, method, location, and tools of the work process. The more autonomy office workers enjoy, the more they are likely to want to control their own working environments, singly and collectively, and the more discretion they are likely to want to exercise over the kind and quality of their surroundings in their places of work.

Interaction and autonomy are strongly correlated with many aspects of office design because they affect workers' expectations about the layout, the work settings – the heights of the space-dividing elements, for example – and their control over environmental services and lighting.

Four types of office work

The dominant organizational mode of the conventional office was 'the office as factory' – a place where individuals processed work, under supervision, at their own workstations. Such work is low in interaction – apart from social chatter – as well as low in the autonomy given to individual office workers. In the USA and the UK a great deal of basic clerical work has either been automated out of existence or been exported to economies where it can be carried out more cheaply. Hence the arrow pointing downwards to indicate that such work is already sifting like sand out of the box. Higher-level office activities of this type are being transmuted – re-engineered – into more intellectually demanding activity where working together and teamwork are all important. In such 'group process' work, interaction increases while individual autonomy remains relatively low. Another persistent, and respectable, form of office work – found, for example, in the legal profession and in research institutes – uses the office as a place primarily for 'concentrated study'. In such offices autonomy is high and interaction low. It is expected, as information technology changes work, that many examples of the offices now identified as being for 'group processes' and 'concentrated study' will tend to converge into what has been called the 'transactional' office where, through deft management of time and space, both interaction and autonomy will be maximized. Out of the top right-hand corner of the diagram is escaping, like steam, the growing amount of office work that is becoming virtual, more or less independent of space and even time.

Hives, cells, dens, and clubs

The diagram identifies four major organizational types and, as a shorthand way of capturing the distinct work patterns and distinctive design features of each, has characterized them as hive, cell, den, and club. 'Hive' because such offices can be compared to beehives occupied by busy worker bees; 'cell' because these recall the monks' cloister or the venerable, highly cellular, offices of the Inns of Court in London;

Below **The workplace forum: the ever-increasing power of technology will eventually lead to the elimination of Individual Processes – unless they are transformed into Group Processes. As Information Technology enhances group competence, so Group Processes will tend towards Transactional Knowledge. Concentrated Study also tends towards Transactional Knowledge, or even home working, while Transactional Knowledge places emphasis on better relations with clients and making full use of all available facilities. The diagram identifies four major organizational types: HIVES, CELLS, DENS, and CLUBS. They are a shorthand way of describing affinities between work patterns, the use of space, and the demands likely to be made by these groups on environmental services.**

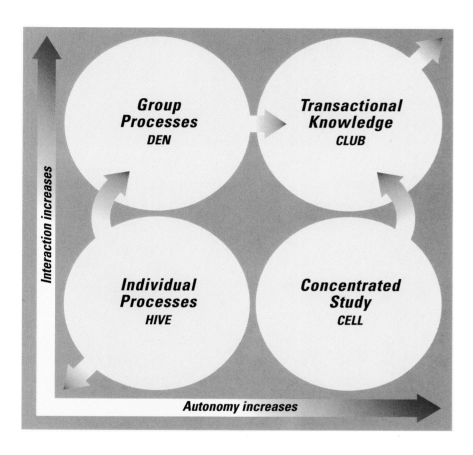

'den' because these are busy and interactive places where it is easy to work informally in teams; 'club' because one of the nearest models to the new transactional office, despite its unfortunate and outmoded élitist overtones, is the old-fashioned gentlemen's club (see page 18). This categorization is, of course, only a convenient simplification. In the real world any organization of any size or complexity is likely to be characterized by a shifting mixture of all four. The terms hive, cell, den, and club can refer either to a whole organization occupying a whole building or to part of an organization occupying a floor or even part of a floor. In most companies there will be found combinations of these work patterns. For example, many have 'back office' staff engaged in data-entry or routine administrative functions – typically accommodated in hives,

or in cheaper office accommodation out of town – while other groups within the same organization are dens or clubs and are more likely to be located in a headquarters office near the city centre. Also, while there are clearly many affinities between certain sectors of work and the types of office – between advertising and dens, for example – the limits of the typology must be recognized since, even within the same professions, there may be sufficient differences in workstyle to preclude straightforward associations between particular sectors and the individual types defined here.

The hive

Hives are characterized by individual, routine-process work with low levels of interaction and low autonomy. Hive office workers sit continuously at simple workstations for long

periods of time on a regular nine-to-five schedule. Variants of hive offices include 24-hour shift working. Workplace settings are typically uniform, open-plan, screened, and impersonal. Typical organizations or work groups include telesales, data-entry or processing, routine banking, financial and administrative operations, and basic information services.

Above right **The origins of the hive office are in industry, where routine, often repetitious tasks were performed under supervision. British Industries – Cotton** *by Frederick Cayley Robinson.*

Right **New kinds of hive office are being created as organizations respond to the growing demand for instant information that has been stimulated by the availability of increasingly powerful data bases. The quasi-industrial environment of this new and intelligently designed IBM office in New York State reinforces the origins of the hive.**

The cell

Cell offices accommodate individual, concentrated work with little interaction. Highly autonomous people occupy them in an intermittent, irregular pattern with extended working days – and often work elsewhere some of the time (possibly at home, at a client's office, or on the road). Each person typically occupies either an enclosed cell or a highly screened workstation in a more open-plan office. Each individual work place must be designed to provide for a complex variety of tasks. The autonomous pattern of work, implying sporadic and irregular occupancy, means that the potential exists for such work settings to be shared. Typical occupiers of cellular offices include accountants, lawyers, management and employment consultants, and computer scientists.

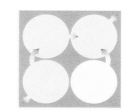

Above left **The perfect environment for the solitary scholar is one in which he has total control of his physical as well as his intellectual environment. St Jerome in his Study by Antonello da Messina.**

Left **The same tradition continues today. In a London law firm, enclosed offices are designed to allow the powerful, self-directed individual as much potential for concentrated work as possible, as well as to protect adjacent colleagues from disturbance. Interior by Baker Nevile Design.**

The den

Den offices are associated with group work, typically highly interactive but not necessarily highly autonomous. Den spaces are designed for group working and often provide a

range of several simple settings, usually arranged in an open-plan office or in group rooms. While the settings are normally designed on the assumption that individual office workers occupy their 'own' desks, such groups also like to have access to local ancillary space for meetings and project work, and for shared equipment such as printers and copiers and other special technical facilities. Tasks are often short-term and intense. Sometimes they are more long-term; and they always involve much team effort. Typical work requiring dens includes design, insurance processing, some media work, particularly radio and television, and advertising.

Above right **Some tasks are inherently collaborative. They are based upon teamwork and have to be carried out with shared resources in a shared environment. The Alchemist's Workshop by Giovanni Stradano.**

Right **The team preparing and presenting continuous programmes of television news at London's ITN offices work in a typical example of a contemporary den. There must be no discontinuity between the newscasters and the people who support them. Architect: Foster & Partners.**

The club

Club organizations are for knowledge work, i.e. for office work that transcends data-handling because it can only be done through exercising considerable judgment and intelligence.

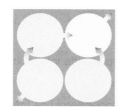

Typically, work in such organizations is both highly autonomous and highly interactive. The pattern of occupancy tends to be intermittent over an extended working day. A wide variety of time-shared task-based settings serve both concentrated individual and group interactive work. Individuals and teams occupy space on an 'as-needed' basis, moving around it to take advantage of a wide range of facilities. The ratio of sharing depends on the precise content of the work activity and the mix of in-house versus out-of-office working, possibly combining tele-working, home-working, and working at client and other locations. Typical organizations include creative firms

such as advertising and media companies, information technology companies, and many management consultancies. What such organizations have in common are highly intellectual staff, open-ended problem-solving, and, above all, constant access to a vast array of shared knowledge.

Above right **The club is essentially an ingenious early nineteenth-century device to allow the kind of people who are now called networkers to share as supportive an environment as possible. It originated in the more ad hoc associations formed in the coffee houses of large cities. Vienna Coffee House *by Ferdinand Wust.***

Left **A late twentieth-century office version of a club allows people to select the work settings they want, when they want them. Chiat/Day, Venice, California. Architect: Frank Gehry.**

Patterns of work and office space

Each of the work patterns characteristic of the four different types of organization implies its own and particular way of using space and furniture. To get the most out of any organization, different kinds of office layouts must be designed to support these patterns. The chart below is intended as a key to the design decisions that follow from this logic. Thus, while hives need relatively simple workstations, cells need richer individual work settings; dens require several relatively simple settings and clubs need many rich and complex ones.

Layouts that best support the different patterns of work are also likely to be used in characteristically different ways over time: more interactive and more highly autonomous work patterns are more likely to lead to time-sharing space – what is often called 'space use intensification' – because occupancy is intermittent or irregular.

Patterns of work, space occupancy, office layout and use of information technology for each of the four organizational types may be summarized as shown in the chart.

	Hive	**Cell**	**Den**	**Club**
Pattern of work	Work broken down into smallest components and carried out by staff who are given precise instructions and little discretion.	High-level work carried out by talented independent individuals (isolated knowledge work).	Project or other group work of a straightforward kind needing a changing balance of different, interdependent skills.	High-level work carried out by talented independent individuals who need to work both collaboratively and individually: work process constantly being redesigned.
Occupancy of space over time, capacity for sharing space over time	Conventional 9–5, but tending towards shift work. Routine timetable, low interaction, and full-time occupancy of space offer little scope for shared space use except for 24-hour shift work.	Increasingly ragged and variable, more extended working days, depending on individual arrangements. If occupancy of space is low, opportunities exist for shared individual settings (enclosed or open).	Conventional 9–5, but becoming more varied by subgroup activities. Opportunity for sharing space over time increases since interactive staff more likely to be away from desks or out of building.	Complex and dependent on what needs to be done and on individual arrangements, but expect high-occupancy pattern of use over extended periods of time. Highly intermittent pattern of occupancy supports shared use of task settings.
Type of space layout	Open, ganged (4 or 6 pack), minimal partitions, maximal filing. Imposed simple space standards.	Cellular enclosed offices or individually used open workstations with high screening or partitions.	Group space or group rooms, medium filing. Complex and continuous spaces incorporating meeting spaces and work spaces.	Diverse, complex and manipulable range of settings based on wide variety of tasks.
Use of IT	Simple dumb terminals or networked PCs.	Variety of individual PCs on networks and widespread use of laptops.	PCs and some shared specialized group equipment.	Variety of individual PCs on networks and widespread use of laptops.

An inevitable direction of development?

The design of the material office and the direction of organizational change are intimately bound together, and must be closely correlated to achieve business success – not to mention business survival.

The first steps in thinking about how this can be done are obvious. Think about organizational structure, work processes, and physical consequences in an integrated, systematic way. The diagrams on the right show two stages in the process of change, from the present-day situation in which most offices are predominantly hives towards a new distribution of office space in which there will be a far higher proportion of cells, dens and clubs. This process involves shifts in the total office population, from lower to higher levels of interaction and from lower to higher levels of autonomy for workers. As this happens, the relationship between the workstyles will change, from the old clerical pattern (hive) in the bottom left-hand quadrant of the top diagram, to more group work (den) or more concentrated individual work (cell). Ultimately, as the diagrams show, both of these more complex forms of workstyles are likely to combine in the most communicative and collaborative work processes and environments (club).

A more practical way of using this form of analysis for a particular project is to identify the relative proportions of organizational types found within one company or location, and then to think through the implications of future change on the relative importance of each within that organization. As the proportions of each of the four types of work change, so will the demand for the different kinds of office layout. In this way, future demand can be anticipated and measured and provision made for the inevitable transition from one mix of office space to another. This technique makes possible systematic planning to accommodate change and is the basis for 'future proofing' office buildings.

In this way business planners can explore, and even determine, appropriate directions for change at the same time as the designers of the physical working environment are stimulated to investigate wider ranges of design solutions. In other words office design and strategic business planning can be integrated to the benefit of both. In this way it is also possible to predict the overall shape of the demand for office space in cities of different economic circumstances.

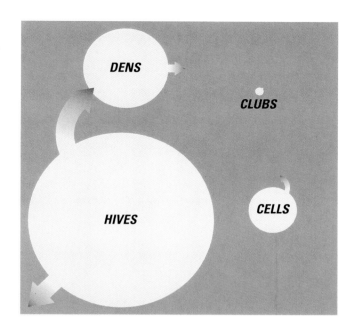

Left **The likely proportion of the four types of office towards the end of the 1990s.**

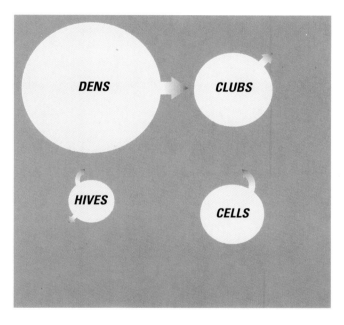

Left **A prediction of how the proportion of the four types of office might change.**

Above **No one organization can be categorized as being completely a Hive, Cell, Den or Club. Most are combinations. Similarly the sum of all offices at any one time must consist of a proportion of all four types. As time goes on this proportion is likely to change. For example, if the vast majority of offices today are Hives, with some Cells and Dens but few Clubs, it is expected that, over the coming years, the proportion of Hives will have significantly diminished in favour of a higher proportion of Cells, even more Dens and a huge increase in Clubs.**

new
directions

New ideas, stimulated by new thinking about the way in which work is done, are reshaping the office environment. Innovation is happening at every scale. New light fittings, such as these ceiling-mounted, adjustable Snakelights that use powerful halogen bulbs, are making possible new kinds of micro environment at the workstation. At the macro scale of building, the traditional relationship between inside and outside is being challenged. In the CLM/BBDO building in Paris the roof above the internal atrium was designed by the architect Jean Nouvel to open when required.

Invention in office design is not happening randomly. Innovations in the design of office furniture, in the ways that heating, lighting, air conditioning, power, and information are distributed in office buildings, and in the configuration, construction, and cladding of the buildings themselves, are all responses, of one kind or another, to new ways of working. These physical elements – the hardware – of office design may be thought to be all-important, but what office buildings actually look like and feel like to the occupiers also has a lot to do with the way in which they are managed. To use an analogy from the world of computers, the software – which in the office takes the form of facilities management – is as important as the hardware of the building itself. This is a profound change for both clients and architects. So the many new ideas in facilities management, in real estate practice and in office location are as critical to the success of an office as the design of any piece of hardware.

The character of the modern office building – certainly one of the largest and, in some respects, one of the most complex of constructed artefacts – can be seen in terms of a dynamic relationship between scale and time and the way in which it is managed. Each of these three elements needs to be understood for the full significance of new developments in office design to be realized. The issue of scale addresses the vast difference between the small and relatively trivial nature of many of the physical components that make up the office interior and the vast, aggregated bulk of many office buildings as a whole. Time is about exploring the difference between the longevity of fixed elements of the building, such as its structure and skin, and the transient nature of many others, such as partitions, furniture, and light fittings. Awareness of how office buildings are managed is critical because even the most sophisticated and superb office environments are useless unless they can be made to work properly at all scales and through time. The importance of managing space through time – the software of office design – is often dangerously underestimated. Hardware – architecture – is where all the status has been in design circles, the route into the magazines, and, eventually, the history books. But the days of the architect as the superhero – or even as the *uomo universale* – of office design are numbered. Increasingly, it is the demands being made by management systems – the software – that are setting the pace for innovation in the hardware of office layout, interior design, environmental services, and architecture.

The systematic coordination of the hardware and software is, of course, essential if office design is to be both

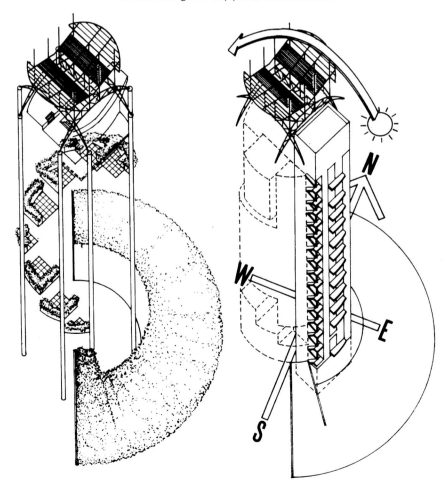

telecommunication companies thought that they could secure new markets by treating each office building as a small utility. The term was soon taken to mean something a little different and, particularly in Japan, usually referred to a building that was as full as possible of integrated electronic technology that controlled lighting, heating, ventilation, elevators, security, and, it seemed, anything else that moved. A somewhat wider view now prevails, seeing building 'intelligence' as the successful integration of *building management*, i.e. fully utilizing the building's physical facilities on a day-to-day basis; *space management*, i.e. managing the use of a building's internal spaces to accommodate change and minimize occupation costs; and *business management*, i.e. exploiting the building to aid the occupier's core business activities, partly through facilitating the storage, processing, and transmission of business information but also through using architecture in its more subtle but no less powerful forms to stimulate interaction, to

*Left **The Menara Mesiniaga Building in Kuala Lumpur, by Hamsah and Yeang, is one of the most 'intelligent' buildings in Malaysia. Its skin is designed to help the building cope with the fierce sunlight of the tropical climate instead of consuming energy to batter nature into submission from behind hermetic façades. In order to do this, the architect Ken Yeang has woven together orientation, sun screens, planting, and office planning – as his sketches (opposite) show. The gardens, on several different floors, also act as a buffer, softening the transition from outside to inside.***

efficient and effective. And it is this amalgamation that underlies the concept of the so-called 'intelligent building'. This term originated in North America in the early 1980s when, after the deregulation of the North American telephone system, developers thought they could add value to property by including one or other of the newly deregulated telecommunication systems as part of the real estate package, while in turn, the enhance the sense of overall cooperation, and to broadcast the right messages to staff and to the outside world. In other words, an 'intelligent building' is one in which architecture and building services are driven as hard as possible to pull people as well as information technology together into one manageable whole to achieve the shared goal of better business performance.

Scale in office design

Design is a vital issue at all scales, from furniture, floor layouts, and environmental systems such as air conditioning, to entire office buildings, and even business or industrial parks and whole city blocks – everything from building components to major segments of the urban scene. The specialisms and skills that are necessary to get office accommodation right at every level range from those of the product designers responsible for luminaires and furniture design, to those of the architects whose job it is to conceive the building as a whole in its setting. There must, of course, be collaboration between them all if any project is to be successfully achieved. At yet another level, city planners play an essential part. The planning and construction of office buildings and quarters, like London's Canary Wharf or Broadgate, or New York's World Trade Center, or Singapore's superbly successful new business environment, are always linked to major issues of politics and economic policy.

The sequence of photographs on these pages of the Hong Kong and Shanghai Bank, seen first as part of the cityscape from across Hong Kong harbour, then as an individual building, then as an agglomeration of structure and services, and then closing in on the details of the interior

spaces shows how enormous, and yet how meticulously detailed this famous building really is. All office buildings are in principle – if not always in quality of execution – the same.

The complexity of each of them is echoed by the varied and changing nature of its users. No organization, no single business relates exactly to a single unit of space for very long. Such neatness is contrary to the messiness and fluidity of organizational life. As boundaries become more permeable and less formal between smaller and larger organizations, between core activities and whatever parts of the business may be out-sourced, between service organizations and those that are serviced, between the networkers and the network, so the need for flexibility increases. Examining both the offices and office organizations of today, we can see that the process of dissolution is accelerating. What matters is to understand, and to manage, an entirely new business reality. Building types, lease structures, rental arrangements, and zoning ordinances that worked in the past are likely to be inhibiting today and suffocating tomorrow – to people, working groups, and businesses.

Office buildings are designed to work on every scale. On the exterior they must relate sympathetically to the urban fabric, as well as being independent and self-sufficient structures. In the interior they must express the values of the organization as a whole, but also work in every last detail such as servicing outlets and seating. The Hong Kong and Shanghai Bank, Hong Kong. Architect: Foster and Partners.

Time in office design

Above **Office interiors, like stage settings, have their own very particular life cycle. This storage system, demountable but domestic, shows how relatively cheap and short-life components can transform the entire feeling of an office interior. Offices, designed for themselves, by Designers Guild, London.**

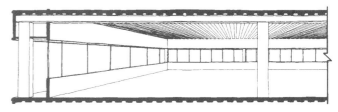

❶ *The building shell. Lifespan: 50–75 years. Structure, cladding (skin).*

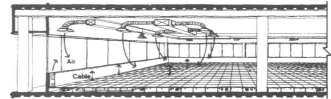

❷ *Services. Lifespan: 15 years. Heat, ventilation, light, power.*

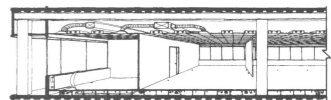

❸ *Scenery. Lifespan: 5 years. Fixed interior elements – ceilings, partitions, finishes, infomation technology equipment.*

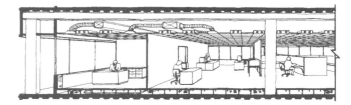

❹ *Settings. Day-to-day rearrangement. Office furnishings.*

Just as the differences in scale must be fully recognized, so the different life-spans of various office components must be understood if business is going to achieve both the long-term and the shorter-term flexibility it would like office buildings to deliver. While big office buildings may look from the outside as if they are meant to last for ever, many aspects of the interior, and even these days of the exterior, are being changed all the time. The contrast between the apparently timeless exterior of the Seagram Building and the seething transience of the interior with its constant turnover of diverse tenants, for example, has already been highlighted in Chapter 1. It is essential that the time cycles are allowed to coexist more or less independently. To assume that everything should last for the same length of time is absurd; to attempt to use only short-term elements to solve long-term problems is inherently wasteful; to have to dismantle long-term structures to solve short-term problems is ridiculously expensive.

The appearance of a building – its construction and fit-out, for example – has a different lifespan from its operation – its environmental services, for instance. Typical lifespans are shown in the diagrams above. Stewart Brand, the inventor of *The Whole Earth Catalog*, in his recent book *How Buildings Learn* has elaborated this idea further and distinguishes between 'site, structure, skin, services, space plan and stuff.' The last is close to what we mean by 'settings' – the highly mobile assemblages of 'chairs, desks, phones, pictures, lamps, ...; all the things that twitch around daily to monthly' that make up so much of the ordinary office worker's experience of the working environment. Brand also draws attention to the opposite end of the permanence scale – the site – which is the only real fixed element in all this temporal complexity because, whatever may happen on or above it,

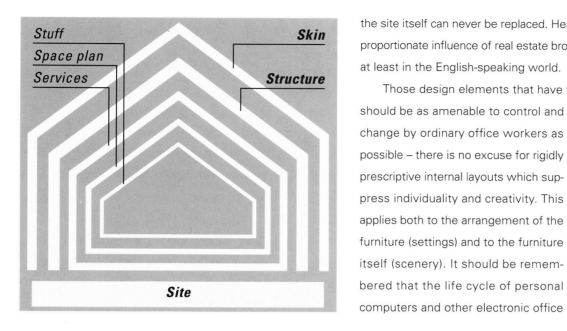

the site itself can never be replaced. Hence, perhaps, the disproportionate influence of real estate brokers on office design, at least in the English-speaking world.

Those design elements that have the shortest lifespan should be as amenable to control and change by ordinary office workers as possible – there is no excuse for rigidly prescriptive internal layouts which suppress individuality and creativity. This applies both to the arrangement of the furniture (settings) and to the furniture itself (scenery). It should be remembered that the life cycle of personal computers and other electronic office

Left **This diagram is based on Stewart Brand's reformulation of the idea of the parallel and independent coexistence of different lifespans in the same building.**

Below **Semi-opaque, easily demountable screens separate work groups without diminishing the feeling of light and space. Offices for Gollifer Associates, London. Architect: Morgan Lovell.**

Above **Ducts and cabling have deliberately been left exposed here to show the importance of the infrastructure of service distribution. Café at Sony's offices, London. Architect: Harper McKay.**

Right **In this conversion, light has been brought into the centre of the office by breaking through the original structure. Greenalls Brewery offices, Warrington, UK. Architect: ORMS.**

healthier environment at the workplace may be abbreviating time cycles even further. The balance of power between employers and employees is changing inexorably everywhere, even in the USA, and the needs of users can no longer be ignored or taken for granted.

The longest-term elements of office design are structural – columns, beams, foundations, roofs, and walls – which means that they are very hard to shift or redesign. They affect the positioning of all other constructional elements, so must be designed to allow for as many servicing and layout options as possible in the future. There is, as Brand has pointed out,

devices is even shorter than that of furniture. Such equipment is always obsolescent and generally replaced within three years.

The most important elements of environmental services such as elevators and air conditioning are usually expected to last about fifteen years. Major refits of office buildings are now very common, and it is generally the upgrading of environmental services that attracts the greater part of the budget. Rising user expectations of a better and a tendency to replace the cladding of outer walls, at increasingly frequent intervals. This is often done for environmental reasons, to deal with solar gain or to improve insulation, for example, but also for fashion – to spruce up office buildings to attract new tenants.

One of Stewart Brand's most important contributions is to question who is actually designing buildings – the original architect or the generations of users who always attempt to modify, add to, and reshape what they have inherited. Design is already a more popular and collaborative activity than many architects would like to admit. Of all the money spent on an

office over its lifespan, by far the greater part is spent on what are often, but wrongly, considered to be the more trivial features of interior design. In comparison with this cumulative expenditure on 'scenery', the one-time cost of the shell is nugatory. By this financial logic architecture should be truly regarded as a minor branch of interior design.

Above **The skin of a building can be a critical environmental filter. Oversailing roofs and sun screens protect the Institute for Child Health, London, from the morning sun. Architect: ORMS.**

The agenda for innovation

The most likely sequence of technical innovation in office design is presented in diagrammatic form on the right. It is, of course, directly related to the lifespans of the elements involved. From the redesign of desks to the restructuring of cities, from rethinking the office timetable to redefining what office location means, these new ideas will shape the whole landscape and timetable of life in the twenty-first century to accommodate not only changing office tasks but also ever more complex networks of interconnected activities.

The first level of innovation is the easiest and quickest to put in place: in facilities management. The second is the design of office furniture and of layouts that can be relatively easily reconfigured to anticipate emerging requirements. This is an area of rapid change: the lead time for new products can be as short as two years. The redesign and installation of new office environmental systems, and of building management systems are longer-term, more technical tasks. Innovative ideas that are emerging for these will affect the design of the heavier and harder-to-shift aspects of office interior design – such scenery elements as ceilings, access floors, partitions. New kinds of skin and shell, which determine the shape of buildings as well as their external experience, take a long time to finance, procure, and construct, however agile the developer or corporate-building owner. The strategic design decisions that must be made about office location, and urban planning as well as about transportation and other kinds of urban infrastructure, are the most time-consuming of all. But making the right decisions is vital if we are to sustain the quality of our lives in our cities and protect our countryside.

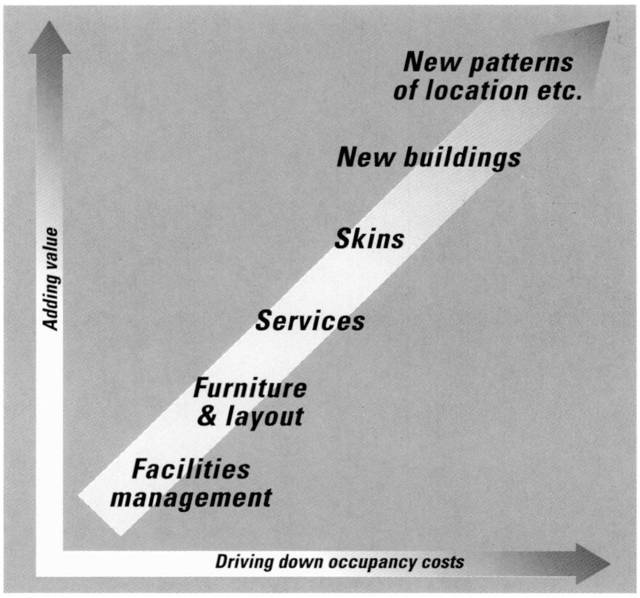

In the UK, even at the height of the last office building boom in the 1980s the annual addition of new buildings to the total office stock never rose above 2 to 3 per cent. Of course, far quicker rates of development are occurring in the rapidly developing cities of the tiger economies of the Pacific Rim such as Seoul, Shanghai, and Singapore. Nevertheless, whatever the rate of development, it would be practically impossible to renew all the office accommodation in a great city in less than twenty years. In the case of older, more mature city fabrics, the period will be much longer. What this perspective of renewal reveals is that, worldwide, the total programme that would be needed to build suitable new buildings or renovate older ones to accommodate new ways of working is both colossal and very long term. Meanwhile, change is badly needed in the detailed arrangements of office interiors by many hard-pressed and rapidly changing organizations – it needs to happen not next century nor next year, not tomorrow but today.

The inventory of some of the most interesting innovations in the field of office design that appears on the following pages acknowledges the importance of varying scales and time cycles, and ensures that hardware and software are given equal attention.

Right **The diagram shows how the dual need to drive down costs (efficiency) and to add value (effectiveness) can be used to establish the agenda not only for redesigning the office but also for rethinking the processes by which office buildings are procured and managed. The vector, reconciling the drive to efficiency and the drive to effectiveness, is used to show the sequence in which changes could be put into effect. Some of the innovations are in the design of the hardware of office design – physical features such as new kinds of environmental system. Others are innovations in software – in the way buildings are managed.**

The diagram can be also be related to the total stock of office space everywhere. When the vector reaches the top right-hand corner, in, say, 2020, an entirely new landscape of the working environment of the twenty-first century will have been created.

Opposite **One-third of the offices in the City of London were rebuilt or radically refurbished in the 1980s in order to accommodate new high-tech needs. This external atrium heightens the contrast between a late twentieth-century building and the surrounding urban fabric representing centuries of accumulated buildings. Alban Gate, London. Architect: Terry Farrell.**

New patterns
of location etc.

New buildings

Skins

Services

Furniture
& layout

Facilities
management

Adding value

Driving down occupancy costs

Innovations in facilities management

Facilities management techniques and procedures have developed tremendously in the last decade. The results include far better understanding of costs in use, better reporting procedures, better monitoring procedures, and, in a few exceptional cases, development of the practice of post-occupancy evaluation, i.e. feeding the experience of buildings in use into the specification of new, more efficient and more effective office accommodation. Facilities management is a dynamic discipline: innovations are intended to give both users and organizations more choice. Of course, not all the ideas that are being developed are so benign. Some are downright retrogressive, even by Taylorist standards. Facilities managers, like architects, are sometimes tempted to deliver what they find easy to deliver – rather than what the clients or users really want. An example is the so-called 'universal plan', which is the imposition of totally standardized workplaces in standardized layouts. The objective is to accommodate change by driving out layout options, a contradiction if there ever was one. Happily, not all developments in facilities management are quite so dumb. Innovations include:

Above and opposite **Skilful facilities management can release the potential of adaptive architecture. Intelligent effort is needed, however, to make best use of the sliding walls lining the atrium, and of the shifting walls and mobile furniture that allow smaller spaces designed for meetings to be used in several different ways. PowerGen's offices at Coventry, UK. Architect: Bennetts Associates.**

■ Improved computer-aided facilities management (CAFM) procedures that allow continuous monitoring of how sensibly and economically office space is being used and occupied. What the computer allows is not just access to large amounts of organizational and spatial data but also a ready means of communicating with users because the visual outputs of data – as well as of plans – are easy to understand. An example is the methods developed by Kreon Cyros, at the Massachusetts Institute of Technology, to manage the stock of office, laboratory and teaching space occupied by that educational institution.

■ Bar coding and other techniques to improve control of inventories of furniture and equipment. Exactly the same techniques that control stock in warehouses and supermarkets can be used in the office to relate the resources of equipment, space, and information technology to changing organizational requirements. As with CAFM, the chief advantage of these is that they allow management to anticipate, and respond more quickly to, emerging user demands – what is good for the user is good for the organization.

■ More precise ways of calculating and reporting the true costs of occupancy to user departments so that they can quickly relate the financial consequences of space-use options to their own overall business plans.

bewildering suddenness. Space-use intensification makes it possible to take a more considered, more statistical approach to the planning of buildings and floor-plates.

■ Computerized simulation to help ordinary office users visualize and appreciate what office layouts and interiors will look like.

■ Better techniques to make office space requirements more popularly acceptable and thus more accurate through involving large numbers of users in creative discussions about better ways of working. People who are involved in creating a better future are much more likely to want to make it work. 'Workplace Envisioning' is the prime example of this. Developed by space planners DEGW in collaboration with furniture manufacturers Steelcase, it involves computer-aided workshops that allow management and staff to work out priorities for organizational change while exploring the spatial and financial implications of these changes.

■ New methods of measuring user requirements, and relating business performance to design; these are described more fully in Chapter 5.

■ New kinds of relationships with suppliers, for example, furniture manufacturers, to permit the leasing of equipment. This simultaneously removes a whole category of non-core capital investment from the corporate balance sheet and potentially improves the quality of maintenance, and of forward-planning for replacement equipment. The same technique is being applied on a grander scale to the leasing of office accommodation and office services to deal with peaks and troughs in demand for office space, so raising facilities management to the level of a long-term business strategy.

■ The abandonment of old-fashioned, status-based allocation of office space in favour of more efficient space use. Andersen Worldwide, for example, has formulated its own global real estate management guidelines (GREMS) to help manage as thriftily as possible its office space at 400 locations. Occupancy costs as well as fee incomes vary widely from place to place. Average occupancy costs per person in each location are related to the income generated by the average fee earner. This is one of the first times that expenditure on property has been routinely related to financial returns on an international, company-wide basis.

■ The beginning of the realization that time-shared workstations, where practicable, not only save space but also remove the necessity of calculating space requirements in relation to constantly fluctuating head counts. Because there is no longer an immutable one-to-one ratio between people and workplaces, space planning is now far less at the mercy of the changes in head count that occur all too often with

Below **The touch-down desks, trolleys, and other paraphernalia needed to support new, more flexible ways of working need careful managing. Barclays Bank, Birmingham, UK. Architect: Sevil Peach Gence Associates.**

Innovations in furniture design and layout

Office work is generally becoming more mobile, more complex, and more plural. And yet there is often the need for some concentrated, individual work in the same place. This has led to one of the eternal conflicts in office design: the need to accommodate communication and interaction as well as individual work. Trying to resolve this has stimulated much new thinking. Innovations include:

Below left **New office furniture has to accommodate more group activities, increasingly obtrusive information technology, and a business environment dependent on the tools of teaching and communication. A custom-made table for Seagrams, in the Ark Building, London.**

Below right **Kyo reconfigurable work surfaces, servicing elements, space dividers, and mobile storage units add up to being one of the most thorough attempts so far to design office furniture that is capable of responding to constant organizational change. Designed by Ben Fether of FM Design, manufactured by President.**

■ The use of modular units on an as-needed basis, in relatively open-plan offices in order to provide busy project teams with shared but immediate access to the enclosed conditions that favour concentrated work. The Steelcase Personal Harbour is the most elaborate example.

■ The so-called 'combi-office' – an older, European attempt to solve the same problem, at layout rather than product level. Small, modular, glass-fronted, individual rooms surround or are immediately adjacent to, spaces for

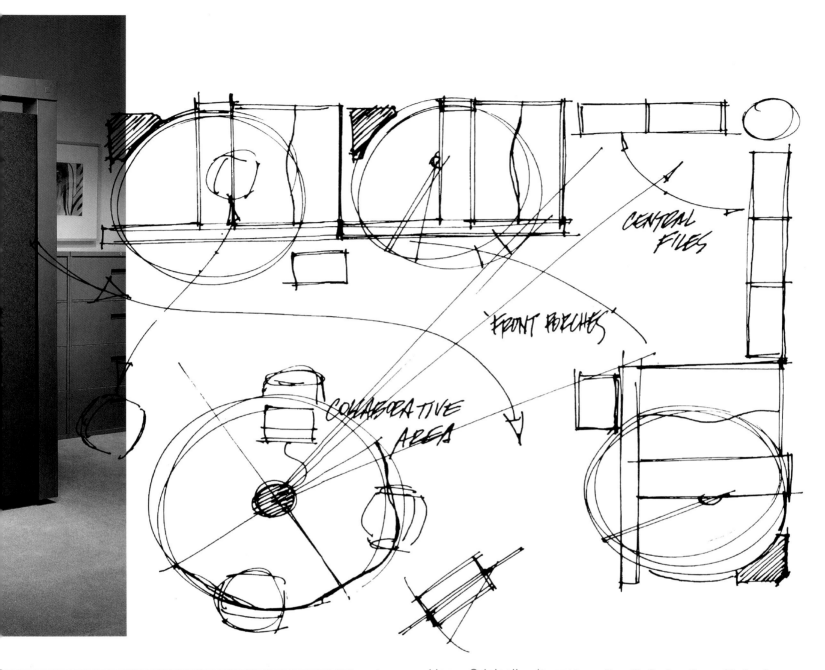

CENTRAL FILES

FRONT PORCHES

COLLABORATIVE AREA

teamworking. Originally it was assumed that the modular rooms would not be time-shared: the social democratic tradition insisted on individual, if egalitarian, workplaces for all. Now sharing the modular offices is seen as practical as sharing the team spaces that lie between them.

■ New furniture for group work, which requires furniture to be very different from the standardized clusters of six and eight workplaces – often called 'six and eight packs' after the beer cans they resemble – that are very often the staple of conventional office planning. Developments include continuous worktops for

Above **The Steelcase Personal Harbour is a freestanding, well-equipped, totally enclosable, 'private workplace' that is designed to accommodate bouts of concentrated individual work immediately adjacent to busy project and group activities – as shown in the sketch.**

Zoning of office layouts to provide optimum conditions for a variety of different work activities. Conventional office design attempted to provide workplaces that could meet any combination of requirements for carrying out work, from the most private and concentrated to the most gregarious and noisy. Even in the past the futility of this design strategy was all too apparent. As more complex patterns of work emerge, failures are likely to become even more apparent. However, once the bond between an individual and a particular work-station is broken, office planning can use zoning, i.e. isolating special areas fitted out for quiet, or for highly interactive activities, or those that depend upon quick access to special equipment – provided office workers are willing to share such specialized resources. The most systematic example is the layouts for Andersen Worldwide on page 178.

Above **As office buildings have become more robust to accommodate change, office furniture has absorbed more functions, including cable-handling. The Mehes range for Ahrend neatly incorporates cable ducts in the table legs. (It is on display in Inland Revenue offices, Nottingham, UK. Architect: Michael Hopkins and Partners.)**

interactive work, such as the lo range produced by Facit; and reconfigurable tables and more mobile furniture for group tasks, such as President's Kyo range, Knoll's Currents range and the Steelcase Strafor TNT nomads.

Storage trolleys and other personal equipment that can be moved quickly from one workplace to another to increase flexiblity of space use, and the mobility of individuals. Examples include the Relay range by Herman Miller, and the Kyo range by President.

■ The first furniture, either imported into the office from restaurant or domestic suppliers, or custom-made, for the vast majority of meetings that are small and informal. A wider, richer vocabulary of furniture for meeting rooms and meeting spaces is also being developed commercially. Yas Hirai's break-area furniture for Kokuyo is an example.

■ Personal computers which are becoming an integral part of office conversations that can range over countries and continents, especially when equipped with video links.

■ More dynamic equipment that supports collective, mobile, often temporary, and highly visual tasks, making display and discussion easy. Wilkhahn's Confair range of lightweight stacking chairs, mobile folding tables, mobile lecterns, white boards and flip charts is an example; Unifor's Move and Flipper chairs and tables, and Vitra's Nexus table are others.

■ The design of convenient, safe, and individual equipment for working at home, such as Vitra's 'office at home' range, and Herman Miller's Relay range.

■ Attempts, ranging from the sophisticated to the wacky, to make office design less corporate and more domestic and diverse, in response to pressure from office workers. An example is Haworth's Crossings range.

Above **The social function of office furniture is increasing. The Interplace break-area furniture was designed by Yas Hirai for Kokuyo after careful observation of employees' behaviour and research into their needs.**

Left **The demand for furniture for meetings, presentations, and demonstrations – like Wilkhahn's folding table, mobile lectern and stacking chairs – is rapidly increasing.**

Far left **As home-working increases, so does the need for furniture that is domestic in feeling but still ergonomic in function. Vitra's 'office at home' includes the Spatio Table, designed by Antonio Citterio with Glen Oliver Low, and the Aluminium Chair by Charles and Ray Eames.**

Innovations in service distribution

Cable and wireless

Despite the increasing importance of information technology, there is still resistance among some developers to thinking about the infrastructure for distributing it. It appears that the need to make office buildings more permeable to cabling of various sorts, to provide adequate volume for the primary, secondary, and tertiary distribution systems of cables and the need to solve the problems that occur at the interfaces between the three systems has still not been fully grasped. There are, however, new products and ideas that can help to resolve these infrastructure problems.

Meanwhile wireless technology has attained enormous spatial significance. No longer do individuals need to be connected to particular workplaces. This opens up the potential, within the office, for people to have access to a much wider range of settings. Combinations of these, each with its own particular environmental characteristics, should enable office workers to carry out a much wider and complex range of tasks. However, structured cabling, saturating the office with outlets for data and power on a predetermined grid, continues to be as important a planning discipline in offices designed for new ways of working as it is for conventional desk layouts. Innovations include:

■ Office furniture, designed intelligently, as a powerful means of supplementing such grids. Desks, like those in the Hannah range for Knoll which have ducts that run under the worktops, can help with more serious distribution of cable for power and data from workstation to workstation in under-serviced buildings

■ 'Hitching posts', still a relatively under-used device, for connecting power and data from secondary distribution in access floors to desk-top height. They can also be used to position the reflectors that are necessary for wireless transmission within the office. Herman Miller, Akerman, Steelcase, Kokuyo, and President all manufacture such devices.

Top **Getting power and data lines out of the access floor and onto the desk has led to the invention of the 'hitching post'. (Seen also on page 82.) Part of the Kyo range for President.**

Above **Taking the lid off the network of cabling that is the modern office: the circular floor outlet at Commerzbank, Frankfurt, could easily accept a 'hitching post'. Architect: Foster and Partners.**

■ Networking and power outlets available throughout the building, including meeting rooms and more unexpected places such as break areas. Such outlets are becoming increasingly available in semi-public places like hotels, airports, and railway stations, as well as in the air and on trains for the convenience of the growing constituency of working travellers.

■ Places to store and recharge mobile phones as an integral feature of the office. Digital, Chiat/Day, Kokuyo, and Sol are all examples of companies that have made this an accepted aspect of their day-to-day routine.

Above **In Kokoyu's Tokyo office, data is transmitted by infrared rays. Cabling may be simplified, but two new elements are introduced: desk-height mobile sensors (seen clearly on the right) and ceiling-mounted emitters.**

Left **The office is becoming more and more the infrastructure of the computer. These are secondary distribution data cables in the access floor at Commerzbank, Frankfurt. Architect: Foster and Partners.**

Innovations in environmental design

Economic as well as ecological pressures are responsible for the striking advances in 'mixed-mode' environmental systems that use both natural and artificial means to make offices habitable. The same pressures have encouraged the use of convection and thermal mass to produce environments that are more energy-efficient than the gas-guzzling office buildings of previous decades and which are also adaptable to many different kinds of use. Such passive systems can be as finely zoned as the

Below **Using physics to ventilate offices naturally creates new external architectural features. Convection towers with louvres which draw cool air through the fabric of the building are the most prominent feature of the roofline at Ionica's offices, Cambridge, UK. Architect: RH Partnership.**

more elaborate, conventional air conditioning to allow for changing patterns of use. The physical results can be handsome; and passive systems can also be much quicker to construct, and simpler to manage, than the highly engineered ones that they are replacing. Innovations include:

■ Exposing the internal building structure, instead of cladding it with suspended ceilings, so that the relatively absorbent concrete acts as a 'radiator' of coolness, helping to stabilize the internal environment, and keeping the temperature down. Sometimes cool air is drawn through the structure at night so that the cooling effect can be enjoyed by the users of the building next day.

■ Drawing cool air through the building by convection, without the use of fans, pumps, or other machinery. Sometimes this is done through special towers, sometimes through staircases, sometimes through the heavy (usually concrete) structure of the roof. These are all examples of the revival of traditional, even ancient, techniques to modify the internal climate of modern office buildings. They contrast markedly with conventional air-conditioning systems which batter, rather than work with,

Above **Stair-towers double as devices to cool the building naturally through convected air movement. Inland Revenue offices, Nottingham, UK. Architect: Michael Hopkins and Partners.**

Left **These whimsical ventilation funnels are in an office partially buried under the green sward at Ready Mix Concrete, near London. Architect: Edward Cullinan Architects.**

Top and above **The recently renovated offices for the Department of Trade and Industry, London. Outside is a new skin; inside a chilled ceiling that exploits the movement of naturally convected air. Simpler construction – for example, ducts above the ceilings are no longer necessary – saved months on the building programme, and also valuable space. Architect: DEGW.**

is a more efficient coolant than air, taking up a far smaller volume to achieve the same effect. Water-chilled ceilings work using the natural convection movement of air, gently cooling hot air as it rises. None of the expensive battery of pumps and fans of conventional air conditioning is needed. Construction becomes simpler and quicker and office workers seem to prefer the results.

■ Mixed-mode office buildings that are designed to meet the conflicting demands of people and machinery. Many office workers, particularly those in northern Europe, dislike air conditioning and want natural and easily controlled ventilation and cooling. Large concentrations of office machines, despite increasing efficiency, still generate large amounts of heat and need artificial air conditioning.

■ Giving individual office workers control over their own internal environments. Air temperature and air movement (as well as the local acoustic environment) may be regulated – with dashboard-like controls integrated in each workstation. The best-known example is manufactured by Johnson Controls. These elaborate, and somewhat clumsy, devices only imitate the

nature. When convection cooling is achieved through an architectural element such as stairs, there is an immediate consequence for the core of the building. In this way the new environmental systems are having a major impact on the planning and the external appearance of office buildings.

■ Using water-cooled ceilings internally to achieve the same effect. Though this requires pumps, these are tiny and use the minimum amount of power. Water

type of control that is built into traditional architecture in the form of windows that can be opened and adjusted. The first approach is typically North American – expensive gadgets used to make cheap space with deep floor-plates habitable in a demanding climate. The second is typically northern European – simple, cheap controls in inherently expensive, much narrower buildings in a more temperate climate.

■ Lighting that can be adjusted, both in intensity and quality, and switched on and off, according to changing individual or group preferences; the increasing demand for this is now being widely met.

■ Proposals, such as Steelcase's Pathways, to combine all the components of the office interior – partitions, ceilings, cable distribution, air conditioning, furniture, and lighting – into completely integrated interior design packages. Such proposals, dominated by the logic of establishing a long-term and robust servicing infrastructure, have important implications for the ways in which clients procure interior design, for the development of design services, and for the degree of control that ordinary office workers can have over their environment.

Left **Johnson Controls, manufacturers of air-conditioning equipment, drew on the example of how drivers and passengers adjust the internal environment of cars when they developed this device. It allows office workers to control temperature and air movement, as well as the local sound level, at their desks.**

Above, left and right **The building skin, with adjustable louvres, was designed to control sunlight and thus allow staff to control the quality of their working environment. The exposed concrete ceiling was designed, because of its mass, to stabilize internal temperatures. Electricité de France, Bordeaux. Architect: Foster and Partners.**

Innovations in the design of the building skin

Conventional office buildings, especially in North America, are usually designed to be hermetically sealed. No one can open a window. The assumptions that lie behind this bizarre practice are that energy is cheap, that the architect's and environmental designer's job is to create a uniformly perfect interior climate that will satisfy everyone; and

Below **This subsidiary atrium lets light deep into the building and also acts as an orienting device. Its internal skin is not sealed, allowing the drama of direct contact with a big, shared space. The Ark Building, London. Architect: Ralph Erskine.**

that the best ways to do this are to screen out the effects of unpredictable changes in the exterior climate and stamp out the possibility of any climate-modifying behaviour on the part of the occupants. Even differences between night and day are, for all practical purposes, ignored — what matters is the provision of constant internal conditions. In this environmentally conscious era such mechanistic, narrow-minded — and fundamentally lazy — assumptions are intolerable.

However, now that architects and engineers are attempting to work with, rather than against, nature, the skins of office buildings are becoming environmentally and architecturally

far more interesting. The aims are to drive down energy costs while allowing users more choice in controlling the quality of their working environments, and to achieve a gentle, enjoyable, and environmentally friendly transition between exterior and interior. Innovations include:

■ New building skins designed to prevent solar gain but to attract as much daylight as possible. Louvres and shades, some of which are adjustable by users, are becoming critically important climate-modifying devices.

■ Well-planted, easily accessible atriums. These have a threefold function: to provide circulation and orientation, to

Above left **The solar-shading fixed louvres were designed to maximize natural lighting with minimal glare or heat gain. Offices for PowerGen, Coventry, UK. Architect: Bennetts Associates.**

Above right **Recladding Sir Owen William's 1930s factory with new kinds of tinted glass helped to renew it in an environmentally friendly way for Boots the Chemist, Nottingham, UK. The building was refurbished for office use by the contractor Amec's in-house design team.**

Above and right **Boldly conceived gardens-in-the-air punctuate the façade of Commerzbank in Frankfurt. These buffer spaces make possible a totally new level of environmental quality and immediacy in this very tall office building. Architect: Foster and Partners.**

bring natural light deep into the building, and to be a socially interactive place. The internal skin of the atrium can be sealed for safety and economy, or left open for social contact.

■ Buffer spaces between the building skin and the interior to create spaces that can have a social function as well as being planted and designed in such a way that they are an important means of modifying the internal climate.

New building shells and new patterns of location

Both in the design of office shells and in the choice of office locations, the beginnings are already evident of what will be very long-term changes made possible by ubiquitous information technology. No longer is it necessary to design a whole office building around the idea of getting everyone there at one time. Not for much longer will it be necessary to design the infrastructure of whole cities around the assumption that office work can only be done if hundreds of thousands of people are prepared to commute at precise hours. Neither offices nor cities need to continue to be monuments to synchrony. Locational trends are clearly toward smaller core organizations, towards networking, towards more people working out of the office more of the time – at home or on the move. Architectural trends in advanced economies are towards fewer, smaller, more specifically designed new office buildings as well as towards recycling existing buildings – turning non-office ones into offices, as well as office buildings to new uses. Suddenly, run-down parts of the inner city become mines of opportunity for new kinds of office organizations. As the old institutional criteria for investment in speculative office buildings dissolve, the potential of recycled office shells, used in different, novel ways, is already having a direct effect on the choice of office location, at least in the inner city.

The real estate industry – for its own commercial reasons – has always tended to over-emphasize the importance of big office buildings. This has been a mistake. The vast majority of office organizations are small and the trend is for even more to become smaller – through out-sourcing, downsizing,

and continuing corporate emphasis on stripping back to the core business. More people are now able to work away from the office more of the time, further diminishing the necessity for the work force to together in one place. This, combined with higher user expectations and the need for better space use, means that both the very deep floor-plates of North America and the uneconomically shallow ones of northern Europe are unlikely to meet future demands. The probable overall trend, in the UK

and then in northern Europe, and eventually in North America, will be towards medium-depth space. Floor-plates of 15 m/50 ft are almost as easy to plan and manage as larger ones: they allow layouts that bring groups of people together rather than isolating them, and can be designed to combine natural ventilation with some artificial cooling.

Above **As new ways of working make it increasingly possible for individuals to choose when and where to work, the concentrated rush that has dominated the lives of millions of commuters for decades will become unnecessary.**

Above **The galleria on the site of the Carl Zeiss plant in Jena, Germany, symbolizes how architecture can help to renew a bankrupt economy. The galleria links retail spaces with offices designed for new high-tech enterprises that are linked to related departments of Jena's university, which occupies the same site under the same roof. Architects: DEGW supported by IBD.**

However, the entire notion that offices are a distinct building type may not be taken for granted for very much longer. A system that involves vast expenditure on buildings which are only partly used for a limited number of hours during weekdays is almost certainly doomed. Indeed, the office tower may soon be as redundant as the steam-powered mill. Both buildings reflect a need to concentrate people in one place at the same time to carry out

repetitive tasks. In the world of offices, this need is increasingly shrinking and there may be few twenty-first century successors to the Chrysler Building, the Seagram Building, and Lloyd's of London. Instead, creative office work will be devolved to any location – a converted warehouse in a city centre, a kitchen in a country cottage, another country – anywhere, in fact, where it makes practical and financial sense for it to be carried out.

Left **Warehouse buildings, such as these in London's Docklands, can make useful offices; others convert easily into homes. New buildings fill gaps to weave a new kind of urban fabric.**

While older, smaller office buildings will be brought back into use to accommodate new ways of working, others will

Above **A new kind of office in an old building: aWarehouse (a compound of 'aware' and 'warehouse') is a cooperative formed by a group of independent young designers who have opted for living and working in a redundant factory in the more bracing environment of the inner city of San Francisco, USA.**

be turned to new uses. Some are already being recycled as apartments, and some converted into mixed use buildings where offices, shops, and housing are accommodated in the same shell. Similar patterns of mixed use were the basis of the urban structure of cities like Paris, Milan, Vienna, and even London in the nineteenth century. The Inns of Court in London provide a wonderful example of how offices can be woven into an interesting, habitable city fabric. When did people forget that the Temple or Grays

Below **Teluride in Colorado, USA, is a mountain-ringed village largely made up of 'electronic cottages'. These are homes for networkers who, confident in modern communications, prefer to maintain a non-urban way of life, organizing both their time and their space in their own way.**

Inn are wonderful examples of office accommodation for smaller organizations? From our new perspective, it has become a critical test of the quality of any building that one can envisage it as suitable for uses other than that for which it was originally built.

The inventive regeneration, for office and other complementary uses, of a wide variety of older buildings ranging from houses to warehouses to factories, is becoming more

Above **The quality of working life in Michael Mainwaring's design office in suburban San Francisco is enormously enhanced by the domestic interior.**

a test of the architectural imagination than devising a glamorous skin for an 80-storey anachronism. Architects must learn to question what their buildings are for, and how they will be used and adapted over time. It is far from wise to attempt to perfect building types whose day has passed.

The most important changes will be at the urban scale. Some commentators feel that the increasing freedom of choice in working times will lead to the death of cities. They imagine that people will prefer the cool virtuality of the electronic cottage and the Internet to less controllable face-to-face encounters with their colleagues in New York's Wall Street, London's West End, or Tokyo's Roppongi. Others argue that fundamentally nothing will change because home-working will simply not be practical for the vast majority of office workers

Top and above **The architect Mario Bellini has converted a turn-of-the-century industrial building in Milan, Italy into a studio for his own practice. Inside, lofty spaces provide a well-ventilated and well-lit ambience. Externally, little has been done to alter the factory's old courtyard.**

for social and domestic reasons. The truth is likely to be more complex. What will happen will be affected by demographic changes such as the breakdown of the traditional family, as well as by the changing nature of work. The choice will not be limited simply to working either at home or in the office.

Many people will choose to work at home, when it suits them, at least some of the time. Others will choose to base themselves almost entirely at home – striking out for meetings only occasionally. Some will cling to their conventional, full-time office bases, although they will come under increasing pressure to justify this option. Yet others will use neighbourhood work centres, as a compromise between home and central city working, in order to keep in touch regularly with colleagues and clients. Most people will learn how to work from a variety of places – from the car, in the airport, in hotels, in clients' offices. Many consultants work in this peripatetic way already. And a new concept in leasing office

space is now being realized where costs are measured on the basis of services by the hour as opposed to square metres/feet per year. Office occupancy, as is demonstrated in Chapter 5, is already less dense and more ragged in timing of occupancy than most people admit.

New patterns of office location are beginning to emerge. 'Edge cities' – the non-planned aggregations of office space, retailing, and housing that are springing up on the beltways surrounding American and Pacific Rim cities – are clearly an option for many for whom car-based mobility is critical. Even today, patterns of commuting, whether in the Thames Valley or Silicon Valley, by no means follow the centripetal patterns that the engineers who built the railways in the UK or the traffic engineers who planned the freeways in California originally assumed. Such quasi-random patterns of movement already tell us a great deal about the amorphous shape of much of the future city.

Left **A turn-of-the-century warehouse in New York, converted into an office and a place to live, exploits the high ceilings and the sheer volume to allow one space to flow into another. Designed by American Design Company.**

Above **Advent Software has brought two floors of a 1930s high-rise office in mid-town Manhattan back to life by slicing through the concrete structure to bring their organization together. Architect: Katherine Huber and Mary Buttrick .**

A new kind of city

The importance of cities will not diminish. However, they will be used in very different and much more entertaining ways. They will provide the essential matrix for the half-planned, half-accidental encounters that are an essential part of our increasingly complex and challenging intellectual and business lives. Cities are great labour markets as well as places that generate intellectual, business, and social stimuli. The new kinds of activity upon which the economies of the future cities will increasingly depend – media, advertising, the pop industry, and, dare I say, architecture – need the densely interactive infrastructure of the traditional city. Cities suit networkers.

This is an argument for the renaissance of city life – although the property industry will have to do its calculations very differently when it relates the supply of office spaces to the demand for them. In the cities of the twenty-first century offices will continue to exist, but will be designed in a richer and wider variety of ways – as streets, villages, colleges, and clubs – to encourage interaction. At the same time 'dead' streets and blocks will be brought back to life by a more social, less time-dependent, more interactive way of working. We must all face the inevitability of designing – and enjoying – different styles of working life, different sorts of city, different types of office, different kinds of home. The challenge that many designers of organizational structures are already facing, and that all designers of buildings and cities will soon have to struggle to address, is an immensely complex phenomenon for which 'teleworking' is merely the crudest shorthand – nothing less than the redesign of the shape of time.

Right **The successful regeneration of what was until the early 1970s the run-down and neglected inner harbour area of Boston, USA, is based upon the intricately networked and complementary nature of a range of activities – retail, tourism and leisure, restaurants, hotels, and housing as well as different kinds of office work.**

Opposite **As information technology supercharges the nature of office work, there is every reason to expect that not only places for living, working, learning and enjoyment will mingle in each city block, but also that the ancient function of city centres – as the best context for the exchange and development of ideas – will be rediscovered.**

the new offices

Innovation in office design starts from the inside and works its way outwards, changing not only the building shell but its relationship to the city. The big transparent terraces in Channel 4 Television's new offices in London, designed by the Richard Rogers Partnership, demonstrate to the world outside what is going on within, and vice versa. The colourful, quirky interior of Chiat/Day's offices in New York, designed by Gaetano Pesce, is designed to accommodate ever-changing shifts between information-technology-based project work and concentrated individual work.

In the world of business, an ability to embrace radical design in order to move forward commercially seems to depend upon four conditions: a powerful financial incentive to seek innovation; the willingness to be excited by the idea that there may be better ways of doing things, and to learn from other corporate and national cultures; the leadership to put new ideas into practice; and, finally, complete confidence in the use of information technology, with the will to push it to the limit.

The current wave of time based innovation in office design began in the late 1980s when these four factors began to converge. Advanced businesses started to reject the past and to seek fresh design responses to their emerging requirements. The case studies in this chapter describe twenty contemporary attempts to create new kinds of office space.

The choice illustrates the organizational dynamic, described in Chapter 2, that is creating the opportunity for big changes in office design. The full range of case studies is presented in the diagram overleaf and shows the shift towards new kinds of hives, cells, dens, and clubs. Some of the cases fit easily and completely into one or other of these organizational types; others, particularly in the longer term, fit less neatly; at least two are hybrids.

Each case study is as distinguished in organizational innovation as it is in design quality. Six come from the United States, five from continental Europe, six from the UK, two from Japan, and one from Australia. They cover a range of organizations that also differ in size: from fewer than a hundred people to several thousand. Not surprisingly well over half are knowledge based, late twentieth-century kinds of enterprises: in information technology or telecommunications, in publishing, advertising or the media, or consultancies. The remainder span a diverse range, including the furniture and construction industries, an airline, two manufacturing companies and a government office – the last, admittedly, of an unusually experimental sort. The organizations occupy a variety of buildings: under half are in new, purpose-built offices; three are in refurbished buildings that were not originally offices at all; five are in classic North American, developer-built, high-rise towers; four are in low-rise buildings more characteristic of the bespoke tradition of northern European office building.

Innovation in office design, as these case studies imply, seems to be happening most rapidly in innovative organizations in the most innovative sectors of the economy. It is significant that none of the case studies is in the financial services industry, that not one is a legal practice, and that there

Seen here are the London premises of Pentagram, an international design firm. Although ten years old, these offices anticipate many of the arguments in this book. The space occupied by designers has often been more innovatively laid out and effectively used than that in most other types of organization. This is because design work is inherently project- and team-based, because the users are stylistically aware people, employed for their creative skills, and because the companies are usually small and relatively impecunious, and therefore rely on originality rather than money.

Left The view from a gallery shows how the extra volume of the double-height space of a converted warehouse has been exploited to house separate project teams. General shared resources, such as the library and central files, are in closer proximity to the workstations than would normally be thought possible.

Opposite Skilful lighting has made the lower-floor project space not only a functional but also a pleasant place to work.

Below The use of full-height glazing makes a small meeting room adjacent to the main project spaces inviting and visible.

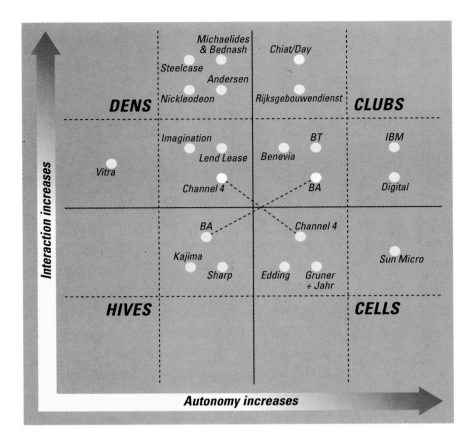

The diagram shows a matrix with the axes "Interaction increases" (vertical) and "Autonomy increases" (horizontal), divided into four quadrants labelled DENS, CLUBS, HIVES, and CELLS, with company names positioned:

DENS quadrant: Michaelides & Bednash, Steelcase, Andersen, Nickleodeon, Imagination, Lend Lease, Vitra, Channel 4

CLUBS quadrant: Chiat/Day, Rijksgebouwendienst, BT, Benevia, IBM, Digital, BA

HIVES quadrant: BA, Kajima, Sharp

CELLS quadrant: Channel 4, Edding, Gruner + Jahr, Sun Micro

Above **Each of the twenty case studies that are described on the following pages has been characterized as a hive, cell, den, or club. Two – Channel 4 Television and British Airways – are obviously hybrids and have been shown as such. Over the years, space-planners DEGW have devised methods to measure how much interaction and autonomy is characteristic of any organization, or any part of an organization, now or, potentially, in the forseeable future. Although it was not possible to take such detailed measurements of the companies that are presented here as case studies, approximate judgments, based on experience and the information available, were made in categorizing each organization into its predominant type.**

is not a single example from the capital-intensive industries of oil, steel or pharmaceuticals. However, even in these relatively conservative sectors there is now some evidence of growing interest in more inventive ways of using office space. Paradoxically, a long record of sustained commercial success seems to be a major impediment to innovation. Change must seem less crucial for businesses that feel themselves to be most secure. (Such security is, of course, an illusion.) Those organizations that are struggling to succeed are the ones who more urgently need to find more inventive ways of using office space more efficiently as well as more effectively.

Some companies may think that lack of funds is a reason for avoiding change. They are wrong. New office design depends absolutely upon thrift – upon the innovative use of the relatively small financial resources allocated to office space to achieve much greater commercial impact.

Finance aside, success in most cases depends upon the the ability to integrate three strands of new thinking: in design, in exploiting information technology, and in managing creative people. For smaller, younger companies, such as Michaelides & Bednash, Imagination and Nickelodeon, managerial integration seems to be easier perhaps because it comes organically with rapid business growth. For bigger, older companies, even for the sophisticated Andersen Worldwide, integrated management demands much more energy, tenacity and diplomacy. Leadership in all companies, large and small, young or old, is critical. In the background of most of these case studies is a powerful individual who was prepared to fight hard for the implementation of a programme of change.

The crucial question addressed in each of the twenty case studies is the degree to which new design thinking has satisfied the priorities of each client. This is why, wherever possible, the direct voices of clients and users are heard, talking about their aspirations, their achievements and their disappointments. The testimony of the architects and designers, while of great interest, is secondary. While every effort has been made to check the facts, the opinions that are expressed are solely mine.

All twenty case studies are ahead of the game in adopting new ways of working. There is, however, a caveat in this evolutionary hypothesis. The majority of the companies are knowledge-based organizations, operating in the most successful and rapidly growing sectors of the economy. They are opening up new options in office design for other types of business to follow. It is also possible that their success signals the closing down of conventional options. What they represent in design terms may be the only viable way forward for knowledge-based organizations in a knowledge-based economy. And knowledge-based organizations may be the only ones that will succeed in advanced economies in an increasingly competitive world.

If this is so, these twenty companies are far more important than they may seem on first sight. Their ways of operating, their business cultures, their extraordinary and innovative office layouts, may turn out to be threatening to some, hopeful to others. More significantly, in aggregate, they represent what the working landscape of advanced economies in the twenty-first century is likely to become.

New kinds of hive

Hive offices are characterized by routine work carried out by individuals who have little autonomy, that is, little ability to determine the way in which their work is done, and whose interaction with each other, on work matters, is intermittent, and not usually critical or conducted at high intensity. Hive office layouts can be traced back to the semi-industrial origins of much office work. Typically they are composed of simple workstations, often arranged in banks of six, eight, or even more work places, with little additional general support space apart from some filing and occasional meeting places. As has already been pointed out in Chapter 2, the simpler kinds of hive office work, under strong international competitive pressure, are either being automated or exported to economies where labour is cheaper. However, it is also true that new kinds of hive offices are being invented all the time as more powerful information technology makes new data-intensive services possible.

Hives abound in Japan. The country's innovative, design-minded culture might appear to be an ideal context for the development of new ways of thinking about the workplace. Yet the typical Japanese office is, by European or American standards, an anachronism – overcrowded, comfortless, lit by glaring fluorescent tubes, dominated by serried ranks of uniform desks, generally arranged on an 'island' plan, and lacking spaces for informal meetings and networking. Moreover, in a country that has led the world in the development of electronics and computer technology, information technology is often sparsely provided. A 1995 survey revealed that only 12 per cent of businesses surveyed had installed full computer networks and 41 per cent were virtually computer-free. Hot desking and the virtual office are all but unknown. Change is, however, coming fast and leading companies are steadily adopting – sometimes a little tentatively perhaps – new ways of working. The two Japanese case studies that follow – Sharp, an electronics company, and Kajima, a design and construction company – represent advanced hive ways of working. Although each is innovative

by Japanese standards, their choice of layout is limited, density is high, and support spaces for meetings etc., though relatively generous, are provided for the whole building rather than integrated into work groups. In this highly conservative context, the innovations at Kajima (clustered desks with low dividing screens, the handsome atrium used for meetings) and at Sharp (clustered desks, staff amenities) are far more significant than they may look: they are very supportive to this particular and continuing working culture.

The British Airways case study is an example of the new kind of information-intensive office – a hive of highly trained people responding, night and day, to queries and data flooding in about complex operations (in this case, managing the logistics of a world airline) through bank after bank of electronic equipment. What is even more interesting is that these quintessentially hive-like operations are integrated with a club-like environment where the airline's highly mobile flight crews and cabin staff are continually being briefed and processed.

The Compass Centre may be Britain's busiest and most intensively used office building. A familiar sight to travellers in and out of London Heathrow, the blue building is a landmark, a shapely, colourful contrast to the generally

British Airways – Compass Centre

Heathrow Airport, London, UK

nondescript mass of buildings which make up the world's busiest international airport. The most obviously distinctive feature is the glass cladding – brilliantly illuminated by night and designed with environmental comfort, as much as aesthetic effect, in mind. (Soundproofing was a clear priority, but the cladding was also skilfully engineered to control heat gain.) The profile of the building may look wilful, but there are sound practical arguments for its highly sculptural form, designed not least to avoid interference with Heathrow's vital radar system.

> *'The Compass Centre,' says Bob Ayling, BA's chief executive, 'is a real airline building – quality space which encourages teamwork and the feeling of belonging to a great international organization. It's an unqualified success for us.'*

The building was developed by Lynton, the developer subsidiary of BAA (the British Airports Authority), specifically for British Airways and houses BA's Combined Operations Centre, the operational base for Heathrow-based flight and cabin crew, with key planning, control, and support facilities. The Compass Centre is the nerve centre for BA's operations worldwide – which involve 15,000 flight and cabin staff, 250 aircraft and 1,000 flights a day, carrying nearly 30 million passengers and 670,000 tons of cargo annually. The building is operational 24 hours a day, 365 days a year. Each day, around 3,000 crew members pass through it, while 1,000 staff are permanently based there, up to 800 being in it at any one time. Many of those who use it are there for only a short time, reporting for a flight or signing off on their return to London. Others are there for their entire working day. Some managerial staff use it as a base, needing work space there for varying periods of time. This complexity of use made for a similarly complex brief, but for BA the new building was seen as a high priority. Before its inauguration, the airline's operations were conducted from nine buildings around the airport and this dispersal of activities was not conducive to achieving BA's prime objective: 'delivering the product to the passenger.' The route to achieving that objective was seen as 'bringing together flight and cabin crew reporting with operations, planning and delivery to promote synergy and ensure that the business of flying passengers is conducted in the most successful way possible'. As BA's chief executive, Bob Ayling, says: 'The Compass Centre was built for the employees, to improve their working conditions and make them feel both valued and part of a wider organization.' With this in mind, the project was developed as a partnership between BAA/Lynton and the airline, and the building was tailored to BA's needs, which included a large area of nearby parking and easy access for crew buses. Since the company could not predict its long-term space requirements, the Compass Centre takes the form of three linked buildings. If the space requirement were to shrink, part of the complex could be separately let, or the whole could be refigured for other users should BA vacate at the end of the 25-year lease.

Nicholas Grimshaw & Partners' impressive building was begun in August 1992 and handed over, in a very basic 'shell and core' condition, in November 1993. Work then began on

BUILDING STATISTICS				
CLIENT: British Airways plc		**FUNCTION:** Combined operations centre of airline		
TOTAL FLOOR AREA: 18,156 sq. m / 194,269 sq. ft	**TOTAL POP.:** 1000 resident / 3000 daily	**OVERALL DENSITY:** 18.2 sq. m per person / 19.3 sq. ft per person		
SAMPLE PLAN AREA (less core): 3,024 sq. m / 32,357 sq. ft	**Circulation:** 34.9%	**Support:** 19.8%	**Cellular:** 7.4%	**Open plan:** 38.0%
CONSULTANTS: *Architect* Nicholas Grimshaw and Partners *Programming* RAN Consultants *Interior Design* Aukett Associates				

Above **The Compass Centre at London's Heathrow Airport is at the heart of British Airways' worldwide operations. Its architecture reflects the rigour of a brief which demanded maximum efficiency and user satisfaction for large numbers of staff engaged in a wide variety of tasks, from piloting aircraft to managing in-flight catering. Flight crews check in here: normally this space would be crowded.**

Left **The operations control room, though packed with technical equipment, is tightly organized. The colour scheme is intended to convey an air of calm amid the continuous activity.**

the fit-out, with Aukett Associates who were BA's lead design consultants for architecture, structural engineering, space planning, and interior design. The £25 million fit-out was completed in the autumn of 1994 and the building brought into operation before the end of the year. During 1992 BA had produced a very detailed brief for the project, covering business needs, the design concept, and space requirements, written by Sam Cassels of RAN Consultants under the direction of Fotoula Karamouzos, BA's project manager for the Compass Centre.

An important issue arose out of the very nature of the project, which brought together staff who had previously worked in separate locations doing very different jobs. How were they to interact, both strategically and culturally? The building should respect their varying identities, but should 'not encourage conflicting sub-cultures to evolve. Thus, while recognizing different approaches and needs, territorial colonization will not defeat the central purpose

Below **The crisis centre, designed for emergencies, is one of the best equipped in the world and available to other airlines when needed. It is also regularly used for staff training.**

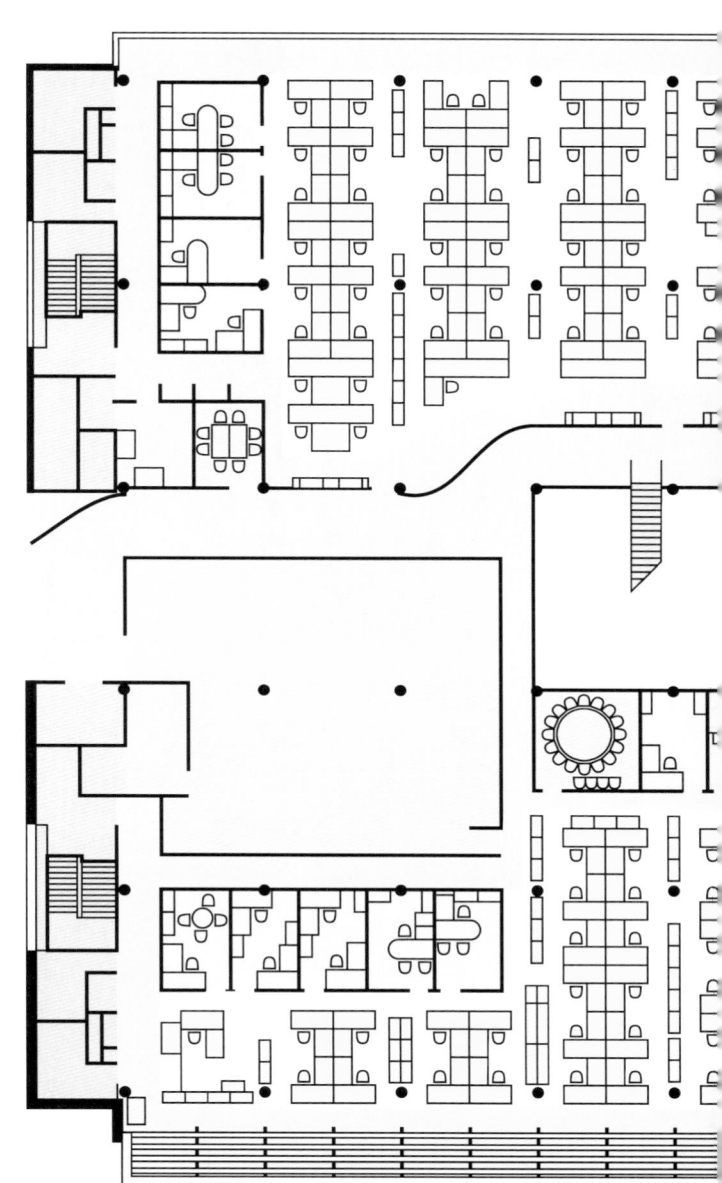

of the building.' User comfort was a high priority so café-like lounges have been set aside for visiting flight crews. The building was to be a 'home for a single flying community with a common purpose' and, again, the emphasis was on breaking down barriers and instilling commitment to a shared task. The main divide was between the 'visiting' staff (flight crew and cabin staff) and the 'residents'. For the latter, the building is an archetypal hive – many work conventional hours – while for the former, it has an element of the club. As well as being allocated briefing and reporting areas, visiting staff, with their very special, peripatetic, and occasionally dramatically rescheduled needs, have shared places to eat, relax, and simply find some quiet at any time of the day or night.

The three-storey complex consists, in effect, of three distinct buildings. These were not conceived as independent

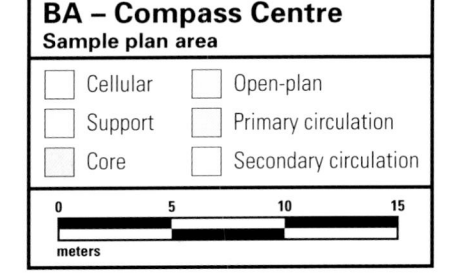

BA – Compass Centre
Sample plan area

☐ Cellular   ☐ Open-plan

☐ Support   ☐ Primary circulation

☐ Core   ☐ Secondary circulation

0   5   10   15

meters

technology is evident as a controlling influence on the tightly planned, operational layouts. The whole space is intended to be flexible and refigurable – all services, including air conditioning, are designed to provide for future change rather than being tied to the needs of existing users. Both BA and Aukett insist that 'this is not just an office building' and stress the variety of tasks carried out in the Compass Centre, from the management of duty free sales to the handling of emergencies throughout the world.

Steve Embley of Aukett says, 'his is a building which is about company culture. It shows how design can reinforce business imperatives. It is, above all, a living place.' A key part of the design brief had been to make the building responsive to users' needs. 'It was a question of carrying people with you in achieving something quite novel,' says Embley. There was close consultation with staff via departmental meetings, a regular newsletter, and a project steering committee. But BA was determined to challenge the accepted ways of doing things,' says Jerry Swift, who acted as project champion on behalf of BA cabin services, 'and it had good reason.' Research had revealed a worrying lack of contact between pilots and cabin crew – a problem that apparently affected many airlines. The flight deck door had been an absolute divide.

Left **The floor plan of the third storey of the central building of the Compass Centre shows two neighbourhoods of open-plan desks for resident staff in the resources and delivery section and the operations control area. These areas straddle the central atrium, which provides a visual as well as an operational link between this floor housing those who programme the schedules of flight crews, and the lower floors where the more transient activity of the crew-handling areas goes on.**

entities, but are linked at each level by a 'street' which passes through the atria of all three. The street and the side corridors running off it define a series of neighbourhoods, each planned for the needs of a specific user group. The central building (Meridian) is the focus for visiting staff, with a secure area on the ground floor (where their baggage is checked in and screened exactly as in an airport terminal) and a reporting and briefing area on the first floor. This is club-like in character, with a variety of layouts and ample seating where crews can socialize, rest, study, or discuss work schedules. In contrast, the office areas are densely populated, with cellular, glass-fronted managers' offices located on the interior street rather than along the window edge – most of the office space is open-plan and densely populated, with little emphasis on privacy. Instant and constant access to information

Swift says that the building 'always meant different things to different people.' The success of the project, he says, lies in the way it reconciles different needs and lifestyles. Andy Cooper, the facilities manager of the Centre, praises the 'sheer convenience of the place. The possibility of chance meetings is one of its great advantages. Previously, people were rigorously compartmented at great cost in terms of both money and convenience.' Cooper says that the objective of making the building 'an enabler for change' has been accomplished. 'Everyone here is aware that we're all in the same business – flying passengers – and that transcends sectional divisions.' The Compass Centre is seen as 'a three-dimensional contract between BA and 12,000 staff.' The building is probably most popular with 'resident' staff, whose work culture was least challenged by its inception and who are now much more obviously involved in the core activity of BA than they were in their old, scattered locations. The purpose of the airline is constantly on view to everyone who visits the Centre.

The Compass Centre was designed to accommodate change and has done so effectively – already a number of the office spaces have been reconfigured. It is also a beacon for change in the company. Indeed, the building has been crucial in fostering a new feeling of community of purpose. It sets the standard for the future, and its success lies behind BA's commitment to its new Harmondsworth scheme to designs by Niels Torp (whose 1980s SAS building for Scandinavian airlines in Sweden, seen on pages 38–9, was such a landmark in progressive office design). Bob Ayling believes that Harmondsworth will embody two important lessons learned from the Compass Centre: 'One, I want an airline building which reflects what BA does – serve customers. Two, it will consist mainly of open-space offices – including mine. There's no excuse for senior managers hiding themselves away.' British Airways staff who don't work in the Compass Centre are envious of those who do. Bob Ayling goes there 'at least once a week, to meet staff and just be seen.' The success of the project is obvious: it provides a good example of a design strategy reflecting and meeting the needs of, and reinforcing, a business strategy and is a significant element in BA's success in the airline business.

Right **Externally, the the three linked buildings that form the Compass Centre are a striking landmark, by day and by night, on the very edge of one of Heathrow's main runways. The form of the building is calculated to cause minimum interference with all-important radar, and incorporates effective sun-screening devices.**

Below **Flight and cabin crew reporting areas are intensively used at all hours of the day and night. They are designed to provide a relaxing and comfortable environment where staff can eat, take a shower, and unwind. They also provide a place where crew members can, and do, meet each other on an informal basis.**

Below **The cross-section shows clearly how the atrium, which is used 24 hours a day, creates a link between the control and resource management functions carried out on the upper floors and the parallel task of receiving, checking, and briefing thousands of transient air crew staff every day.**

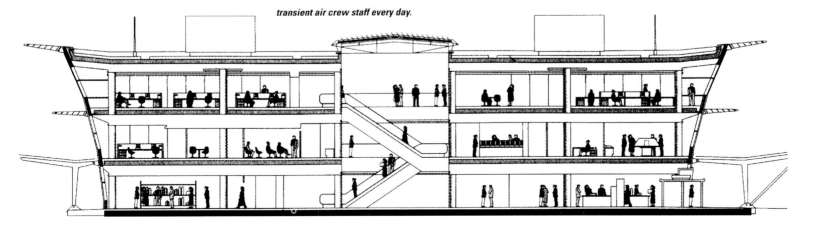

Sharp

Makuhari, Japan

When it was completed in 1992, the 80th anniversary of the foundation of the company, Sharp's building in Makuhari was seen as something of a symbolic landmark; but more importantly, the building reflected new ideas in Japanese workplace design. Haruo Tusji, Sharp's president, wanted to create a building of inspirational quality, a twenty-first century monument embodying the company's credo: 'the harmony of man and technology.' It should be an inspiration to the creative thinkers of the future, Tusji declared, and provide above-average working conditions for the highly skilled staff. The 21-storey building houses the Tokyo research and development base of electronics giant Sharp Corporation – which operates in 34 countries worldwide.

> *'We did not think of the building in the traditional way – commissioning a design architect and a construction company, but we ourselves considered its use, design, and systems, in the way that we think about one of our new products.' says Tetsuo Kusakabe of Sharp.*

When the building was being planned, Sharp organized a consultative process via a series of seven staff committees, involving more than 80 individuals out of a total staff of 800, and its managing director, Kiyoshi Sakashita, insisted that 'the most important point in making decisions is to have the consensus of all involved.' A Sharp project manager, Tetsuo Kusabe, worked closely with developers Shimizu throughout.

Sharp is a leading light in the development of electronic (and particularly liquid crystal) technology and the Makuhari building has many 'intelligent' features – cashless vending, for example, in the cafeteria (it displays not just the price but also the number of calories on the plate), an automated guidance system for visitors, cable television monitors, fully integrated information technology provision, and a highly sophisticated security system. Kiyoshi Sakashita was in overall charge of the design process and he believes that the completed building reflects Sharp's core beliefs – the value of teamwork and close attention to detail, and quality of product. 'The company's ideas are clearly reflected in the building,' he says.

Large, column-free office floors provide considerable scope for flexibility and change and the traditional 'island' layout has been avoided in favour of clumps of staggered cubicles, so that staff do not have to face each other. Services are distributed via zones along the edge of each office floor, avoiding the intrusion of core plant rooms. Cabling is highly flexible. Since the office space and furniture is standard, departments can expand or contract within the various floors as the need arises – the space can be modelled to their specific needs and there are three basic layout patterns. There is a permanent exhibition showcasing products on the second floor, to which the public has access – 200 or more people come daily. The large auditorium is also made available for public use when not required for conferences, but is used daily for presenting new research to the various teams working in the building. Other conference rooms, with personal screens at every seat, and the restaurant are located on the fourth floor.

By Japanese standards, the interior design at Sharp's Makuhari office is both varied and carefully tuned to the character of various areas of the building. Colour is used boldly.

DEN	CLUB
HIVE	CELL

BUILDING STATISTICS

CLIENT: Sharp			**FUNCTION:** Multimedia research and development			
TOTAL FLOOR AREA: 44,521 sq. m / 476,375 sq. ft		**TOTAL POPULATION:** 800	**OVERALL DENSITY:** 55.65 sq. m per person / 595 sq. ft per person			
SAMPLE PLAN AREA (less core): 990 sq. m / 10,590 sq. ft		**Circulation:** 17.0%	**Support:** 72.0%	**Cellular:** 0%	**Open plan:** 11.0%
CONSULTANTS: *Architect* Shimizu Corporation						

Above **The atrium is a key feature of the building, and as the entrance to the building, is designed more to impress than to act as a meeting place.**

Left **The architecture is highly expressive and the lobby has a temple-like monumentality. It provides a powerful focus to the entire building, which contains a generous provision of shared space, some of which is also made available for limited public use.**

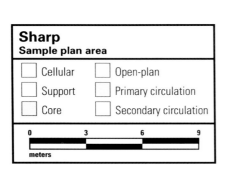

Sharp
Sample plan area

☐ Cellular   ☐ Open-plan
☐ Support   ☐ Primary circulation
☐ Core   ☐ Secondary circulation

0   3   6   9
meters

Right **The floor plan of the fourth level of the 21-storey building shows the concentration of formal meeting and conference facilities, most of which are located on lower floors in order to be near the entrance. This is characteristic of most major Japanese corporate office buildings. (The upper floors, not shown, are typically more uniformly planned at relatively high densities.)**

Below **The typical Japanese 'island' layout has been abandoned and partitions provide an element of privacy and autonomy. The furniture is of exceptional quality .**

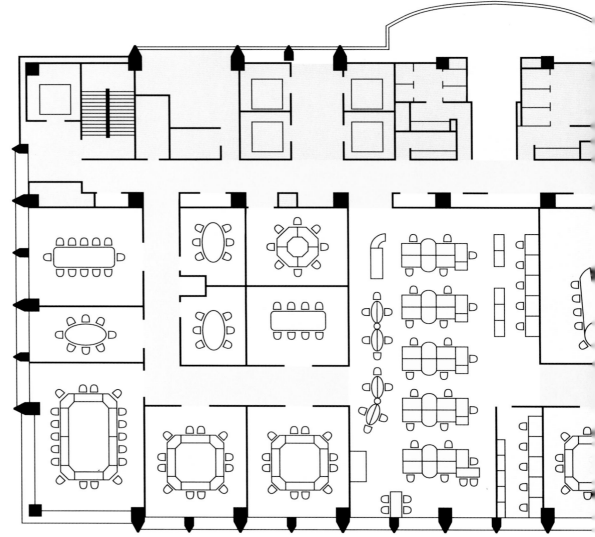

A special signage system was developed specifically for the building by Kiyoshi Sakashita's design team and incorporates colour coding for the various areas, public, private, and high security. Small kitchen areas are provided on every floor and are places to relax and socialize in. On the 21st floor a VIP suite, decorated in traditional Japanese fashion, provides for executives and important visitors. Externally, the Makuhari building is unappealing, making little impact on a new industrial and research suburb – full of relatively undistinguished buildings – where 150,000 people currently work. However, its interior breaks new ground, not least in the concessions it makes to individual preference and user comfort in a country where neither are normally high priorities.

Tetsuo Kusakabe, the senior Sharp manager responsible for overseeing the Makuhari project, sees it in terms of integration – bringing together people previously spread across a number of sites, to form a multimedia research division,

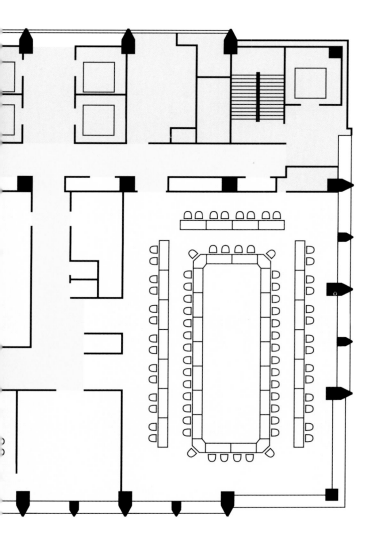

embracing many disciplines. 'The building supports our work,' he says, 'because it includes so much of our core thinking – not to mention our systems – in its design.' Kusakabe believes that one of the prime strengths of the project was its in-built adaptability. 'It's rather as if it were a building meant to be tenanted – we didn't over-customize the spaces and therefore they can readily be changed,' he says.

The integrated communication and information system in the building is a triumphant success for Sharp, simultaneously serving the company and demonstrating the quality of its products – no member of staff can remain ignorant of what is going on in the research and development division and in the company generally. (Flat-screen computers have the incidental benefit of reducing the visual clutter in offices. Sharp is remarkably paper-free.) Tetsuo Kusakabe sees the building as a reflection of the company's ever-changing technological agenda.

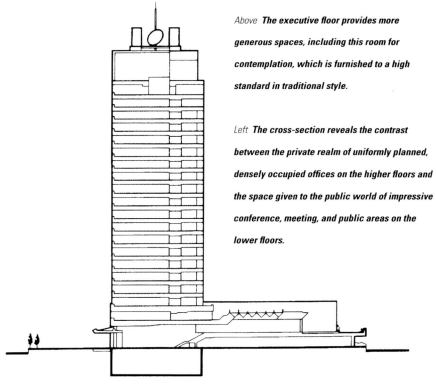

Above **The executive floor provides more generous spaces, including this room for contemplation, which is furnished to a high standard in traditional style.**

Left **The cross-section reveals the contrast between the private realm of uniformly planned, densely occupied offices on the higher floors and the space given to the public world of impressive conference, meeting, and public areas on the lower floors.**

Kajima – KI

Tokyo, Japan

In its own way a landmark in the process of change, the KI Building, developed by the Kajima Corporation, was built at the height of the 1980s boom and embodies the expansive mood of the period. The intensive use of information technology made it a pioneering 'intelligent building' and even today, it remains exceptional for the degree to which information technology is integrated into the designs. In addition, the in-house architects looked long and hard at the humanist tradition of northern Europe when conceiving the imposing central atrium and, unusually for Japan, the space is used not just as a showpiece, but also as a place for interaction and informal meetings.

Kajima is one of Japan's biggest design and construction companies with in-house engineering, architectural and research departments, and when the building was completed in 1989, it was a flagship, a demonstration of what Kajima could achieve for its clients. Located close to central Tokyo, in an attractive inner suburb, the building makes a relatively restrained impact on its setting and still commands respect for its sheer professionalism and polish.

Still on the leading edge of Japanese office design, the building is now seen to provide Kajima with the basis for moving towards a different use of space – for more intense, individual work, as well as for more group work.

KI is impressive, but Kajima, like much of Japanese business, is now looking ahead, focusing not so much on how its buildings look as on how they perform. Seita Morishima, who heads the 80-strong architectural team at Kajima, believes that the KI project would be very different today. As he says, 'Now the philosophy is: what about the inside?' Like Kunihide Oshinomi, head of Kajima's design studio, he thinks the atrium is the most successful element in the whole building.

It is heavily used by staff for informal meetings and also provides a place where visitors can be received – and suitably impressed. 'It is open, not glazed-in like almost every other atrium in Japan, and well planted,' says Morishima, 'and the jungle effect is good – most things in Japan are generally overly controlled.'

The atrium also provides a focus for the offices which look into it. These are arranged, however, in traditional hive-like patterns: ranks of semi-screened workstations fill deep (up to 25 m/270 ft) floor-plates. The furnishings are of above-average quality but the layouts are, by European or American standards, crowded. Kunihide Oshinomi feels that the rigid layout is increasingly at odds with the creative work which the company wishes to encourage. 'The design of the current office is very static, an aesthetically oriented design. The whole space remains traditional.' he says, 'We now have to satisfy two different needs: intensive and interactive. So we need not only more personalized, individual space, but also space where it is easier to communicate with others.' Oshinomi recognizes that the vast open spaces of Japanese offices could hardly be a greater contrast to the traditional northern European cellular plan. What is needed, he believes, is a Japanese development of the idea of the 'combi-office'.

Morishima is also arguing the case for 'a more open, communicative pattern of space – with more scope for group discussion.' KI certainly does not provide much space for teamwork, for discussion and debate – there is nowhere

DEN	CLUB
HIVE	CELL

BUILDING STATISTICS

CLIENT: Kajima Corporation			**FUNCTION:** Construction and design company		
TOTAL FLOOR AREA: 30,000 sq. m / 321,000 sq. ft		**TOTAL POPULATION:** 1100	**OVERALL DENSITY:** 27.3 sq. m per person / 292 sq. ft per person		
SAMPLE PLAN AREA (less core): 2,075 sq. m / 22,203 sq. ft		**Circulation:** 33.0%	**Support:** 29.4%	**Cellular:** 0%	**Open plan:** 34.0%
CONSULTANTS: *Architects* Kajima Construction Company and Midi Consultants					

Above **The canteen has a club-like quality and provides an attractive staff amenity with a terrace looking out over Tokyo suburbs.**

Left **The atrium, although large, is surprisingly intimate. It makes a powerful statement about the prestige of the company but also, and more importantly, provides a meeting place for staff and clients. It is lavishly planted and provided with elaborate water features. There is also a 'fragrance control' system to perfume the air (though this has not been used recently on economic grounds).**

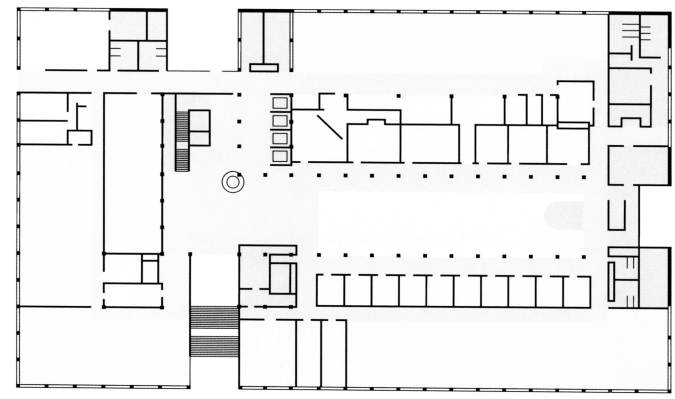

Right **The floor plan of the entrance level of Kajima's offices shows the base of the central atrium which is filled with small tables and chairs used for informal meetings. On either side of the atrium are banks of more formal meeting rooms, with open-plan office space on the perimeter. (More conventional hive-like offices occupy the 4½ floors above.)**

Kajima – KI
Sample plan area

☐ Cellular	☐ Open-plan		
☐ Support	☐ Primary circulation		
☐ Core	☐ Secondary circulation		

0   5   10   15
meters

Below **Because the building occupies a site with big level changes, the otherwise uniform office floors are occasionally relieved by high ceilings and double height spaces.**

among the workplaces where designs can be shown and discussed by a design team, for example, and this is now seen as a serious deficiency.

But space planning and facilities management are fledgling professions in Japan. Oshinomi feels that those who do practise them have a lot to learn and are fixated by the ideal of uniformity rather than a concern for the needs of a specific business operation. Morishima concurs with this view – during the boom years a great deal of attention was paid to the look of buildings, too little to how they worked.

There was no time, it seemed, for analysing what the space was for. Now Kajima's clients are rapidly turning their attention to operational issues. Morishima points to a basic difference between the Japanese and the Western approach and explains that 'Structural organization to achieve a task is not very evident in Japan.'

The lessons learned from KI are informing a wider analysis in Kajima and other companies about the role of the office building, and one can expect a very fundamental questioning of what once seemed to be the immutable foundations of office design and business practice in Japan. Technology is solving the difficulties inherent in Japanese orthography. In a changing business world, Kajima's experience at KI has shown that there is a limit to the usefulness of a would-be all-purpose model. Oshinomi admits: 'Frankly, we need to find more flexible office furniture systems, and even a new office style which includes home, remote or satellite offices. We must recognize that we can now work separately yet be networked together.' In Japan, as elsewhere, standardization may be on the way out, and diversity on the way in.

Innovation
in the cell

In cell offices the predominant work mode is concentrated and individual. There is usually – but not always – little interaction between the highly autonomous participants. Completely enclosed office rooms or highly partitioned enclosures accommodate a wide variety of individual tasks. Cell offices have an even longer history than hives and are particularly associated with the legal profession, universities, and research institutes. In all these contexts high status and highly autonomous individuals have long been accustomed to relying on individual rooms to protect them from distraction. Cell-like enclosures, i.e. those with high but not full-height partitions, have been the staple of much North American office planning since the late 1960s. Such bull-pen layouts have never had much merit and are likely to have even less in the future.

In northern Europe, direct pressure from an office work force able to influence the shape of its working environment through statutorily constituted Workers' Councils has encouraged the building of offices composed more or less entirely of identical, interchangeable, individual cells. These are very different from the status-rich, differentiated cell offices in the North American mould. In one of the two German case studies, Gruner & Jahr, huge numbers of cellular offices, supported by common meeting areas, are arranged along the network of 'streets' that holds this very large building together. In the case of Edding, interactive common support spaces are surrounded by glass-fronted enclosed offices. A similar basic pattern, combining individual enclosures and shared open-plan space, is found in Sun Micro's new offices in California. This is a North American example of a new business that has worked out, from first principles, that while cell offices are right for certain kinds of tasks, they need to be supplemented by open environments to support interaction, teamworking and the sharing of resources. One striking difference between the German and the North American examples is that the space in Sun Micro's offices in sunny and temperate California is much deeper and generally further

from daylight than would be acceptable in the greyer climate of Hamburg or Hanover.

Time-sharing of workstations is possible and is becoming more common. In the North American system of 'hotelling' – not used so far at Sun Micro where individual room 'ownership' is highly prized – cell offices are programmed to be interchangeable so that they can be reserved and time-shared, just like hotel rooms. 'Hotelling' is likely to increase as innovations in information technology change the ways in which office work is done and dissolve the assumption that if there is one person there must be one desk. This will lead to space allocation by zoning specific kinds of office activities into specific kinds of office space – the basis of the club office. Shared or not, the demand for cells is likely to continue to be an important component of office design. In this context the Channel 4 headquarters in London is an interesting hybrid, combining cells for solitary workers with team spaces, or dens, for those who work in groups.

Edding

Ahrensburg, Germany

The competition for building Edding's new headquarters was won by architects whose entry was based on their conviction that the dictum 'a house must be like a small town, or it is not really a house' could equally be applied to offices. This dictum, expressed by the well-known Dutch architect Aldo van Eyck but based on a saying of Palladio, underlay the concept of a building that provides for individual needs and preferences but also sustains the working community.

The 1988 brief had specified the combi-office. This concept, first seen in Sweden in the 1970s, originated as an attempt to resolve the conflict between the demand for privacy and the need for more teamwork and better communication. When completed in 1990, Edding's offices were claimed to be the first such complex in Germany. In effect, they combine cells, allocated to almost everyone irrespective of status, with common space for shared office equipment, meetings, and project work.

> *Addressing the problem of combining concentrated, reflective work and spontaneous interaction in the context of demanding project work led to the development of a solution that accommodates both: the combi-office.*

Founded in 1960, pen manufacturers Edding previously occupied two buildings in Ahrensburg. While staff numbers hovered around 90, these remained adequate and most people were happy with their traditional format – heads of departments in their own rooms, most staff two or three to an office and only specialist teams in shared space. The growth of the company underlay its decision to relocate to a new building. Brunswick-based architects Hans Struhk & Partners' building, designed for 160 staff, has an informal, accretive character, though its architectural expression is entirely modern with metal and glass façades on a concrete frame. At its heart is the two-storey galleria or 'street' which connects the blocks of offices. Rigorous, even spartan, in character, the street comes to life in use and is a place for informal meetings and social contact. People are actively encouraged to circulate along the split-level galleries and frequent use of the staircases is almost unavoidable. (Edding, like other companies, was struck by the fact that sedentary office workers will almost always use elevators if they are available, yet seek 'healthy' exercise by running or working out in their leisure hours.) The galleria provides access to, and views into, all the working areas.

The two blocks (one of two, and the other of three storeys) contain nine combi-office zones. Individual offices, generally 4.2 x 2.4 m/14 x 8 ft, and with clear glazed screen walls, are permanently allocated to individuals. Each contains a worktable, a mobile filing cabinet, shelves, and cupboards, and a small desk area for a visitor. The traditional etiquette applies: if the door is closed – an uncommon occurrence – it is assumed that the occupant is anxious not to be disturbed. Outside is the 'common zone', equipped with conference tables, fax and photocopy machines, special typewriters, banks of filing cabinets, and a kitchen/coffee area. The handful of senior executives enjoy superior facilities – double-size rooms, individually furnished, with a view over the landscaped area in front of the building. As usual, the move into new offices was the occasion for updating the company's technology. The level of information technology use is high for all staff (said to be between 40 and 65 per cent of total

DEN	CLUB
HIVE	**CELL**

BUILDING STATISTICS				
CLIENT: Edding AG		**FUNCTION:** Headquarters of pen manufacturer		
TOTAL FLOOR AREA: 4,450 sq. m / 47,615 sq. ft	**TOTAL POPULATION:** 160	**OVERALL DENSITY:** 27.8 sq. m per person / 297.5 sq. ft per person		
SAMPLE PLAN AREA (less core): 1,529 sq. m / 16,360 sq. ft	**Circulation:** 35.3%	**Support:** 42.4%	**Cellular:** 22.3%	**Open plan:** 0%
CONSULTANTS: *Architect and Interior Design* Struhk and Partners with Goede & Palesch *Programming* Congena				

Above **Office space is essentially cellular, with workstations permanently allotted to individuals, but glazed partitions encourage a feeling of openness and transparency.**

Left **The two-storey 'street' is the core of the building, and the galleries and staircases which form circulation routes also provide locations for informal encounters. Good use of natural light is an important aspect of the scheme.**

work time), and cable ducts were designed for high flexibility. However, since the use of laptop computers is still limited, there is little access to information technology in meeting rooms.

The building houses a variety of activities – sales, accounts, purchasing, and general administration. In most departments, conventional working hours still apply. Only in the export department do staff work early and late and few people, other than sales staff, work to any significant degree outside the building. The heavy emphasis on staff amenities is typical of Germany. Natural light permeates the entire building and

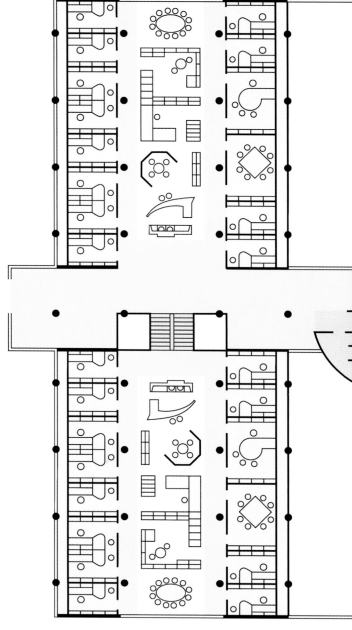

*Below **Office cells provide for a high degree of user control over working conditions. Ranged along the edge of the building, they have opening windows. The high-quality furniture is by Martela of Finland.***

opening windows are fitted throughout. Air conditioning is provided only in plant rooms. (There are complaints of over-heating in summer, despite the provision of sun screening and blinds.) Furniture by Martela of Finland is designed for user convenience – its crisp and functional mix of metallic and wooden finishes is echoed in the no-nonsense fit-out of the offices as a whole.

Edding is an excellent example of the cell office, brought up-to-date in the business climate of an enlightened, medium-sized and clearly very prosperous German business. But how well do the cells really work for a changing organization? Both the management and users of the building report positive benefits from the move – transparency, openness, space,

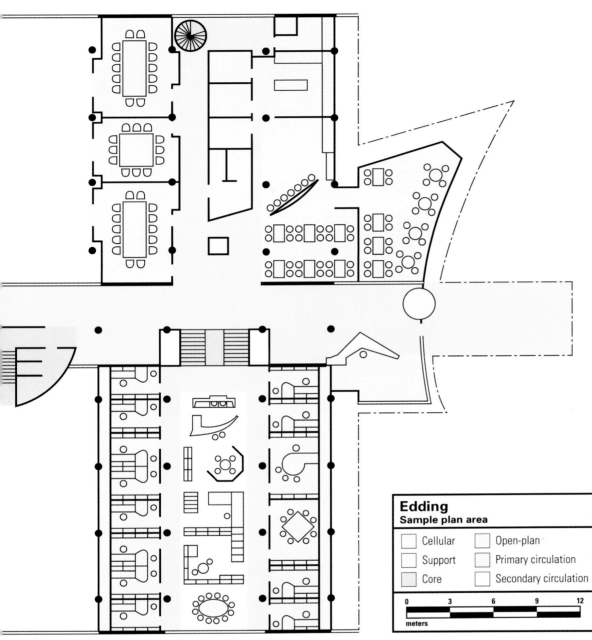

Left **The floor plan shows the upper level of the four two-storey pavilions that make up the Edding building. Three of the pavilions are designed as combi-offices with more or less standard-size, glass-fronted, individual office rooms on either side of the central space, which is used to accommodate shared equipment and facilities. The ground floor of the fourth pavilion, seen at the top right, is given over to major meeting rooms and the staff restaurant. The pavilions are linked by a double height 'street'.**

Edding
Sample plan area

☐ Cellular		☐ Open-plan
☐ Support		☐ Primary circulation
☐ Core		☐ Secondary circulation

0   3   6   9   12
meters

privacy, and scope for concentrated work, and for interaction and informal contact with colleagues. Many staff were apprehensive about the new premises, but most are now pleased. A study by the Fraunhofer Institute of Stuttgart found that the new building out-performed its predecessors in almost every respect, though, surprisingly, the majority view was that the company's old buildings were more private and yet at the same time were more encouraging to informal communication. The needs of departments do, of course, vary widely. In accounts, 90 per cent of work is individual rather than collaborative; in management, the proportion is 60 to 40 per cent. Sales staff report that 90 per cent of their internal meetings tend to be informal, yet for managers half of all meetings have a formal character. The fact that office provision is so uniform throughout suggests that, despite the extensive consultation that went into the project, and despite the real control individuals have over their lighting and ventilation, individual discretion in workspace design was, in the end, subordinated either by Edding or its architects to the overall look and consistency of the building.

Edding is convinced, however, that its decision to retain highly cellular office space was correct. Interchangeability of workplaces to help facilities management is important as is the elimination of unnecessary and wasteful status distinctions. The defects of the project seem to lie in the under-use of the common areas of the building, which are perceived as

Right **The building provides a high-quality environment with good use of natural light. Planting and the use of water soften its impact on the external landscape.**

lacking in privacy and comfort and sometimes noisy. The lack of partitions and rather hard aesthetic does not help. The architects' aim to provide a 'family atmosphere' has not been entirely achieved: the common areas are seen as inappropriate places to arrange meetings with clients, while individual offices are too small for more than two people – their very smallness risks them being confrontational rather than comfortable. There is a general conviction in the company that the common areas must be more effectively used and that

the staff must adopt more mobile ways of working. This implies a greater reliance on laptops and portable technology.

Edding's approach has always been to involve staff closely in decisions about their workplace, and they now expect further changes. There is a clear leadership role, which rests with management, in determining what they should be. There is also the issue of to what extent the building – and the combi-office concept on which it is based – can cope with change. So far, that question remains largely unexplored.

Below **The cross-section shows how individual office rooms, book-lined and intimate, look out on to a central, common area used for shared activities, equipment, and filing.**

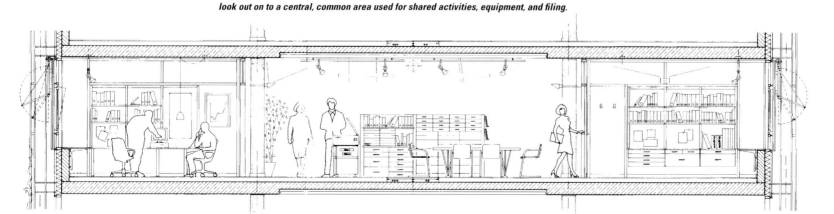

Gruner + Jahr

Hamburg, Germany

When it was searching for new premises, Gruner + Jahr emphatically did not want a typical office building, but a centre for encouraging creative work. To make its business successful and to attract the talented staff it required, it decided to provide as wide a range of amenities as possible for itsemployees, with a variety of spaces for work and relaxation, in a building that would be integrated into, rather than set apart from, Hamburg as a whole.

Gruner + Jahr, the media and magazine publishing empire, producers of an extraordinary range of magazines in Germany, including *Stern*, first expressed its principal objective – to bring all its Hamburg operations, divided among a number of buildings, under one roof – as early as 1978. In 1982 they identified the Baumwall quay site. In the port area that had still not recovered from severe damage in the Second World War, the site was little more than a traffic artery dominated by the overhead tracks of the U-Bahn. An invited competition was held in 1983 and the Munich office of architects Steidle + Kiessler were the winners. Construction took place in 1987–90 and was part of a renaissance of that part of Hamburg, whereby the port was reconnected, by an area of green public space, to the city centre.

The completed building is typical of much progressive commercial architecture in Germany – uncompromisingly modern, with metal and glass cladding on a concrete frame, but somewhat less gymnastic and demonstrative in character than the high-tech work of, say, Richard Rogers. The architects were understandably keen to pay homage to the building's maritime location and there are clear references to the cranes and warehouses of the adjacent port. The scale of the building, effectively a massive 'groundscraper', was carefully considered, while its form, a series of long blocks terminating in gable ends, provides a memory of the traditional Hamburg warehouse. The architecture is workmanlike and straightforward, rather than highly expressive or extrovert, though a tower (known as the 'toboggan') provides one external point of identity – inside, it houses a series of conference rooms.

The building is more notable, perhaps, for its considered relationship with the city. A walkway, taking advantage of changing levels and linking St Michael's church to the quay and Baumwall U-Bahn station, passes straight through Gruner + Jahr and gives access to shops and a café as well as to the company's entrance lobby (seen as a public space). Transparency was a key objective: the building should be intelligible, rather than forbidding, to users and to the public. The use of streets and courtyards to define internal space is crucial in this respect, breaking the large building down into tangible neighbourhoods.

The brief demanded a building for 2000 employees with every opportunity for collaboration and interaction between departments. In tune with the ethos of the company – profit-sharing, non-hierarchical, stressing self-government and individual responsibility – the project was rooted in close consultation and research into the needs of future users. The

> *Gerd Schulte-Hillen, Gruner + Jahr's chairman, insists that 'one of the principles of modern management is that individuals' needs should be taken into account as much as possible and that their requests should be considered when their workplaces are being designed.'*

DEN	CLUB
HIVE	**CELL**

BUILDING STATISTICS				
CLIENT: Gruner + Jahr AG & Co		**FUNCTION:** Headquarters of publishing and media company		
TOTAL FLOOR AREA: 60,000 sq. m / 642,000 sq. ft	**TOTAL POPULATION:** 1950	**OVERALL DENSITY:** 30.8 sq. m per person / 330 sq. ft per person		
SAMPLE PLAN AREA (less core): 5,531 sq. m / 59,182 sq. ft	**Circulation:** 30.3%	**Support:** 7.6%	**Cellular:** 58.6%	**Open plan:** 3.4%
CONSULTANTS: *Architects* Steidle + Kiessler with Schweger + Partners				

Above **The cellular form of the space – everyone has his or her own small office – reflects a strongly expressed preference among staff and is seen as encouraging creative individual work.**

Left **The complex is planned around a grid of top-lit internal corridors that run into larger 'streets', which are the focus for interaction and personal communication as well as a physical link between the wings of the building.**

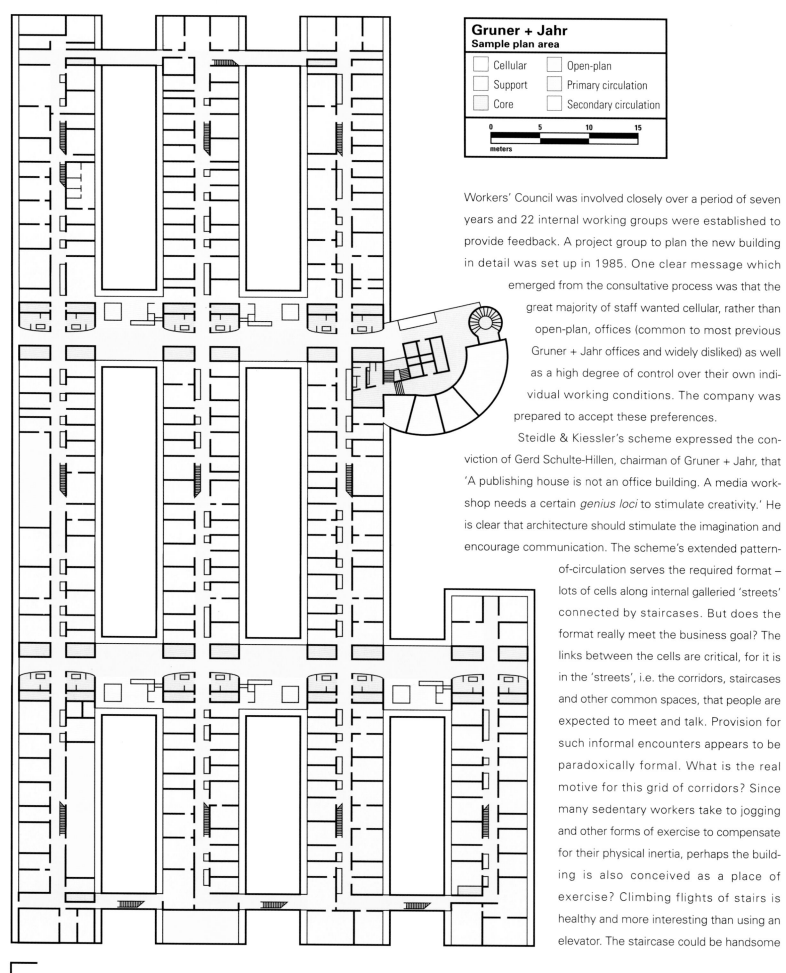

Gruner + Jahr
Sample plan area

- ☐ Cellular
- ☐ Support
- ☐ Core
- ☐ Open-plan
- ☐ Primary circulation
- ☐ Secondary circulation

0   5   10   15

meters

Workers' Council was involved closely over a period of seven years and 22 internal working groups were established to provide feedback. A project group to plan the new building in detail was set up in 1985. One clear message which emerged from the consultative process was that the great majority of staff wanted cellular, rather than open-plan, offices (common to most previous Gruner + Jahr offices and widely disliked) as well as a high degree of control over their own individual working conditions. The company was prepared to accept these preferences.

Steidle & Kiessler's scheme expressed the conviction of Gerd Schulte-Hillen, chairman of Gruner + Jahr, that 'A publishing house is not an office building. A media workshop needs a certain *genius loci* to stimulate creativity.' He is clear that architecture should stimulate the imagination and encourage communication. The scheme's extended pattern-of-circulation serves the required format – lots of cells along internal galleried 'streets' connected by staircases. But does the format really meet the business goal? The links between the cells are critical, for it is in the 'streets', i.e. the corridors, staircases and other common spaces, that people are expected to meet and talk. Provision for such informal encounters appears to be paradoxically formal. What is the real motive for this grid of corridors? Since many sedentary workers take to jogging and other forms of exercise to compensate for their physical inertia, perhaps the building is also conceived as a place of exercise? Climbing flights of stairs is healthy and more interesting than using an elevator. The staircase could be handsome

in itself and, perhaps, a good place to show works of art. But are these business ideas?

The architects, focused on designing the perfect individual working environment, were aiming for one that was 'domestic', with privacy yet plenty of scope for interaction and socializing. It was assumed – and it has turned out to be the case – that few people would choose to close their office doors (unless they needed to have a confidential discussion) so the cells are not closed. People wander freely in and out of colleagues' offices. Some groups in some departments (for example, magazine picture departments) share den-like open-plan offices – still extremely modest compared with the grand scale of North American dens – since their work is interactive by its very nature. Those who work in these group or team spaces, however, feel that they are less privileged

than those allotted cellular offices. The latter average 14 sq. m/150 sq. ft of space and are simply – 'boringly', according to some users – furnished. There have been some complaints that the desks (by Gesika) are not adjustable and not ergonomically efficient. However, the majority of employees lucky enough to occupy the cellular offices generally remain adamant that the format works well.

Many of the cellular offices have doors opening on to an external walkway as well as opening windows, so that natural ventilation is plentiful. 'Green' policies, as applied in Germany,

Above **The architecture has clear roots in Hamburg's nautical traditions – as seen to strong effect in this meeting-room tower.**

Opposite **The floor plan of main office floor shows the same basic pattern throughout: with a few exceptions, individual office rooms line the long corridors. The two main 'streets', seen running horizontally, are intended for social and business interaction, and meeting spaces are provided at the crossroads. Conference rooms are concentrated in the big semicircular tower.**

demand a high degree of energy efficiency, with largely natural ventilation. In most areas, air conditioning is provided only in a supporting role, to be switched on in very hot weather – the exceptions are kitchens, photographic laboratories, and other specialized areas. In the cellular offices, users can control the air conditioning by means of wall-mounted switches. Sun shading on the south, east, and west façades takes the form of external awnings at the upper level and external venetian blinds lower down. Internal venetian blinds are standard. Even so, some occupants report problems of overheating in summer.

Right **The very large building is effectively broken down into a series of medium-rise sections, linked by glazed bridges.**

A strong cultural, and even political, agenda underlay the form of the building reflecting a determination to cater for employee preferences to a degree that is especially typical of Germany, the Netherlands, and Scandinavia and that would be seen as eccentric in, say, Britain or the United States. This approach has certainly had the effect of producing a complex, idiosyncratic building – with attendant problems of maintenance and management. A few years into its life, user reactions vary. Privacy and quietness are highlighted as its strengths. The natural light and views out are also appreciated. Not surprisingly, given the overwhelming length of the corridors, some staff

Below **The external form of the building makes references to both dockside warehouses and ships. This 'media city' is part of a major reconstruction of a run-down quarter close to the centre of Hamburg.**

members complain that they are 'endless' and about the amount of walking needed to go to the lavatory or to get a cup of coffee. Some feel that the communal areas take up too much space – and the restaurant is widely felt to be rather bleak. Yet these amenities were intended to stimulate the interaction which was such a key objective of the project. There is a widespread feeling that a greater range of dedicated meeting and conference rooms should have been provided, and that more comfortable, relaxing shared spaces are needed for team- and shared work.

The idea of the building as a 'media city' implies public as well as private space, and perhaps the sense of community is underplayed in the building. Yet it is a popular workplace, with a strong sense of identity. Its weaknesses might have been predicted, but its strengths are proven. Merely bringing together everyone in one place was an enormous advance – Gruner + Jahr feels that the company is now a far more communicative community than ever before, and that this is reflected in the business.

Below **The cross-section shows the walkways and staircases that, in the words of the architect who planned them, 'do not bring just storeys and functions together but also the users of the building.' Major conference and meeting rooms are concentrated in the tower.**

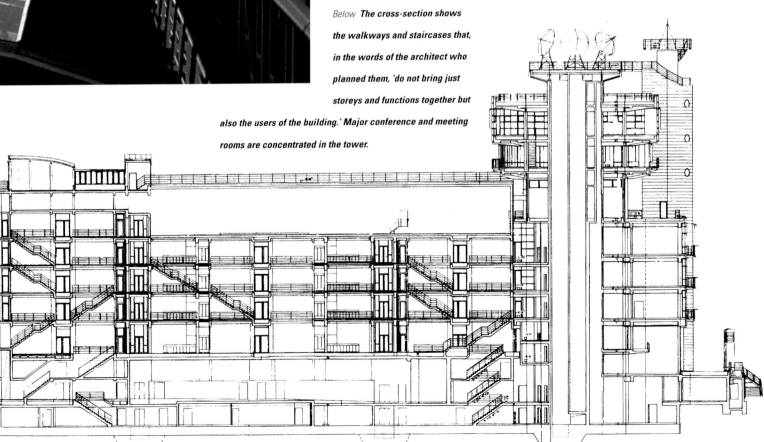

Sun Micro

Palo Alto, California, USA

'It's not just a matter of physical changes,' says Ann Bamesberger, manager of work effectiveness at Sun Micro, 'it's the organizational dynamic that really counts.' This thinking underlies the company's continuing

experiments in reorganizing its office space. Sun Micro, one of the largest manufacturers in the world of computer hardware and software, is heavily committed to research and product development and employs a large number of highly qualified technologists and engineers. It is also a player in a very competitive global market and needs to monitor that market constantly and address changing consumer needs in order to maintain its position. Engineers, managers, and marketing staff must be in close contact. It became clear that this imperative was not being satisfactorily met, necessitating a change in the physical setting of these employees' working lives. Not only was one department housed several miles away from the rest of the company, but virtually all the office space was of a cellular nature, since the conviction has always been that research and development staff need privacy and calm to pursue their projects. Sun Micro had commissioned several studies which suggested that more interactive space was needed throughout the organization and that the traditional cellular office had its deficiencies. Typically, a member of staff would spend 30 to 40 per cent of the working day away from his or her desk. Corridors and staircases were the scenes of many informal discussions of the sort which characterize teamworking.

The process of change began within the marketing and communications (Marcom) team. Until 1995 this team had occupied another building in Palo Alto, some distance from the rest of Sun Micro in the city's Menlo Park – the implication being that its outward-looking concerns were divorced from those of the technical staff. One of the aims of the project was to challenge that assumption, and certainly one of the immediate advantages of the move to Menlo Park, where Sun Micro already had seven buildings, is that Marcom staff can easily meet managers and engineers by walking from one building to another rather than driving several miles. The building which has housed the group since 1995 is part of the campus designed by architects Backen, Arrigoni, & Ross to standard American industrial park specifications: two to three storeys high, with 30.5 m/100 ft-deep floors and fully air-conditioned. (Building deep and using air conditioning is cheaper, in purely financial terms, even in temperate California, than adopting 'greener' approaches to servicing.)

The Marcom team is concerned with Sun Micro's communications to the outside world, to potential customers. At the time it moved the group had 46 staff. It has since grown. It includes graphic designers, writers, and marketing and advertising managers, as well as others whose skills might equally be at home in an advertising agency, and its work is more collaborative by definition than that of other Sun Micro employees. The group formed the ideal subject for an experiment in more interactive working.

The Marcom team occupies less than half of a typical floor on the campus. This was fitted out and space-planned

> *'We wanted to bring marketing and engineering folks together, get them to talk to each other and quit their ivory towers,' says Ann Bamesberger of Sun Micro.*

DEN	CLUB
HIVE	**CELL**

BUILDING STATISTICS					
CLIENT: Sun Microsystems			**FUNCTION:** Objects / products (OP) group of computer manufacturer		
TOTAL FLOOR AREA: 2,512 sq. m / 26,884 sq. ft		**TOTAL POPULATION:** 65	**OVERALL DENSITY:** 38.6 sq. m per person / 413 sq. ft per person		
SAMPLE PLAN AREA (less core): 2,512 sq. m / 26,884 sq. ft		**Circulation:** 32.6%	**Support:** 29.2%	**Cellular:** 38.2%	**Open plan:** 0%
CONSULTANTS: *Architect* Backen Arrigoni Ross *Interior Design* Bottom Duvivier					

Above **Sun Micro's experiments in workplace design combine cellular offices – full of technology – with heavily used team spaces.**

Left **The numerous break areas were deliberately planned by management as places to encourage interaction. They are frequently used for informal business meetings and discussions as well as for social purposes.**

Right **A typical floor plan shows the heavy concentration of small, standard-size offices. These have sliding glass fronts and are arranged so that they are adjacent to more central communal 'activity' or support spaces.**

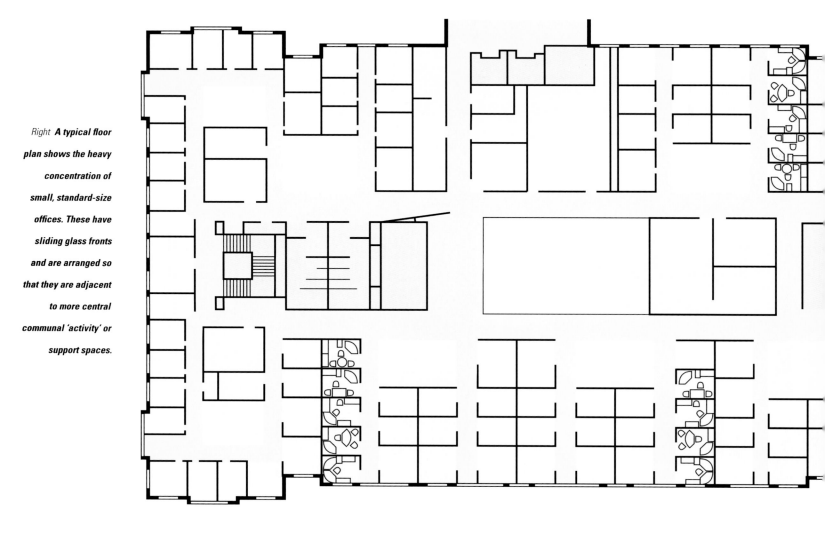

Sun Micro
Sample plan area

☐ Cellular	☐ Open-plan
☐ Support	☐ Primary circulation
☐ Core	☐ Secondary circulation

0	5	10	15

meters

by San Francisco architects Bottom Duvivier. In effect, the team now occupies a form of combi-office consisting of cellular offices surrounding a shared space, with a good provision of break areas. Unsurprisingly, the use of information technology is universal. Screens are everywhere although laptops are not generally used (Sun Micro does not make them).

Although Marcom inaugurated Sun Micro's attempts to break down the monopoly of the cellular office, all staff there retain small, fully enclosed offices, generally about 2.4 x 3.6 m/8 x 12 ft. However, the new group-work areas are so heavily used that some group members have questioned whether the cellular offices are needed at all. Considerable efforts were made to improve the furnishings of the individual offices, to give more flexibility, and glass doors (generally open) encourage a feeling of transparency and communication. Furniture is free standing and adjustable. Wall-hung

storage systems can also be freely adjusted and provide a mix of shelves, storage areas and paper-trays, encouraging neatness and order (though there is no official clean desk policy). Some staff feel that, given the non-technical nature of their work, a naturally ventilated building would have been preferable. In general, however, the project is popular with users and the attractions of the well-landscaped and highly social campus compensate for the longer journey times many face in going to work there. (Though some, used to working in a normal urban environment, found the site's isolation and the security imposed rather irritating.) The relocation has made communication between departments much stronger, while the refit has achieved the successful collaborative working within the Marcom team that the company wanted.

Extending the new approach to fit-out beyond the specialized areas of marketing and public relations to the core activities of the company was a more difficult proposition. But this process is now under way. The recently completed (1996) refiguring of the objects/products (OP) group, which

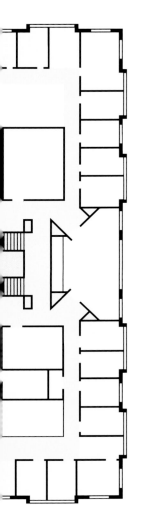

includes 50 software engineers and 15 product-marketing staff, was a significant step forward. The project was undertaken after a study by a Los Angeles-based company, Iometrics, which applies psychological research methods to the study of the workplace. The aim was to understand the needs of a specific group within the company that was felt to require strong feedback from customers. At a preliminary stage there were interviews with staff, focus groups, and general meetings and a survey was carried out.

According to Bamesberger, the aim was 'maximum collaboration, while still enabling the necessary heads-down work that software engineers perform.' Company vice president Richard Green, responsible for the OP group, wanted to achieve a new sort of space which would encourage such contacts. Like the Marcom layouts, the result is a North American version of the combi-office. The layout is designed to provide the quiet space that many staff still demand – glass walls to the individual cellular offices break down visual barriers but still shut out noise and interruptions. The shared group spaces that are immediately adjacent to the cell offices were the subject of particularly close user consultation: everyone recognized how much the cellular offices were liked, but there was a strongly perceived need to persuade people to venture out of them on occasion. According to John Duvivier, the solution – which was to manage the timetable rather than the space to make sure that interaction happens –

emerged from the views of the users, guided by the architects. The longstanding tradition of weekly 'all hands' meetings at Sun Micro created the right climate for fertile user feedback. 'They were great occasions to meet people and chat,' says Duvivier.

Duvivier regards the finished space as 'an experiment still, not a final solution.' Flexibility provides for physical changes. Many staff have already personalized their offices. 'They're a creative bunch – nearly all Ph.Ds – the creators of the future,' says Duvivier. 'They like their own space and their own identity within the company.' (They were allowed to select their own office furniture.) Duvivier defines the finished project as 'purposeful, interactive, rather serendipitous,' but admits that it is, in essence, a compromise.'It had to be that way – you can't force creative people into a mould they find uncomfortable.'

The success of the OP project is still being assessed. Ann Bamesberger doubts that the high level of interaction envisaged at the outset has yet been

Below **The emphasis in the fit-out has been on informality, as seen in this meeting area – the company seeks to encourage interaction between staff whose specialized work tends to be highly individual in nature.**

Above and below **Sun Micro's experiment in interaction focuses on the open-plan team spaces. One of them is seen here in three distinct roles. The furniture is lightweight and portable so that these spaces can be easily reconfigured – in contrast to the cellular offices seen on the right.**

achieved. 'People pursue their own ways of working, designing, creating and we have to empower them to do that,' she says. But has the project been good for the business? 'It was very costly and whether it represents value for money has yet to be seen,' Bamesberger admits. 'But people can see that it's something different and new and they respect what we're trying to do.' She also says that the spaces are less flexible than she'd hoped – 'it costs money to change things, whatever anyone says.'

Sun Micro is now working on two or three new 'campuses' and a parallel 'teaming' initiative has been taken in their offices in Farnborough in the UK. The experiments at Menlo Park are providing valuable feedback for their planners. 'We'd do the same again, in a sense,' says Bamesberger, 'but there is a limit to the degree to which buildings can change behaviour. People get together and interact quite naturally at home, even in conferences and meetings. In their normal working environment, they always seem more constrained. You can't easily mix people whose approach to work is so different, not without major organizational changes.'

Ann Bamesberger believes that the advent of the virtual office will have a major impact on Sun Micro – staff will only meet together for tasks which need to be interactive. This sounds like a strong move towards the idea of office as club. 'All this is coming – and soon – and we must face it,' she believes. 'Perhaps buildings will count for a lot less – good management and the proper use of technology are equally important. You can bring people to a building, but you can't control the way they use it. At best, a building is just one leg of a three-legged stool.'

New kinds of office – the den

In den offices the emphasis is on interactive group work. The teams that work in them are not necessarily highly autonomous – although they are beginning to control their mode of operation and the use of their resources more and more. Consequently den activities are becoming much more complex and are likely to require a wider range of settings. Given this definition of the den, little sharing of individual workstations is expected. As time goes on and technology develops, this is likely to change.

Meeting the plural and changing demands of group working is critical to the design of successful dens. Projects are rarely the same. Often several projects are worked on simultaneously in the same place; sometimes people work on more than one project in parallel but in different places. Dens tend to be environments in which no outcome is entirely certain, no resource completely bookable. Hence some redundancy of provision is inevitable, despite the most skilled programming and scheduling.

Lend Lease Interiors and Imagination and, to a lesser extent Vitra, and the team spaces in Channel 4, are typical of the kinds of environment that creative organizations are tending to make for themselves. They are busy and often crowded. Great attention is paid to the accommodation of project work, sometimes to the detriment of the quality of individual workstations. Consequently, in quantitative terms the proportion of space devoted to meeting and project areas tends to be high. Sometimes, as in Nickelodeon, Steelcase, and even Vitra, considerable architectural prominence is given to the apparatus of these areas.

The computer is becoming a working partner in these creative offices. At the centre of the Steelcase office is a kind of 'war room' in which audio-visual technology plays a very visible, almost Disney-like role. At the other end of the scale, Michaelides & Bednash, in its intimate, low-budget, central London conversion, has made the centre of its office a big communal table at which everyone sits, at any time, in any order, to use the ubiquitous and vitally important laptops –

the new medium of work. Nickelodeon and Andersen World-wide are very different in style, but share intense pressure to achieve interaction throughout their entire organizations. Elaborate attempts have been made in both cases to ensure that a wide enough range of shared settings is available to complement carefully designed individual work settings. In the following case studies, significant differences can be observed in the balance of space allotted to group rather than to individual activities, in dens rather than in hives and cells.

To achieve similar but changing management objectives, superb new offices have been sometimes built, as for Channel 4 and Vitra; on other occasions the effort has been entirely internal and remedial, making better use of existing standard office buildings, as in the Lend Lease, Steelcase and Nickelodeon cases. In two examples, Michaelides & Bednash and Imagination, wonderful dens have been created out of buildings that were not originally intended to be offices at all: a rag-trade sweatshop and a school respectively.

Michaelides & Bednash

London, UK

'The table was the key idea, the focus for a network of ideas,' says architect Simon Henley. 'They had to be convinced, of course, but now it seems the only sensible way to work.' Michaelides & Bednash, based in the

West End of London, is a relatively new and markedly youthful company which operates in the rapidly developing world of media entertainment and advertising. Its core skill centres on its research-based understanding of how the media engages people. This knowledge is used to develop campaigns for advertisers and also to provide a basis for the company's involvement in the development of television programmes. Michaelides & Bednash is, in other words, about communication, ideas, and interaction; and its partners wanted a working environment that expressed their own clear-cut ideas on the advertising business as well as the company's particular identity, and also served its practical, day-to-day needs.

> *'Flexibility is the idea,' says partner George Michaelides. 'The office is a blank canvas, something to work on. This place challenges people to behave differently from those in a typical office space – they cannot hide in their cubbyholes here.'*

According to George Michaelides, one of the two founding partners, 'We wanted not just space, but a culture of work – it's what separates winners and losers.' Although there was no formal brief as such, the partners' ideas for their new office space were rooted in a vision of participatory work which implied transparency, teamwork, and a lack of obvious hierarchy, and included phrases such a 'original, not just better' and 'reassuring, not combative'. 'They said what they wanted very clearly,' explain architects Buschow Henley. 'They wanted to look well established and secure, but also informal and innovative,' says architect Ralph Buschow. 'The space had to reflect a lot of ideas.' Secrecy,

says Michaelides, is the very antithesis of what the firm is about. He finds the idea of partners and senior managers shutting themselves away in private compartments both offensive and inappropriate to the operations of the company. The two partners believe in leadership, and this belief underlay the office project in which they had a firm hand. However, they reject the idea of 'managers' and 'ordinary staff'. Michaelides insists that 'Nobody here is ordinary. We like extraordinary people.' The company is a closely knit team; there are just twelve people: eight media strategists, two PAs, a receptionist, and an accountant.

The location, a floor in a handsome, steel-framed 1920s factory building in Great Titchfield Street, was discovered after a long search. The architects were thrilled by the building, solid and decent in itself and with fine views of William Butterfield's magnificent High Victorian church of All Saints, Margaret Street, a monument they greatly admire. The floor acquired by their client was relatively narrow in section with exceptional natural lighting, without excessive solar gain in fine weather. Opening steel windows provide completely adequate ventilation. The space was superficially, unnattractive: carpeted, dingily decorated, and filled with 'hideous' light fittings. Stripping out revealed its qualities. Replanning focused on the aim of keeping the space as open as possible, though lavatories, a tiny kitchen (staff are encouraged to use the local cafés and restaurants), space for coats and a couple of conference rooms were needed.

DEN	CLUB
HIVE	CELL

BUILDING STATISTICS				
CLIENT: Michaelides & Bednash		**FUNCTION:** Media company		
TOTAL FLOOR AREA: 308 sq. m / 3,300 sq. ft	**TOTAL POPULATION:** 10-20	**OVERALL DENSITY:** 30-15 sq. m per person / 300-150 sq. ft per person		
SAMPLE PLAN AREA (less core): 300 sq. m / 3,210 sq. ft	**Circulation:** 40.2%	**Support:** 43.4%	**Cellular:** 0%	**Open plan:** 16.4%
CONSULTANTS: *Interior Design* Buschow Henley				

Above **The office consists essentially of one large room, fitted out stylishly but quite minimally to produce a generous and enjoyable work place.**

Left **All staff work at a single table, 20 m/66 ft long and extending the full length of the office. They choose their place in line with the task in hand – there are no allocated workstations.**

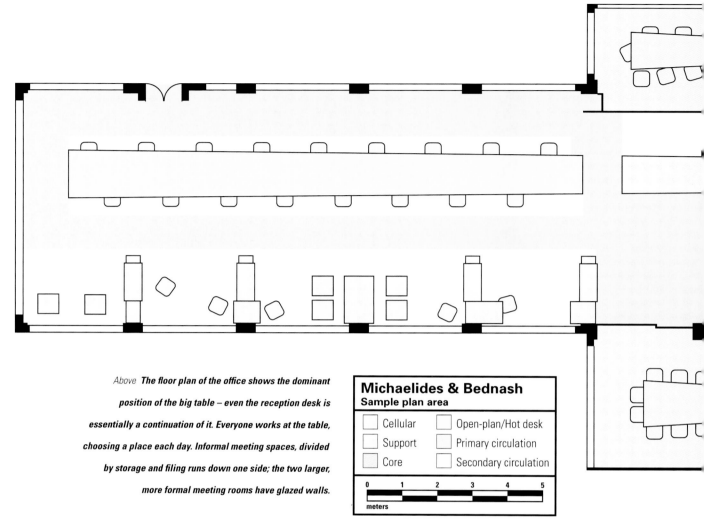

Above **The floor plan of the office shows the dominant position of the big table – even the reception desk is essentially a continuation of it. Everyone works at the table, choosing a place each day. Informal meeting spaces, divided by storage and filing runs down one side; the two larger, more formal meeting rooms have glazed walls.**

Michaelides & Bednash
Sample plan area

☐ Cellular		☐ Open-plan/Hot desk
☐ Support		☐ Primary circulation
☐ Core		☐ Secondary circulation

0   1   2   3   4   5
meters

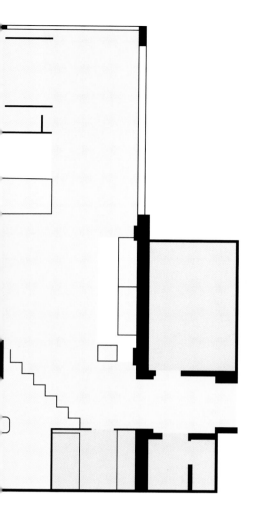

One basic need of Michaelides & Bednash is a place where people can work together. 'We are not and cannot be a virtual office,' says Michaelides. 'We need to be together quite a lot of the time. We can't work in isolation.' He compares the job the company does to that of the teams of writers who concoct television sit-com scripts: 'They sit around, for days on end if necessary, and throw ideas, lines, jokes at each other – it's collaborative by its very nature. That's how it works.'

This is where 'the table' fits in. Buschow Henley suggested that the new office should be configured around one big table, where everyone would work. 'At first, their reaction was sceptical, to say the least,' says Simon Henley. 'We did have to convince them.' The architect's relationship with the client was a 'continuous dialogue', both cordial and intense throughout. Buschow Henley is itself a new practice and the job received hands-on treatment from partners Ralph Buschow and Simon Henley. 'We worked with the partners in Michaelides & Bednash and with their whole office,' says Henley. 'There was a strong element of leadership, in that

the partners had a very clear view of what they wanted from the project. In some ways, it seemed absurdly simple, but then that, in a sense, is an image of the firm itself.'

Michaelides & Bednash's 'big table', 20 m/66 ft long, stretches the entire length of the office. Only the receptionist has a separate desk, and that too is within the main working space. The partners see no reason why a reception area should be an 'in between' zone, cut off from the rest of the operations. The table looks like a long rectangle, but actually gets wider at the far end. If people want to work alone they may move to that end, whereas a group of people collaborating on a project may gather round the narrow end. There are no fixed workstations: people plug in their laptops at any convenient point. They sit where it suits them: there is no pecking order. The 'big table' is in itself anti-hierarchical.

Above **A converted 1920s industrial building in London's West End provides a piquant context for the new office. The essentially light and airy quality of the interior is being maintained – the company actively discourages the accumulation of paper files.**

Far left **Informal meeting areas off the main space offer an alternative work setting and a place to think and relax – though there is no physical separation from the general office area.**

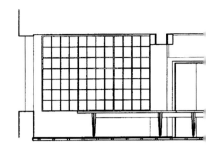

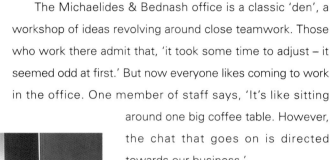

Below and opposite below **This conference room, used for internal and client meetings, is located close to the entrance. As the architect's conceptual drawing shows, visitors enter the main space obliquely, initially encountering opaque glazing, so that there is a sense of surprise when the corner is turned and the view into the room opens up.**

The Michaelides & Bednash office is a classic 'den', a workshop of ideas revolving around close teamwork. Those who work there admit that, 'it took some time to adjust – it seemed odd at first.' But now everyone likes coming to work in the office. One member of staff says, 'It's like sitting around one big coffee table. However, the chat that goes on is directed towards our business.'

Inevitably the success of the project depends on good interpersonal relationships: people have to respect other people's space. In fact, if anyone wants to work quietly or to have a private telephone conversation, they can withdraw into alcoves, formed by shelving, off the main space. The office is not frantic or noisy: it has an air of calm and order. This is helped by the absence of heaps of paper. As far as storage was concerned, Michaelides & Bednash decided to be ruthless: there are just four filing cabinets and no plans to acquire any more. The policy is not to keep material in hard copy, but to rely on electronic storage. The two meeting rooms are seen as free standing interventions into the space rather than separate compartments. The smaller one has huge pivoting doors which are like a retractable wall. The larger meeting room is glazed in such a way that what is going on inside can be seen from the main office, while translucent panels screen the view in from the entrance area.

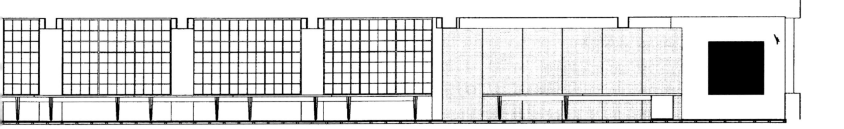

Michaelides & Bednash are still, after two years of occupation, '100 per cent happy' with the office. 'The place and the company seem to belong together,' says Michaelides. He concedes that a substantial growth in numbers could make it unworkable, 'but we don't want to grow that big. I think we're the right size now. Some companies in our field grow beyond their natural size and run out of steam.'

Although, as Simon Henley points out, the budget was quite modest, Michaelides & Bednash is a highly memorable, well-crafted space, with detailing and fittings to match. The client wanted the architects to achieve a closely coordinated look, and even commissioned them to design its stationery – the standard notepad is long and thin, like the famous table. It is hardly surprising that the table has become the predominant image of the company. It is both a symbol of team-working and an eminently practical device well suited to the work that goes on in the office. George Michaelides sees it as 'the antithesis of the virtual office' – being together, he says, is what makes the company tick. The Michaelides & Bednash table would not work for many of the companies featured in this book.

The office space is very specific to the business it houses (though many clients, it seems, go away asking why their own offices cannot be more like this). But it comes close to the ideal setting for collaborative office working, encouraging people to do things rather than constraining them. It gives the impression of being a place where users have some control, rather than being controlled by their surroundings. 'It's good because we kept it simple,' says George Michaelides, who believes that, 'Every office should be a place where you'd like to live.' The space could, indeed, adapt to another use very easily. The same could be said of most user-friendly office environments. Michaelides has memories of a visit he made many years ago to the newsroom of national daily newspaper. The energy and collective effort he saw there made a deep impression on him. In their cleaner, leaner world, the Michaelides & Bednash office embodies those qualities. The company has created the perfect office loft in the city, superficially simple, but rich in ideas about the future of the work place as a place for people.

Above **The architect's cross-section through the office shows the big table stretching the length of the room, and the reception area fronting one of two glass-fronted conference rooms.**

Vitra

Birsfelden, near Basel, Switzerland

'Liberal ... with contradictions and the breath of real life,' as Vitra's chairman, Dr Rolf Fehlbaum, describes the building, the Vitra headquarters was designed by Frank Gehry, one of the most creative and original figures

on the world architectural scene in the 1990s. The highly expressive buildings of this California-based architect have a strong international appeal, not least because of his ability to respond to a great variety of contexts. The Vitra furniture company is a natural Gehry client, innovative and committed to high standards in both design and the working environment. Rolf Fehlbaum has a strong personal interest in architecture and has been responsible for commissioning a number of new buildings on the company's main factory site at Weil-am-Rhein, Germany. These include works by Nicholas Grimshaw, Alvaro Siza, Tadao Ando and Zaha Hadid, as well as a factory building and Vitra Design Museum by Gehry. Visitors are welcomed there: around 40,000 come annually. The company's site at Birsfelden is close by, but across the Swiss border. The former factory there (built in 1957 as Vitra's first production base) has been revamped as a centre for product development and research. Vitra's headquarters is adjacent, in a building designed by Gehry and houses staff previously based at several undistinguished buildings in the town.

According to Fehlbaum, it was regarded as imperative that product development and administration were near neighbours: 'We all need to be in close touch.' The site, in a suburb of Basel, was 'quite sensitive,' says Fehlbaum. A large corporate-style building could look seriously out of place. But

> *'We wanted an open and transparent building, bringing together people who were previously hardly in contact with each other,' says Vitra's chairman, Dr Rolf Fehlbaum.*

Vitra specifically did not want a corporate look; it asked Gehry to design 'something rather more informal – something spontaneous not slick.'

Gehry's building, completed in 1994, consists of a central 'villa' distinct from, but linked by bridges to, the main office wing, part of which is let to the drug company Hoffmann La Roche. Vitra knew from the beginning that it would not immediately occupy all the space, though provision is made for the addition of a further block of offices, should it ever be required. The villa contains a reception area, a two-room restaurant which spills out on to an external terrace in fine weather, and a variety of meeting rooms plus a well-equipped audio-visual room. The complex is not just the 'front door' to the building but also a social focus for those who work there, not only Vitra's staff but those of tenants, who can also use the communal spaces and reserve the meeting rooms. 'And they are very much used,' says Fehlbaum. 'They are firstly social spaces, but equally they encourage informal business meetings and the exchange of news and ideas.' The meeting rooms form wings (or 'ears') to the villa – none is rectangular and each one is very different in basic form, decoration (strong colours are used), and furnishing. The atrium itself has comfortable chairs where more informal meetings can take place, but people often stop to chat on the bridges looking down into the space. The staff cafeteria has a prime position overlooking the terrace and a forest beyond. Fehlbaum believes that a building – corresponding perhaps

DEN°	CLUB
HIVE	CELL

BUILDING STATISTICS

CLIENT: Vitra International AG		FUNCTION: Headquarters of furniture manufacturer		
TOTAL FLOOR AREA: 6,450 sq. m / 69,015 sq. ft	TOTAL POPULATION: 200	OVERALL DENSITY: 32.25 sq. m per person / 345 sq. ft per person		
SAMPLE PLAN AREA (less core): 902 sq. m / 9,651 sq. ft	Circulation: 20.8%	Support: 24.8%	Cellular: 22.7%	Open plan: 31.7%
CONSULTANTS: *Architect and Interior Design* Frank O Gehry & Associates, Inc.				

Above **The meeting rooms, mostly situated in the entrance building, are varied in character and furnished to a very high standard, reflecting the importance to the company of interactive space.**

Left **The main entrance is a meeting place, where staff can relax or conduct informal business meetings. In winter, an open fire provides a focus, a symbol of the benign and supportive family atmosphere of the company.**

Right **A typical meeting room features Vitra's own furniture and one of the highly individual light fittings designed for each room.**

Above **Highly expressive and colourful, the architecture is used to support a quest for better office design.**

Opposite, below **The office space is largely open-plan with some cellular elements – effectively a lively version of the combi-office. Teams are brought together in den-like spaces.**

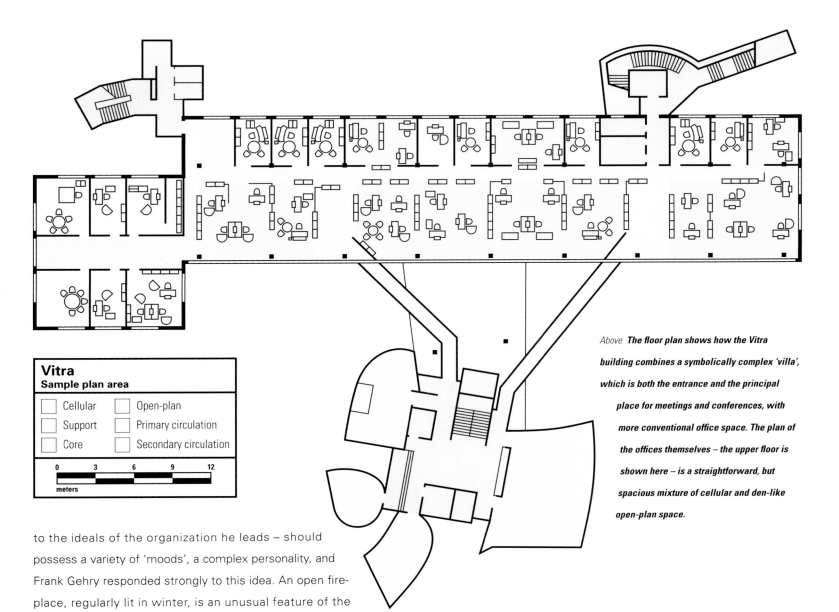

Vitra
Sample plan area

☐ Cellular	☐ Open-plan	
☐ Support	☐ Primary circulation	
☐ Core	☐ Secondary circulation	

0   3   6   9   12
meters

Above **The floor plan shows how the Vitra building combines a symbolically complex 'villa', which is both the entrance and the principal place for meetings and conferences, with more conventional office space. The plan of the offices themselves – the upper floor is shown here – is a straightforward, but spacious mixture of cellular and den-like open-plan space.**

to the ideals of the organization he leads – should possess a variety of 'moods', a complex personality, and Frank Gehry responded strongly to this idea. An open fire-place, regularly lit in winter, is an unusual feature of the atrium. The villa is a place for thought and discussion – the ideas are progressed back in the offices. The former concentrates all the visual shocks and surprises; the office wing, in contrast, is understated, rationalist.

The architecture of the Vitra offices is radical, but the actual office space is a straightforward mix of open-plan, semi-open space, and cellular offices, with the hierarchy expressed in terms of private offices for senior management. There is a frank acceptance of rank and position in the company, but within a social democratic ambience. Management style is markedly relaxed and informal with a strong personal touch. Paternalist values are not far away in what is, of course, a family company. All workstations are allocated since most staff work regularly in the office. The open-plan space is well above average in quality; the floor-plate is fairly shallow, so there are good views out, and the

Right **The Vitra headquarters building juxtaposes the highly sculptural reception and meeting-room area, with a more straightforward and rational office wing.**

Opposite, below **The dichotomies in the building between the rational and the expressive, between outgoing and internal, between meeting places and workstations, are made very clear in the elevations.**

Below **A roof plan of the villa shows the way in which meeting rooms are canted out from the central space.**

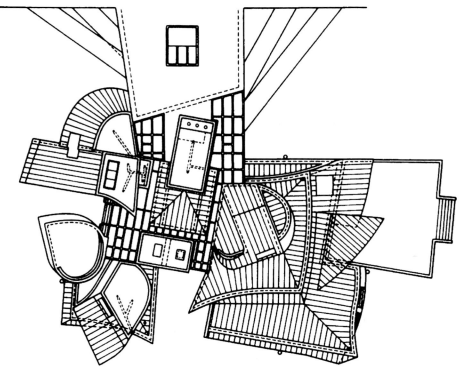

space enjoys generous natural light. There is considerable scope for rearranging the open areas and altering the balance between open and cellular space by moving or removing flexible partitions. Rolf Fehlbaum worked closely with Gehry and his team throughout the project, from the initial conception down to the choice of furniture and decor (including the extraordinary shapes, decor, and light fittings in the meeting rooms). There was consultation with staff, but on a relatively formal basis – Fehlbaum took a clear lead throughout the project: 'I doubt if this building would have emerged from the normal consultative process. There had to be a clear idea behind the project, one that would not be compromised. We'd do exactly the same again.'

The building is clearly felt to be a success. 'I can see very few faults in it,' says Fehlbaum. 'We get a very positive feedback from staff – people really like working here. People are often here working late at night and they feel at home in the

and has a clear view of its own image, mission and future, Vitra resembles Imagination, and Michelides & Bednash. However, the company differs from many others in that it is privately owned and moderate in size.

Its offices, exactly like its publicity material, reflect the company's identity as stable, caring, a little paternalistic but totally committed to quality and prepared to take risks. 'We could have given staff a package of 'extras' – fancy carpets, desks, and so on – in their offices,' says Fehlbaum, 'but we chose to do something that improved life for everyone. We want people to enjoy their work place and what they do in it.' At the same time, Vitra wanted 'to make a statement about what this company is – a lot of creative individuals'. Frank Gehry gave Vitra a building which works very well, within the bounds of a family rather than an organizational brief, but which is, perhaps more importantly, an excellent image-maker for a company that

building. There's nothing of the bleakness of the typical office block – it has a domestic informality which is part of its success.' The success of the Vitra headquarters reflects, as is so often the case, the involvement of one person who had the authority to help form the designs working closely with the architect. In this way, and in that it is good at what it does

achieves a rare marriage between art and commerce. Vitra is anxious that creativity – at the heart of its business as a world leader in furniture design – should spill over into the way the company is run. Its headquarters is a creative 'den', defiantly anti-corporate in spirit, with no pretensions to egalitarianism but a firm commitment to encouraging new ideas.

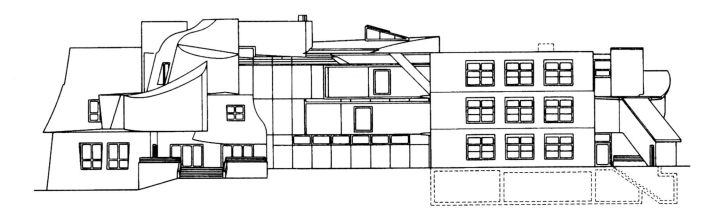

Imagination

London, UK

Imagination's striking headquarters reflects the company's ethos as 'a multidisciplinary creative consultancy, an ideas factory, not a media production line,' as Gary Withers, who founded the company twenty years ago, defines it. 'Nothing is impossible' is his motto and Imagination is dedicated to proving him right. Its aim is to 'harness our unique and unparalleled creative resource to conceive and deliver truly innovative and effective brand experiences on behalf of our clients.' Over the years, Imagination has launched Ford cars, lit Richard Rogers' Lloyd's Building (see page 32), designed the Dinosaur Gallery at the Natural History Museum in London, given BT (British Telecom) a new corporate identity, and staged the spectacular opening ceremony for the Broadgate office development in the City of London (see page 43).

Before it moved into its new premises in Store Street, Bloomsbury, in August 1989, Imagination had previously been located in Covent Garden, an area that was very convenient and popular with staff. However, the building had become grossly overcrowded – indeed, some staff had had to be decanted and housed in other buildings nearby. It was also highly compartmented, with people on a number of floors and poor communications between departments. A larger premises was needed, but the company was determined to stay in central London. An entirely new building was one possibility and several exploratory schemes were prepared by Withers' chosen architect, Ron Herron. Quite detailed plans were also produced for the conversion of a building in Battersea – on the outer edge of Imagination's preferred location area – but they proved abortive. Late in 1987 a former Edwardian school in Store Street was 'discovered' and identified as Imagination's new home.

The school consisted of two tall blocks separated by a narrow yard. 'We needed space,' says Alex Ritchie of Imagination, 'and preferably open-plan space, which we'd lacked, to promote better communications within the company.' The way in which the two buildings were joined to make the appropriate space was spectacular and helped achieve Imagination's other objective: 'to create a really striking showcase building, stimulating for clients and exciting for staff,' as Ritchie puts it.

The transformation of the old building was to be the late Ron Herron's major built work of architecture. It reflects concerns that had been evident in his work over a quarter of a century, dating back to the time, in fact, when he was one of the founders of the pressure group Archigram, which was the most radical voice in British architecture during the 1960s. Flexibility was one of the foundations of the Archigram credo, as was a taste for the transient and the demountable. Conventional architecture, Herron and his colleagues argued, imprisoned people whereas their own revolutionary approach to design could liberate and empower. The Imagination project embraced these ideas. A great Teflon-coated PVC roof covers the yard between the two existing buildings, turning it into a lofty atrium which is the focus of all activity in the company. A series of lightweight, vertiginous metal bridges links the two wings at every level. The refigured ground floor

'The building patently works,' says Alex Ritchie of Imagination. 'It's proved highly adaptable to our needs, which change all the time.'

DEN	CLUB
HIVE	CELL

BUILDING STATISTICS					
CLIENT: Imagination Ltd.			**FUNCTION:** Design and communications consultancy		
TOTAL FLOOR AREA: 6,000 sq. m / 64,200 sq. ft		**TOTAL POPULATION:** 230	**OVERALL DENSITY:** 26 sq. m per person / 279 sq. ft per person		
SAMPLE PLAN AREA (less core): 750 sq. m / 8,051 sq. ft		**Circulation:** 23.9%	**Support:** 18.7%	**Cellular:** 0%	**Open plan:** 57.4%
CONSULTANTS: *Architect and Interior Design* Ron Herron					

Above **A strong emphasis on interaction and the exchange of ideas lies at the root of Imagination's work ethic. Meeting rooms, like this one on the mezzanine floor, are combined with a preponderance of open-plan space.**

Left **The complex brings together two converted Victorian buildings, which are linked by a spectacular atrium, crisscrossed by lightweight bridges. It is seen as reflecting the perceived image of the company: futuristic, innovative, constantly surprising. A meeting room is squeezed in on the first landing.**

contains a reception area, the board room, staff restaurant, and one of the heavily used exhibition areas (extending into the atrium). A mezzanine area, to which one is led via a steel staircase, rests on top of the board room. The basement (which already existed) houses photographic and sound studios, a video-editing suite and a staff gymnasium. The upper floors are given over to offices and to design studios.

Right **Bridges connect the offices, which are a mix of open-plan and cellular, on both sides of the spectacular central atrium that was once an open-air school yard.**

Here the floor-space is a mixture of group or den-like spaces and a few enclosed offices and meeting rooms. Gary Withers himself has a suite on top of the streetfront building; and the Imagination Gallery, self-contained and used both to display Imagination's own projects and for guest exhibitions and other events, is located on top of the other wing, contained within the same fabric-covered roof-structure as the atrium.

Withers was closely involved in the project throughout, working with Ron Herron and job architect John Randle. The schedule was tight: just twelve months from the start of work on site to occupation. 'The project was run like an Imagination project,' Randle recalls. 'The pace was fast and furious.' Withers and the architects met or talked on the telephone at all hours and weekend meetings were common. Everyone was heavily involved. Withers had a clear vision of the building he wanted and, though he consulted colleagues on the detailed needs of their departments, he remained in sole charge of the project from the client side. 'The client was one man,' says John Randle. There was little scope, given the schedule, for rethinking and revisions. Any issues which arose had

Opposite, below **Imagination's founder and chairman, Gary Withers, runs the company from a penthouse office, a rooftop retreat where many of the company's ideas emerge.**

to be resolved without delay. Many of the contracts were unconventional, designed to avoid any delays. In technical terms, says Randle, the building was far from sophisticated. Servicing was somewhat 'basic', while provision for information technology systems was built in as the project proceeded and is far from advanced.

Alex Ritchie says that there is little in the building that anyone would change, were the project to be done again. A standing team is responsible for rearranging the open-plan floors, which were 'half planned' by Herron, when the need arises and all fittings are designed to be moved easily. One major problem which Imagination faces is that its continuing success has led to a growth of staff numbers. There are now

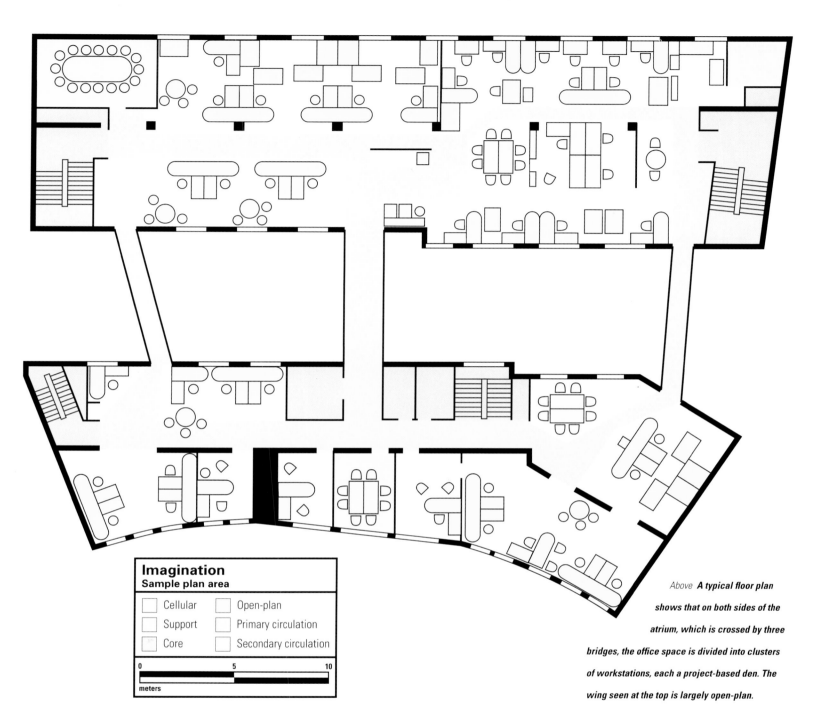

Imagination
Sample plan area

- ☐ Cellular
- ☐ Support
- ☐ Core
- ☐ Open-plan
- ☐ Primary circulation
- ☐ Secondary circulation

0   5   10
meters

Above **A typical floor plan shows that on both sides of the atrium, which is crossed by three bridges, the office space is divided into clusters of workstations, each a project-based den. The wing seen at the top is largely open-plan.**

more than 230 and, 'We are running out of space,' admits Ritchie. But there is scope to colonize parts of the atrium.

A typical open-plan office at Imagination is a lively place, a classic, somewhat overcrowded, den with a strong creative 'buzz'. Screens and filing cabinets help to provide personalized spaces but there is little privacy and no obvious demand for it. The image is one of informality and interaction. Drawing boards are as much in evidence as personal computers and CAD stations. The Imagination team is essentially interdisciplinary and ideas are its business. Some staff find the high level of noise in the offices distracting and the hard acoustic does not help. To others, however, it is part of the character of the company. Nor could the offices be called tidy. Despite an injunction from the management to avoid clutter, many people sit among heaps of paper and storage facilities are deliberately minimal. The building relies on a mix of natural and mechanical ventilation: opening windows on the street wing and opening windows plus a mechanical exhaust system on the rear wing. There are frequent complaints that the latter is too warm in summer and adjustments to the system do not seem to have entirely solved the problem. Indeed, with its limited views out (on to the backs of buildings in the adjacent square) the rear wing offers the least desirable working spaces in the complex. Nonetheless, the Imagination headquarters seems popular with staff, who generally warm to the strongly interactive character of life there. The excellent staff facilities including a stylish restaurant and bar, which

Above **The billowing fabric roof of the atrium has a sculptural quality; its practical advantages include low cost and the provision of a benign, day-lit internal environment.**

Right **The initial sketch of the new roof, by the architect Ron Herron, shows the dynamic effect obtained by the use of an innovative fabric covering.**

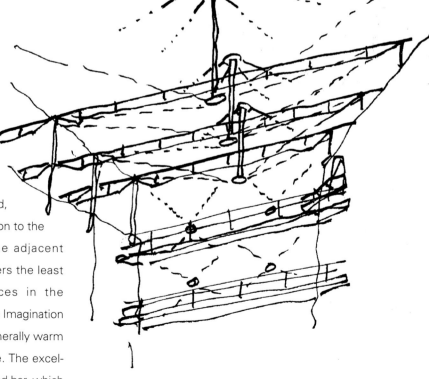

what it would look like at the beginning.' Gary Withers' role in its creation was critical and he retains a strong affection for it – witness the enormous efforts taken to create spectacular displays, inside and out, every Christmas. It is seen as a potent resource, vital to Imagination's success and worthy of proper maintenance. The practical issue is that the roof has a limited life span and has already been replaced. The complex is nonetheless a memorable place to work in and it would be hard to believe that the power of the place does not set a strong stamp on the work that comes out of it.

is useful for entertaining as well as pure subsistence, and the gymnasium help. The staff tend to be young and flexible in their approach to work. Imagination has a non-hierarchical image. Senior staff are generally integrated into the space occupied by their departments. There are only a few car-parking spaces for the entire building. Most of the staff travel by public transportation, or bicycle, or motorcycle.

The image of Imagination is now inseparable from its striking headquarters. This is simultaneously a design and a managerial achievement. The building remains, eight years after its completion, a stunning object with the power to impress anyone who enters it, not least Imagination's clients, though John Randle believes that 'the image came out of the finished building – nobody was quite clear

Below **A cross-section shows how the two buildings are linked at each level by bridges and united by the fabric roof that also effectively adds another floor to the block on the right. This top-storey space is used for exhibitions and conferences and often let to outside organizations. The basement and ground floors are given over to parking and other shared amenities and services. In between are the main floors of project space.**

Channel 4 Television

London, UK

'Moving here,' says the general manager of Channel 4 Television, 'was a key event in our history. We've learned about new ways of working. The building is about communication and interaction. And it's a practical success.'

Before the company moved into its new headquarters in Horseferry Road, Victoria, Channel 4 occupied six buildings in the 'Fitzrovia' quarter of London. It was founded in 1982, and by the late 1980s the management had concluded that relocation was inevitable and vital. First, the Channel faced the need for major renewal of its technical hardware, a long-term investment that had to have an assured location. Second, the division of staff into a number of separate buildings created considerable problems of communication and discouraged the informal social contact seen as important in a 'creative' organization.

'We didn't consciously set out to make a statement with this building,' said Michael Grade, when he was chief executive of Channel 4, 'but its look and its functional aspects are very much in tune with what we are.'

Channel 4 does not make its own programmes. It is essentially a 'publisher', buying in material and transmitting it. The main business of the company is commissioning programmes from independent production companies, with the creative, legal, and financial work that that entails. Advertising sales, publicity, transmission, and general administration account for most of the other jobs at the Channel.

The decision to commission a custom-made building was made following an exhaustive survey of existing schemes, either completed or in the pipeline, that might be customized for Channel 4's special requirements. None was found suitable. The Richard Rogers Partnership scheme was chosen after a two-stage invited competition. One clear objective from the start was to avoid any suggestion of extravagance. Channel 4 wanted to be seen as a thrifty organization.

The key player on the client side was Frank McGettigan, Channel 4's general manager, who saw the building as a vital tool in encouraging new ways of working and a new spirit in the company. He was very conscious of his responsibility for overseeing the project and accounting to the board, and was determined that Channel 4 would get the right building at the right cost. The latter issue led to some 'vigorous' discussions with the architects as the project proceeded.

The scheme was, in fact, somewhat scaled-down from the competition-winning design. The atrium, in particular, was reduced: there were fears that an over-large lobby would look showy and extravagant. In the event, the space is a little cramped and, indeed, there is a slight feeling that the dimensions of the building generally are less than generous. Perhaps the richness and complexity of Rogers' architectural vocabulary heightens the sense that a great deal is being packed into a quite limited space.

The technical space, to house transmission equipment, is at lower ground level, and the building's one production studio occupies a 'black box' that extends down into a further basement level. The office space on the upper floors is a mix of open-plan and cellular, the balance being specified by the client. Management and associated offices are housed in cells overlooking the dramatic glazed atrium and are definitely an executive domain. Other departments,

BUILDING STATISTICS						
CLIENT: Channel 4 Television			**FUNCTION:** Headquarters / transmission centre of television company			
TOTAL FLOOR AREA: 15,000 sq. m / 160,500 sq. ft		**TOTAL POPULATION:** 550	**OVERALL DENSITY:** 27.3 sq. m per person / 292 sq. ft per person			
SAMPLE PLAN AREA (less core): 1,894 sq. m / 20,266 sq. ft		**Circulation:** 21.4%	**Support:** 11.8%	**Cellular:** 43.0%	**Open plan:** 23.8%
CONSULTANTS: *Architect and Interior Design* Richard Rogers Partnership						

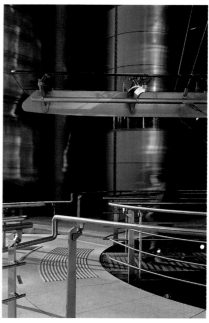

Above **The building is well crafted in a high-tech style which is seen to be in keeping with Channel 4's image.**

Left **The building makes a strong statement about the company's image, which was described by Michael Grade as being 'not really establishment ... a bit anarchic.' A generous public piazza seems to invite passers-by to step inside the transparent atrium, while a landmark tower sgnifies the building's broadcasting function.**

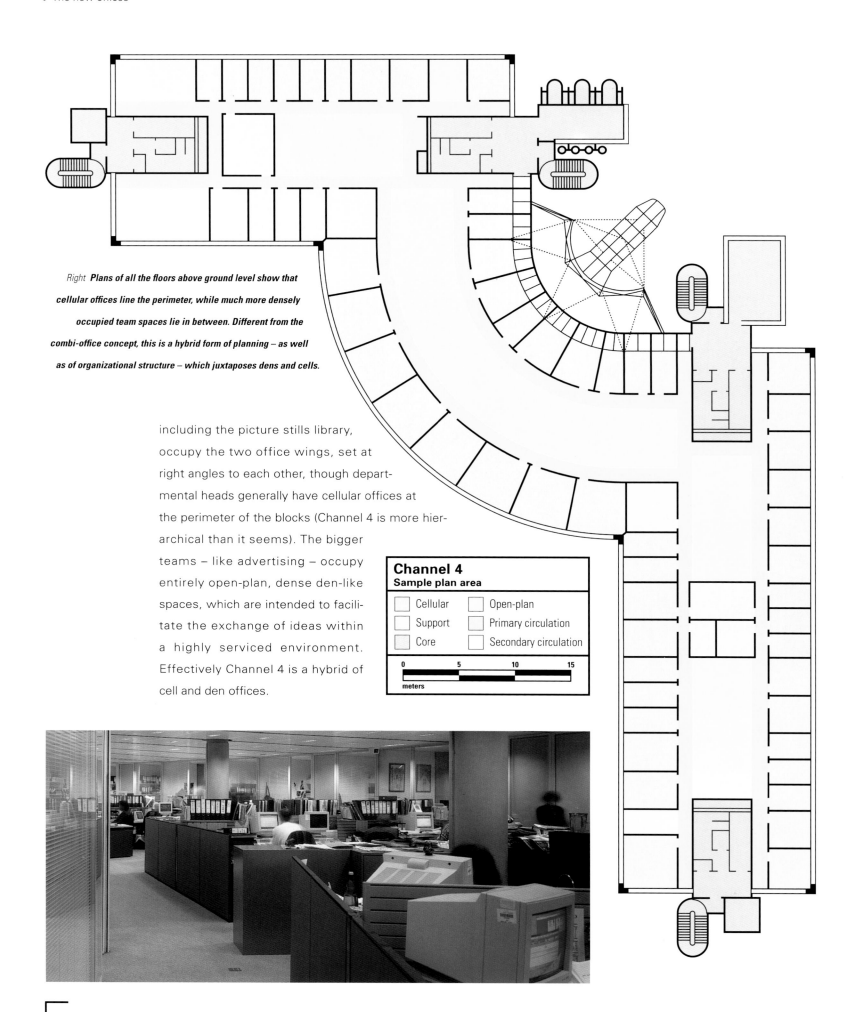

Right **Plans of all the floors above ground level show that cellular offices line the perimeter, while much more densely occupied team spaces lie in between. Different from the combi-office concept, this is a hybrid form of planning – as well as of organizational structure – which juxtaposes dens and cells.**

including the picture stills library, occupy the two office wings, set at right angles to each other, though departmental heads generally have cellular offices at the perimeter of the blocks (Channel 4 is more hierarchical than it seems). The bigger teams – like advertising – occupy entirely open-plan, dense den-like spaces, which are intended to facilitate the exchange of ideas within a highly serviced environment. Effectively Channel 4 is a hybrid of cell and den offices.

Channel 4
Sample plan area

☐	Cellular	☐	Open-plan
☐	Support	☐	Primary circulation
☐	Core	☐	Secondary circulation

0   5   10   15
meters

meetings to protracted late-night telephone conversations.

Andrew Morris of Richard Rogers Partnership, project architect under RRP director John Young, says that the working relationship was good: 'They were capable of making decisions and sticking to them. It was a clear-cut process.' The close involvement of McGettigan, as a very senior manager with the full support of the Channel 4 board, was important in this respect. 'It was seen as my project,' says McGettigan, 'and I was charged to ensure that we led it.' The launch of the project coincided with a period of uncertainty for the Channel. The building needed to be seen as a good investment, with potential for subletting should the need arise. 'We wanted to avoid a very specific building,' says Gill Monk. In the event, Channel 4 has thrived and continues to occupy the entire space.

McGettigan worked closely with Gill Monk (head of personnel and administration). They held regular meetings to discuss the project with all the departments (by their nature, very disparate in character – Channel 4 is a mix of 'suits' and 'jeans'). Alongside basic issues such as space allocation, sensitive topics like smoking policy were debated. Some matters, however, were not up for debate. The decision to opt for a sealed, air-conditioned building was taken at top management level (though air conditioning was essential only in sensitive technical areas). Staff were given little control over lighting levels, another issue that has led to some criticism since the building's occupation. Furnishings were chosen by Gill Monk in consultation with the architects. Monk was a decisive client, making clear, for example, her total opposition to demountable partitions which, she claims, do not provide adequate sound insulation. She wanted a 'thoroughly professional look'. McGettigan and Monk attended weekly meetings with the architects and other professionals. There were also many informal contacts, ranging from breakfast

Frank McGettigan feels that the objectives behind the project have been 'very largely' achieved and that Channel 4 broadly got the building it wanted. He praises the 'terrific attention to detail' of the architects, which was vital to the success of the project. Architecturally, the Rogers design is a powerful statement about the Channel's special identity. The look of the building appears to have a wide appeal – coming into it in the morning is 'always a special experience', and the building helps to 'sell' Channel 4: it is seen as an impressive place to bring potential buyers of advertising time, for instance. It also works well in practical terms. The plan of the building does necessitate lengthy walks between certain departments, but management believes this is well and good: people meet in the lifts and atrium and the sense of isolation some experienced in Fitzrovia is a thing of the past.

Above **The glass and steel atrium is a spectacular and richly detailed, if relatively tight, space; it forms an impressive point of entry as well as a waiting area for visitors.**

Opposite, below **The open-plan office space is fairly conventional: a somewhat crowded den, occupied by teams.**

the green square beyond and access to an external terrace for eating out in fine weather. The aim was to create a high-quality place, not only for eating but also for meeting. Modest business lunches take place there, saving the company money and staff time – there is scarcely a restaurant of any quality in walking distance of Horseferry Road. There is a coffee bar which is open when the restaurant is closed and Gill Monk sees the space as important in generating a sense of community during the long working days. It is also useful for the occasional large party.

The office space at Channel 4 is transitional, as opposed to highly innovative, but it reflects a pattern of work in which senior executives deal with the outside world and other staff have to work in intense collaboration to service a television channel. The separation of senior managers from the working departments could be seen as conservative. However, it is emphasized that an 'open door' policy prevails and executives rarely pull down the blinds to exclude views into their offices. The insistence of most departmental heads on having cellular offices reflects not only the status-oriented nature of the television industry, but also how the jobs of managers tend to be outwardly oriented compared with those of the project teams. Channel 4 sees itself as radical and democratic in

Above **Many of the cellular offices overlook the atrium and are accessed via open walkways which allow a view into the offices, breaking down any impression of secrecy.**

The staff restaurant was seen as an essential feature of the building – formerly Channel 4 had never had a canteen. It is located on the ground floor – but slightly below the level of the main atrium so that views out are not compromised. It was deliberately given a prominent location, with views to

nature, but has not broken down old ways entirely. Some heads of department would like more privacy and complain about inadequate soundproofing.

The open-plan offices have good daylighting but are crowded, with lots of technology, screens, and filing cabinets – there is paper in abundance. There are some complaints about ceiling heights and lack of environmental control. Frank

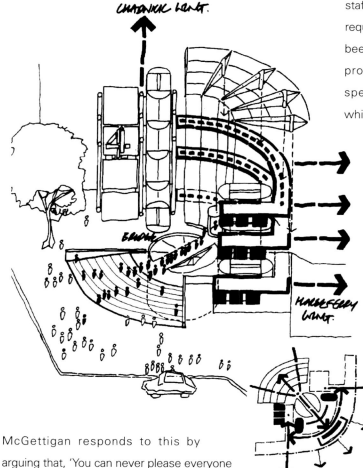

staff, some departments have moved or changed their space requirements, and a number of additional cellular offices have been created. That this has been achieved without serious problems is a tribute to the original specification of the internal fit-out, which was designed to be flexible.

Most of the departments within the organization feel that they have better and more generous space than they had in Fitzrovia in which to pursue their various functions. The consultation process appears to have produced the desired results in this respect. The views of individual staff vary a great deal: many feel that the open-plan floors are somewhat cramped and uninspired. Most Channel 4 employees are critical beings, but few would want to go back to the old offices, even given their more desirable location.

The Channel 4 building is seen as an exciting place to work. If it has practical failings, these probably reflect an understandable caution within the organization in the face of financial uncertainties. The building provides the Channel with a spectacularly memorable image that acts as a symbolic heart for the organization – and a place where the many independent producers and film-makers who create the programmes can find a point of identity. It is also a powerful and positive urban statement, embodying Richard Rogers' conviction that 'commercial' buildings can contribute something positive to the public domain. It is an act of confidence which has paid off.

Left **As seen in his sketch, Richard Rogers' strategy for the building, provides for a high degree of transparency, with views in from the street and views out from the offices into a landscaped garden.**

McGettigan responds to this by arguing that, 'You can never please everyone – if we had opening windows, people would disagree about whether they should be open or shut. As it is, some people complain that the building is too hot, others that it is too cold!' But McGettigan believes that 'if people here weren't happy, you'd soon hear about it.'

While no major changes have been required since the building opened in the summer of 1994, some replanning of office floors has been necessary to accommodate additional

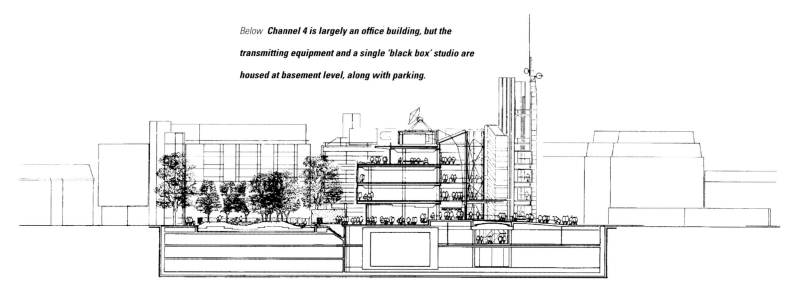

Below **Channel 4 is largely an office building, but the transmitting equipment and a single 'black box' studio are housed at basement level, along with parking.**

Nickelodeon

New York City, USA

The objective of the new offices was to bolster the spirit – adventurous, lighthearted but intensely inventive and innovative – which had made the company a success and to counter any tendencies towards static, corporate thinking. 'They wanted offices that were playful and conveyed a sense of self, a sense of family and a sense of home' say the architects, who explain that the brief demanded an 'anti-corporate – positively anti-hierarchic' look. The client was Nickelodeon, the television network, which was launched in the early 1980s from a single room with six employees. Now it broadcasts children's programmes by cable to over 60 million homes and has 53 per cent of the American children's TV market. Moving its headquarters to four floors of a 1970s office tower off Times Square was necessitated by the rapid growth of the organization.

> *'It's a unique place that probably wouldn't suit anybody else, a mix of private and open spaces with a character that tells you what Nickelodeon is all about,' said Geraldine Laybourne, the company's former president.*

The commission for the company's new headquarters came to California architects Fernau & Hartman through a rather uncommon channel. Nickelodeon's former president, Geraldine Laybourne, the driving force behind the project, got to know the practice when they designed her new house in Telluride, Colorado, in the heartland of telecottaging (see page 98). Fernau & Hartman were subsequently invited to compete for the Nickelodeon job against a clutch of big East Coast firms with plenty of experience in commercial and corporate architecture. They emerged the winners, but worked with Kohn, Pedersen, Fox of New York as associates in the project.

This was to be Nickelodeon's second move in a few years, and there were still fond memories of the channel's original premises. 'Their first loft offices had been crowded, creative, communicative,' says Richard Fernau. 'They wanted to recreate that character and retain their vitality and particular identity.' The architects' dynamic aesthetic, challenging the formality and rigidity of classic modernist layouts, was in tune with the aims of the client. Fernau says that, 'The idea behind it all was a creative, open democratic environment.' The architects developed this idea, in democratic fashion, in discussion with as many people as possible at Nickelodeon. There were many workshops, dinners with specific departments and the executive team, and a number of general gatherings open to all staff as the move was being planned. 'We met so many people, and got lots of good ideas,' says Laura Hartman. Having been hired 'to find out what was needed – and get it right', the architects were anxious to have the backing of the staff. 'Connectedness' emerged as a common priority – this extended in multiple directions: within, and also beyond, the confines of the office building, to visitors and to those who work there intermittently. Making the best use of any available daylight was another priority. This strengthened the argument for open-plan offices throughout, with internal divisions made as transparent as possible.

David Kau, Fernau & Hartman's project architect, got to know the character of the company. Programmes are not made in the building. Nickelodeon has studios elsewhere in the city and is, in any case, a commissioner more than a large-scale maker of programmes. But programmes are previewed

DEN	CLUB
HIVE	CELL

BUILDING STATISTICS					
CLIENT: Nickelodeon			**FUNCTION:** Headquarters / production centre of television channel		
TOTAL FLOOR AREA: 11,215 sq. m / 120,000 sq. ft		**TOTAL POPULATION:** 400+	**OVERALL DENSITY:** 28 sq. m per person / 300 sq. ft per person		
SAMPLE PLAN AREA (less core): 2,250 sq. m / 24,000 sq. ft		**Circulation:** 29.5%	**Support:** 23.5%	**Cellular:** 8.5%	**Open plan:** 38.5%
CONSULTANTS: *Architect* Fernau & Hartman ***Executive Architect*** Kohn Pedersen Fox					

Above **Though most space at Nickelodeon is open-plan, there are a number of enclosed meeting rooms – this one forms part of the spectacular 'Crate', the multilevel stack of conference rooms (seen left).**

Left **Slicing through three floors of a standard Manhattan office building and then connecting them with a glazed staircase and the 'Crate', a central pyramid of meeting rooms, was symbolic and practical: its aim was to make the company more transparent and interactive.**

Above **Staff at Nickelodeon tend to be young and adaptable – teamwork comes naturally and the space is in tune with the ad hoc – but purposeful – mood. The space has been designed with an extraordinary disregard for the orthogonal discipline which has shaped so many conventional North American offices.**

at the Times Square building, auditions take place there and creative brainstorming sessions are held daily. 'The staff were generally young, very into teamwork, very adaptable. Spontaneity was a high priority. If ideas weren't encouraged and allowed to blossom, Nickelodeon wouldn't flourish.' Not all of the 400-plus staff are permanently based in the building; around 15 per cent are 'seasonal', brought in to work on specific projects that may last weeks or months. Many people work part-time and hours are often irregular.

The Times Square/Broadway Viacom Building, a standard office shell not designed for creative work, was itself a potential problem. How could a sense of identity be instilled into three large, identical floors. Besides this, when an organization's working space is divided, especially between floors, communications and 'connections' suffer. The divisions between the floors needed to be eroded. The architects' proposal to cut a series of holes through them to link the three floors was agreed to. (In the USA, landlords tend to be far

Right **Views and routes across the building are carefully protected to encourage easy communication and avoid any feeling of claustrophobia at the centre of the large floors. Partitions are kept low and too many rigid right-angles are avoided.**

more responsive to users' requirements than they are in, for example, the UK.) A staircase, glazed to increase visibility and maximize daylight, connects the floors. Within the space sits the 'Crate', a three-storey, pyramidal bank of conference rooms. The largest, at the base, is over 180 sq. m/1,900 sq. ft. From the outside the Crate looks like a single volume. Continuity between the floors is also emphasized by objects such as the 'fins' – walls used as pin-up boards – found at the same points on the west and south of each floor. The fins are heavily used; people tend to congregate near them so they form the focus for innumerable impromptu meetings.

Left **The floor plan shows one of the four floors occupied by Nickelodeon in a typical high-rise New York building. Most of the open-plan and cellular offices are placed on the perimeter, with support spaces arranged around the entrance from the core. Three floors have been brought together by breaking though them to create a glazed staircase and stack of meeting rooms seen, arranged diagonally, in the lower right-hand corner of this plan.**

Nickleodeon
Sample plan area

☐ Cellular	☐ Open-plan
☐ Support	☐ Primary circulation
☐ Core	☐ Secondary circulation

0	5	10	15

meters

The key to Fernau & Hartman's architectural strategy lay in the issue of communication and connections. The spaces in the building are intended to encourage *ad hoc* communications: departments may commandeer spaces for meetings. Large 'barn doors' can be used to shut off spaces for conferences and presentations. The application of castors to much of the furniture allows people to configure the spaces according to their individual requirements. The aim was to provide a great variety of places to work, meeting the functional needs – and even the moods – of the diverse work force. Some departments are less flexible than others, so there are formal as well as informal spaces. Kitchen areas, each with a 'diner' attached, are heavily used for meetings as well as for eating. The diversity of materials used – timber, steel, cork, laminates, ceramic tiles, papier mâché, rubber, carpet, and glass included – is equally intended to express heterogeneity and spontaneity. 'They're honest, natural, ordinary ' materials, nothing corporate,' says Richard Fernau. 'Old-style corporate offices tend to impose one uniform look on everyone.'

Opposite, above **A bold use of colour and striking forms adds to the distinctive quality of the interior, which draws on the imagery of the studio.**

The architects sought to 'learn from the spatial sensibilities of New York City', creating a 'multistorey landscape' with its own 'streets', 'monuments', and 'neighbourhoods'. They speak of 'an interior architecture for an urban condition.' The sense of place in the building was to extend beyond its skin: the views out, particularly east and west to the Hudson and East Rivers, are spectacular. In a conventional corporate tower, they would be the preserve of executives in private perimeter cells. At Nickelodeon, they are there for all to enjoy as they use the various spaces – open workstations, not private offices, dominate the edge of the building. Moreover, views out are rigorously safeguarded by the layout of neighbourhoods and streets, so that nobody can fail to be aware of the location at the legendary heart of a legendary city. Each neighbourhood within the building has a character as distinct as that of New York's Soho or Little Italy, and staff move from one to another to use the different facilities that each offers. Again, the urban analogy applies: these are not closed ghettos, but lively places where people meet to do business and socialize. They contain spaces (given names such as Mediaplatz or Piazza del Popolo) which have a similar function, in microcosm, as public spaces in cities.

Oposite, below **The architects' cross-section shows the way in which three of the floors occupied by Nickelodeon are linked by a new staircase and the stack of meeting rooms known as the 'Crate'.**

Like Gaetano Pesce's Chiat/Day offices – also in Manhattan – which formed, in fact, a constant point of reference, Fernau & Hartman's Nickelodeon, is colourful and stimulating, without resorting to what Fernau calls 'fixed smile kid's stuff. The client's view was that "Nick is kids. It doesn't need to pretend".' Once inside, it is hard to believe that this was a very run-of-the-mill commercial block. The 'buildings' within the landscape of the interiors –

there are more than 20 of them, built of contrasting materials and boldly coloured, are available to all staff for meetings. Some departments have highly customized spaces. For example, 'Nick Jnr', which makes programmes for pre-school children) has toddler-scaled spaces where adults have to crawl through the doors.

When the project was conceived some staff feared the imposition of an arbitrary 'look' unrelated to practical needs, but the willingness to experiment and take risks while avoiding affectation eventually won general support. There is a feeling among the staff that in this new space the company has been able to return to its creative roots.

Since the first stage of the project was completed in 1995, Nickelodeon has expanded on to another floor of the Viacom Building, where it is clearly rooted for some time to come. Fernau & Hartman say that there is plenty of scope for change in the offices, though so far changes have been limited. Many partitions are movable, but some areas of the building are fixed, with permanent features as in a city. Richard Fernau insists, however, that the success of the project – Nickelodeon is going from strength to strength – 'is not just about the look of the thing.' It is, he maintains, a result of the way in which the new offices reflect the way in which the organization operates. The spontaneity, the informality, and the sense of a common goal have been renewed by breaking down architectural and organizational barriers. This is a solid business achievement albeit expressed visually in an extraordinary way.

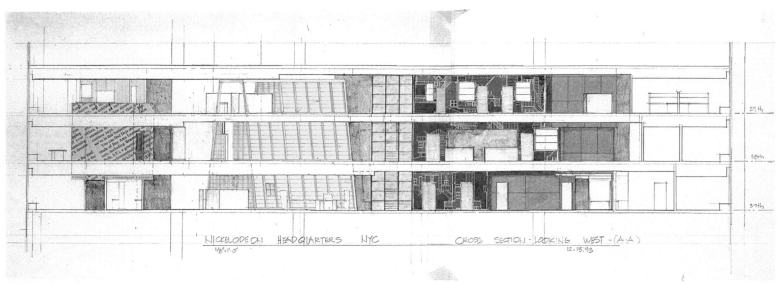

NICKELODEON HEADQUARTERS NYC   CROSS SECTION · LOOKING WEST · (A·A)
1/8"=1'-0"   12·13·93

Steelcase

Grand Rapids, Michigan, USA

The 'leadership community', a new approach to the use of office space for the company's top management which Steelcase established in 1995, was designed for a high measure of both interaction and autonomy. It represents

a radical and very visible move for the company, probably the world leader in office furnishing and fit-outs, and reflects the philosophy of Steelcase's president and chief executive officer, Jim Hackett. 'Team management is what matters,' he says. 'We changed the way we work because we had to. Why sit in a traditional office when doing so is limiting your leadership?'

'I felt that management needed a new focus,' explains Hackett, 'and you have to change places to change ways of thinking.' The move from the previous Steelcase executive suite on the fifth floor of the company's corporate headquarters (a building dating from 1983) to an area occupying half of the fourth floor involved evacuating a maze of cellular offices and conference rooms, a maze in which executives were lost and invisible in private office rooms of up to 75 sq. m/800 sq. ft with secretaries outside in communal spaces. In the new, completely refigured area (20 per cent smaller than the previous executive floor), apart from enclosed conference rooms and 'enclaves' for private meetings, the space is arranged as a series of open 'neighbourhoods' for the 26 top executives of Steelcase and their assistants. Over 80 per cent of the total area is now support space, 20 per cent 'owned' – before the transformation, the proportions were exactly the opposite. Choosing this den-like form of office was a deliberate step by Steelcase's

'The results are double the success we thought they would be,' says Jim Hackett, Steelcase's president and chief executive officer. 'You meet people. There are lots of chance encounters, casual discussions, exchanges of ideas – that's what drives a business.'

top management away from hierarchy and towards interaction. Hackett recalls his contacts with the world of finance. 'When you met bankers, say in London, you'd find that they lived a totally hierarchical existence. Being promoted meant moving from one room to another or to a different building. I wanted a different sort of office to work in a new way.'

The essential idea behind the 'leadership community' project was to instil the idea of teamworking into the company. The 'team' was to be understood as including not just the top executives but everyone in the working community. Far from being a fad, Jim Hackett argues, teams are the way to get things done and 'community' is not a fanciful conceit but a strong business concept. The community consists of around 50 people, including the company's leaders – leadership being another idea central to the project.

Jim Hackett was closely involved in the project at every stage. His analysis of the company's problems, actual and potential, reveals a holistic view of the process of management. Anthropology – understanding people's values and culture – as much as space planning or technological change, underlay the project's genesis and implementation. It was led and managed in-house by a team chaired by Hackett and coordinated by Jim Lawler, Steelcase's director of facilities management. The team included Dan Wiljanen, the company's president of human resources, designers, office technologists, and the expert organizational development psychologist Fritz Steele. It isn't surprising to learn that the

DEN	CLUB
HIVE	CELL

BUILDING STATISTICS					
CLIENT: Steelcase Inc.			**FUNCTION:** Senior management team in furniture manufacturers headquarters		
TOTAL FLOOR AREA: 2,383 sq. m / 25,500 sq. ft		**TOTAL POPULATION:** 50	**OVERALL DENSITY:** 48 sq. m per person / 510 sq. ft per person		
SAMPLE PLAN AREA (less core): 1,892 sq. m / 20,200 sq. ft		**Circulation:** 17.6%	**Support:** 43.5%	**Cellular:** 0%	**Open plan:** 38.9%
CONSULTANTS: *Interior Design* In-house *Programming* Fritz Steele					

Above **In the centre – both physically and operationally – of Steelcase's 'leadership community' offices is a superbly equipped meeting/information area, a sort of 'war room' where global sales campaigns are planned.**

Left **Senior staff, once used to big private offices, now find themselves in a far more open environment. Folding screens like these can be used to shut off rooms for quiet private work or small meetings.**

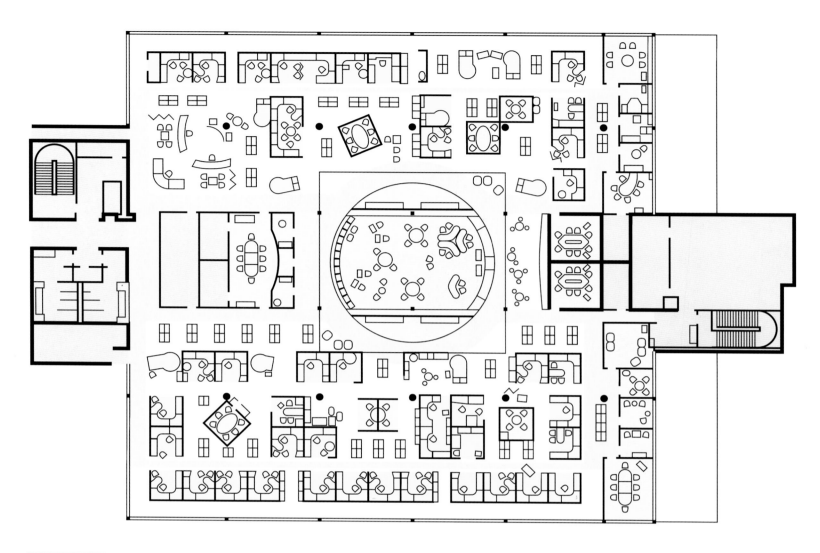

Steelcase
Sample plan area

☐	Cellular	☐	Open-plan
☐	Support	☐	Primary circulation
☐	Core	☐	Secondary circulation

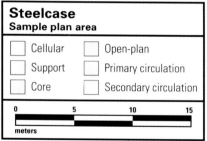

0   5   10   15
meters

Above **In the middle of the top floor of Steelcase's headquarters is the circular operations centre which visually, and operationally, dominates the whole floor. The floor plan reveals the wide variety of different work settings – project spaces, meeting rooms or areas for concentrated work available as needed – that are placed around it.**

company has commissioned a similar, post-occupancy analysis of the project.

The first moves were made in February 1995, when focus-group sessions began. 'We took staff stage by stage through the whole thing,' says Hackett. 'The project team wanted to understand the whole process in social and psychological, as well as physical and organizational, terms.' As the designs for the new space took shape, the consultation became more detailed. Finally, a full-size plastic foam mock-up of the space was constructed in Steelcase's factory. This rather extravagant prototype – Steelcase is a furniture company – took four months to build and was used as a basis for testing and comments. The new facility was completed and occupied shortly before the end of 1995.

'The whole process taught us a vast amount about how people work,' says Jim Hackett. There are no private offices. The central area includes an operations centre where information about company performance and objectives is displayed. From here, executives identify the tasks that need to be done and go out and do them – all are highly mobile and the office is the place where they meet and exchange ideas. Executives are grouped around the central space in quadrants, arranged according to activity (for example, sales orders and product development) rather than status. Each quadrant contains a mix of team space and allocated workstations that use a variety of Steelcase products including Personal Harbours, with some stations set aside for visitors. An area

company is not in question. But the absence of an intuitive designer, with the ability to make a place rather than merely lay out space, is very apparent. The interior is somewhat bland and lacking in a specific character that expresses the nature of the

*Left **Workstations use the company's own innovative furniture. Seen here, towards the back, is the versatile Personal Harbour, a freestanding office module (see also page 83).***

business. Steelcase's location, in a middle-size city with relatively low property values, has allowed it to be extravagant in space-use in a way that is shocking to those used to more crowded cities. This is clearly reflected in the layout. More importantly, the leadership community might have

where the need to respond to change was most obvious was that of information technology. Instead of being tied to fixed workstations – though each has a home base – staff are liberated by mobile phones and laptop computers. 'The conference table has to be computer-linked. It isn't a place to get away from your computer,' says Hackett.The Internet, he adds, offers even larger opportunities for interaction.

The 'leadership community' is, inevitably, a showcase for Steelcase's own products. The technical know-how of

gained character, intensity – and perhaps even greater effectiveness – if space had been more at a premium.

The project was not a one-off exercise, but a pilot for other projects in the company. 'This is not a concept whose relevance is confined to an élite,' Jim Hackett argues. 'The executive community was asked to take the lead, as it properly should. We are now looking at extending this approach to the whole company.'

'It's seen as an enjoyable place to work,' he says 'We get a really positive feedback from the staff, which is satisfying. Perhaps the best proof of how well it has worked lies in the upturn in our business. We feel that the leadership of the company has the right resources to make it work at maximum efficiency. And the project is closely linked to our core business: developing new products, which means ideas.'

*Left **Lavish kitchen and refreshment areas are strategically placed immediately adjacent to the operations centre and are good places to meet on a casual or an ad hoc basis.***

Andersen Worldwide

Chicago, USA

'This is a project which shows that traditional notions about the correlation between hierarchy and physical space are being not only challenged but, in some senses, reversed,' says Despina Katsikakis of space planners DEGW,

who was a key player in Andersen Worldwide's relocation, completed late in 1996, to 225 North Michigan Avenue, Chicago.

Andersen Worldwide, the 'umbrella' group which heads the 100,000-strong Andersen auditing and management consultancy organization (divided into Arthur Andersen and Andersen Consulting), employs 1,100 people in its Chicago headquarters. It was based for some years in two buildings in the Loop area, one of them a 1960s office tower, the other a converted department store. In geographical terms, the organization has not moved very far, but in terms of work practice and business philosophy the change is radical and reflects Andersen Worldwide's belief that 'what you do is more important than who you are,' as John Lewis, chief financial officer for the company, puts it. Lewis believes that creativity and productivity are encouraged by setting aside conventional notions of hierarchy and place. 'It's somewhat like a newsroom, isn't it?' a television interviewer who has just seen the new offices once asked Lewis, who liked the comparison. 'It's certainly a great place to meet people.' he replied, 'and today meeting people informally is a vital part of work – you don't achieve things by sealing yourself away in a cell.'

John Lewis sees the project as a matter of 'breaking down the silos', the vertical and highly divisive departmental compartments in which partners, senior managers, and other staff worked, and introducing communication and openness in new layouts designed to bring different people and diverse skills closer together. In Andersen Worldwide's old buildings, says Lewis, there was a perceived lack of communication. Hierarchy, it seemed, mattered more than business effectiveness and this was seen as an increasingly serious issue.

The entire Andersen organization is actively promoting change. Andersen Worldwide, as the hub of the Andersen empire, is about knowledge and it needs to harness the knowledge of everyone in the organization, encouraging creativity and the desire to learn and innovate. The physical corollary is treating work space as a flexible tool, not as a mysterious and intractable series of constraints. The walls come down as the old hierarchies are challenged and lose their meaning. Nobody is rooted to one spot, day in, year out. Nobody has a right to a fixed place. The workplace must support and serve the worker, not prescribe his or her life, and the worker must learn to use the space effectively for his or her needs. So out go the old cellular offices, including those for the vast majority of partners. In Andersen Worldwide's old offices the spaces at the corners of the building, with views out on both sides, were traditionally reserved as management's private domain. Now these areas are all earmarked as project areas and conference spaces, used by everyone, while partners and managers are much more closely integrated with their departments. Enclosed offices have been drastically reduced – from 300 to 60. The new

> *'Change management was what made the project a success,' believes Bill Johnson, Andersen Worldwide's director of administration. 'It's not just about physical space, or new technology, but better use of human resources.'*

DEN	CLUB
HIVE	**CELL**

BUILDING STATISTICS

CLIENT: Andersen Worldwide			**FUNCTION:** Headquarters of auditing practice and management consultancy		
TOTAL FLOOR AREA: 23,365 sq. m / 250,000 sq. ft		**TOTAL POPULATION:** 1,100	**OVERALL DENSITY:** 21 sq. m per person / 227 sq. ft per person		
SAMPLE PLAN AREA (less core): 3,458 sq. m / 37,000 sq. ft		**Circulation:** 17.0%	**Support:** 40.4%	**Cellular:** 12.9%	**Open plan:** 29.5%
CONSULTANTS: *Interior Design* Skidmore Owings & Merrill *Programming* DEGW International Limited					

Above **The enclosed meeting rooms, one of which is shown here with an open door, are intended for concentrated conferencing and interaction. Photographed before the building was occupied and fully furnished, the open space forms part of the general office area.**

Left **Open, reconfigurable project areas are designed for informal meetings. At the centre of the table is a 'hitching post', used to distribute cabling. This area, on the corner of the building, would once almost certainly have been reserved for an enclosed executive office.**

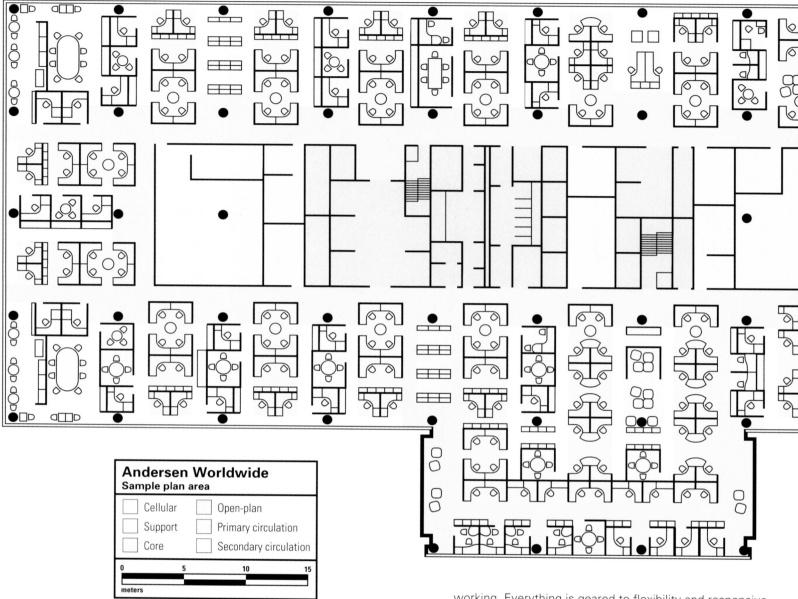

Andersen Worldwide
Sample plan area

☐	Cellular	☐	Open-plan
☐	Support	☐	Primary circulation
☐	Core	☐	Secondary circulation

```
0          5          10         15
████████████████████████████████
meters
```

Above **A typical floor plan shows the basic space-planning discipline. There are clear major circulation routes parallel to the core. Perpendicular to the core are zones of small, individually owned 'home base' workstations that alternate with space that supports a far wider range of concentrated individual and shared group activities.**

headquarters, on five floors of a tower designed by Mies van der Rohe that was chosen for its relatively large floor-plates, represents a 30 per cent reduction in space from the old premises – this big annual saving effectively paying for the relocation and the new fit-out in only three and a half years. The new layouts give practically all members of Andersen Worldwide their own 'home base' workstations, but also allow unprecedentedly easy access to parallel and adjacent neighbourhoods i.e. adjacent zones of additional, shared support settings that allow staff to switch easily from private work to informal conferencing and net-

working. Everything is geared to flexibility and responsiveness – project teams can set up conferences or activity areas at short notice within a few metres of their own workstations, using movable furniture, laptop computers, and mobile telephones.

One aspect of changing practice which Andersen is pursuing with evangelical zeal is 'the paper purge'. When it moved, the organization disposed of 79 tons of paper (it was, of course, recycled). Any tendency to hoard paper is now actively discouraged. Fewer filing cabinets mean more space for people and fewer barriers to interaction. If there have to be filing cabinets – and the organization cannot be paper-free – they should be both movable and managed.

Andersen Worldwide's relocation could be interpreted as merely a matter of space-saving, another response to financial pressure in a highly competitive field. Cutting occupancy

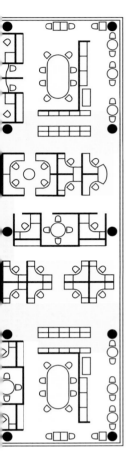

Left **The main circulation route, which runs from end to end of the building on both sides of the core, gives access to all the office neighbourhoods.**

Below **This reconfigurable meeting area in the centre of a floor is located close to an open-plan office neighbourhood, glimpsed on the left. There is provision for pin boards, as well as to hang white boards for meetings.**

costs was, of course, one of the most important objectives behind the project. (It proved impossible, in fact, to fit everyone into the North Michigan Avenue building – further space had to be taken a few blocks away for around 150 staff.) But the move was much more closely linked to the search to find new ways of working which integrate people, information technology, and physical space to achieve better and quicker results for customers. Andersen was determined to carry its employees with it. Despina Katsikakis says that an 'enormous' amount of participation underlay the success of the project: 'Change management involves abandoning the old rules – all to do with imposing solutions on people – and getting to know what people want.' Katsikakis and her team met around 80 per cent of the staff in a series of workshops, focus groups, and open design sessions. It wasn't just a matter of asking people to describe their ideal working environment: most find it hard to be very definite. Instead, they were offered a series of options and asked to comment, contradict or, above all, improve on what was being proposed. One very real fear was that there would be no privacy or calm. The flexible but mixed space which has resulted from the project is designed to assuage such concerns. Katsikakis worked very closely with John Lewis as well as with Andersen's director of administration Bill Johnson, and with a 25-person project-user group, containing representatives of all departments, which met regularly. There were also separate project teams overseeing the physical construction of the new offices and the installation of more responsive and powerful computer and telecommunication technology.

Bill Johnson never underestimated the likely resistance to the move and the changes that accompanied it. There was predictable resistance from some executives and from managers in the middle levels of the organization, he says. 'Some of them are still very much adapting to the change but the culture shift we'd hoped for is happening.' Most staff, however, like the new space and there is no doubt in the company that it

Below **The cafeteria is positioned to take advantage of the best views. The ceiling is a fanciful touch in an otherwise sober interior.**

reflects new business goals. Johnson believes that there is now greater awareness on the part of staff about the objectives and possibilities of the whole company – people are given more responsibility, more challenges and are more able to exercise judgment and initiative.

The refit of the North Michigan building was planned by DEGW in association with the Chicago office of architects

some respects, the North Michigan fit-out was technically less radical than had been hoped for. Plans to install entirely demountable walls, with lots of glazing, throughout the office had to be abandoned because of shortage of time in favour of a more conventional, fixed 'drywall' arrangement. It is not yet clear how far this will inhibit change in the future. Bill Johnson believes that the project already provides for a great degree of diversity, given that people can work in groups or withdraw into enclosed spaces to write, think, or conduct telephone conversations. What has been provided is a planning infrastructure that can cope with today's den-like pattern of high interaction and medium auton-

omy, but also accommodate the migration towards more club-like working that Andersen Worldwide predicts for many of its working groups.

Left **In a typical office neighbourhood workstations are laid out in an informal manner, the continuous worksurface helping to make the area as flexible as possible.**

'There is space for collaboration and space for privacy. The only deficiency, as far as I can see, is that we slightly underestimated the area of conference space needed,' says Johnson. In a sense, however, the fact that the fifteen-room conference area – not to mention the huge number of smaller interactive settings – is now constantly in use is a sign of success. John Lewis insists that, 'It's a matter of people organizing themselves to book the space they need – again, it's about changing the way we think and not expecting everything to be exactly as it was in the past.'

Already, changes – monitored by extensive and ongoing post-occupancy studies – are under way in the new space as work patterns and technology change. That more and more people are using laptop computers suggests that a further breakdown of fixed layouts could be desirable. The most positive feature of the project is its frank reflection of changed ways of working. Mies van der Rohe's building was designed for the work patterns of the 1960s, when vice presidents sat in big closed offices hogging the perimeter while the rank-and-file were segregated into smaller, viewless work places deeper within the building. The refit for Andersen Worldwide proves that an apparently dated building can be reborn for the new ways of working in the late twentieth century. John Lewis sums up the success of the project in this way: 'The way we think and the way we work has changed and will change more. Change is now permanently written into the agenda for Andersen Worldwide.'

SOM (Skidmore, Owings & Merrill) and the project was implemented under the supervision of SOM. There is nothing luxurious or showy about the new offices – the clients of the headquarters are all fellow members of the Andersen organization and do not need to be impressed. 'If anything, the fit-out is a little spartan,' says Bill Johnson. But it has a wide significance. 'Neighbourhood' space is seen as the future. In

'We want our office to be a prototype of how to get it right. We want an environment that supports people working together and reflects our culture of openness, individual account- ability, and participative management.' It

Lend Lease Interiors

Sydney, Australia

would be hard to find a more definite statement of intent. Lend Lease Interiors evidently wanted to make crystal-clear its objectives at the start of the refurbishment project for its offices in the Australia Square Tower in central Sydney. The company's letter, inviting eighteen architectural and design practices to submit proposals, emphasized its need 'to respond quickly to shifts in our business and manage change. Our people need to be learning continually – and the workplace must also be flexible and adaptable. The richness of interaction at work will be a critical part of this learning process, as much as our business systems and technology.'

This experimental project proves the benefits of involving busy users in rethinking how and where they best do their work. The result of extensive consultation is a choice of work settings that allow project groups to work more productively.

Lend Lease Interiors is part of the Lend Lease Corporation, a leading Australian public company providing integrated financial and property services to clients round the world: the interests of its component companies include property funding and development, project management, construction, and interior design, as well as engineering design for industry. Lend Lease anticipates sustained growth for all its businesses and has a clear strategy for achieving this which implies harnessing the talents of its staff to the best possible effect.

Lend Lease has occupied part of Australia Square for some years. The building is a 1960s landmark, designed by Modern Movement master Harry Seidler on a circular plan that creates interesting, but somewhat challenging, interiors.

The project provided for the relocation of the New South Wales operations of Lend Lease Interiors and Civil & Civic (another Lend Lease company, specializing in new building construction) – 190 staff in total were involved – on the sixth, seventh, and ninth floors, each around 1,000 sq. m\10,700 sq. ft. The successful contender for the design strategy commission was the Sydney practice Bligh Voller, working with space planners from architects DEGW, while Lend Lease Interiors themselves acted as project managers. The project took a year to realize, staff moving into the refurbished floors in September 1995.

Lend Lease Interior's broad objectives for its own offices were clear from the start, but they were much more fully defined as the project proceeded. In essence, Lend Lease Interiors wanted a den – to introduce more project spaces, more support, and workstations that could be adapted to a variety of individual requirements. Flexibility was to be a priority. Interaction was the ultimate aim: 'information sharing rather than information hoarding'. The work place, Lend Lease Interiors believes, should be 'enjoyable and stimulating'. A three-month study period, during which Bligh Voller/DEGW and Lend Lease Interiors' project managers assessed the nature of the company's work and its future accommodation needs, helped to fine-tune the brief for the project. Fundamental questions were asked. Who really needs fixed space in the office of the future? How much of the paper filing in any office is really vital? Out of the management and

DEN	CLUB
HIVE	CELL

BUILDING STATISTICS					
CLIENT: Lend Lease Interiors Pty Ltd.			**FUNCTION:** Project management division of property corporation		
TOTAL FLOOR AREA: 1,000 sq. m / 10,700 sq. ft		**TOTAL POPULATION:** 56	**OVERALL DENSITY:** 17.9 sq. m per person / 190 sq. ft per person		
SAMPLE PLAN AREA (less core): 1,000 sq. m / 10,700 sq. ft		**Circulation:** 19.0%	**Support:** 34.0%	**Cellular:** 4.5%	**Open plan:** 42.4%
CONSULTANTS: *Interior Design* Bligh Voller *Programming* DEGW International Limited					

Above **The team bays allow users to work together as well as separately.**

Left **What was the sixth-floor showroom, with an impressive coffered ceiling, is now the centrepiece of the project. The space is particularly interesting because of its height and geometry. The ingenious layout reconciles the circle and the triangle and keeps clear views and circulation routes open at the same time as providing a variety of work spaces.**

staff workshops, staff survey interviews, and other research came some firm recommendations. There should be 'team bays' containing workstations, with centralized storage areas for papers. Enclosed booths would cater for concentrated individual work, while 'war rooms' would provide for brainstorming project meetings, alongside a range of meeting rooms. The project also had to provide for good circulation within the work space, allowing the floor plan to work well for late twentieth-century needs. The sixth floor was a particular challenge. Seidler had designed it as a showroom, with a ceiling height of 4.8 m/16 ft beneath the strongly modelled coffered concrete ceiling.

Katherine McPherson of Bligh Voller says that the design background of many of the Lend Lease staff helped in the

Opposite **The floor plan of the sixth floor shows how the bold imposition of a triangular pattern of circulation makes sense of a circular floor-plate with a big central core. It provides a logic for locating a wide range of specialized supplementary settings – project areas, meeting rooms, social places – near everyone's workplace.**

Below **Staff work in groups in open-plan areas which encourage teamwork and interaction.**

development of the project. 'We had virtually daily meetings with Lend Lease Interiors – as both client and project managers,' she recalls. Lend Lease Interiors wrote the outline brief, providing the key inputs on business strategy, information technology, human resources, and construction matters, while DEGW produced the stategic brief as well as the detailed space budget based on focus groups and extensive interviewing, Time Utilization Studies and Workplace Envisioning workshops.

Sue Wittenoom of Lend Lease Interiors explains that the briefing was done not on a hierarchical basis – by managers only – but by a group which represented 'a vertical slice of the organization, one representing all peer groups.' Lend Lease Interiors, she says, 'is highly participatory.' In fact, virtually all the members of the group had plenty of experience of fit-out projects. When it came to taking quick decisions, these were made by a specifically designated group of three people. Daily coordination and management of the project

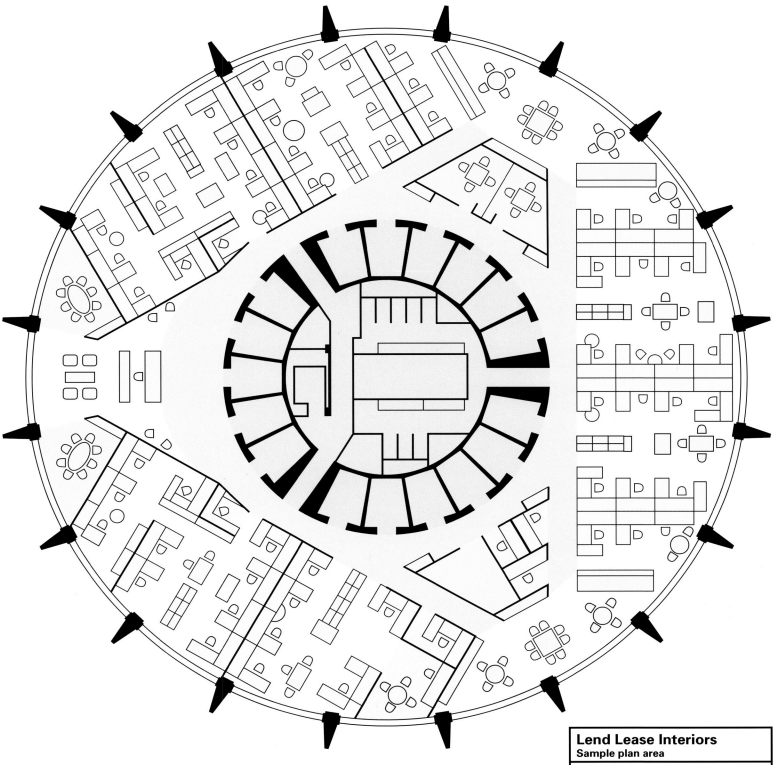

was the task of Norman Herfuth, Lend Lease Interiors' project manager, who integrated specialist inputs.

A great deal of attention went into the fit-out, extending from the overall layout to the detailed design of workstations, the whole programme being informed by the credo which Lend Lease Interiors set out at the beginning of the project. Work areas were designed for flexibility: any area can be demounted and reconfigured without compromising the group support facilities. All work elements can be readily rearranged: the use of a small range of basic components and the configuration of services facilitate this operation. There is plenty of scope to rearrange teamwork areas at short notice. All staff are arranged in groups and individuals have only minimal storage space; most storage is

Above and below **The well-equipped refreshment area was designed to be used not just as a place to escape from work, or to turn one's back on colleagues, but also as an additional resource for networking or simply getting on with the task in hand. The layout of the entire office is intended to allow staff the widest degree of choice in how, when and where they carry out their work.**

concentrated at the central 'team bay'. Each floor has an escape zone, in the form of a 'green room' complete with dishwasher and refrigerator, where staff can hold informal meetings, socialize over an end-of-work drink – or hold a leaving party.

Sue Wittenoom reports that transforming these offices into highly equipped dens has been a striking success. A post-occupancy analysis, conducted by DEGW, highlighted increases in performance of up to 41 per cent over that in the previous office space. Revenues for the group increased by over 30 per cent in a year, with no corresponding increase in the number of employees. The transformed space has proved to be very flexible, though Lend Lease Interiors tends to move people rather than furniture and fittings. 'We see the future in terms of moving people in a behavourial sense,' says Wittenoom, 'encouraging them to use the space differently.' But Lend Lease Interiors does not see the project as a finite thing, rather as a stepping stone to further learning, part of a strategy for change. 'If anything,' says Wittenoom, 'the project could have gained from using

movable furniture for even more flexibility, currently limited by the use of highly serviced systems furniture.'

Within the workplace, however, staff have a great degree of freedom to choose the setting in which they want to work. In some cases, this may mean working at home on an assignment which demands a high level of concentration. This approach, Sue Wittenoom insists, 'is a pretty good alternative to individually regulated "micro-environments". But you can never account for individual taste – we still get people complaining about distracting noise when quiet rooms are vacant and ready to use just feet away.' Overall the impression is of a busy and stimulating workplace.

Lend Lease Interiors started out on the Australia Square Tower project wanting 'a new workplace to support the re-engineering of the way we work.' The organization feels that it has achieved what it set out to achieve and carried its staff with it. '"Work" is defined more broadly,' says Sue Wittenoom. 'It's much easier to interact with colleagues. The general feeling is strongly in favour of the new arrangements.' The project brought together a group of people and a place and made the marriage work. Empty desks are now a thing of the past. The space is made to work hard at the same time as being an agreeable, interactive working environment. While respecting the distinct character of Seidler's building, the Lend Lease Interiors project has created new offices which are relaxed and informal, but equally purposeful and highly efficient, a humane space for the business needs of the twenty-first century.

New kinds of office – the club

Club offices are characterized by high levels of both concentrated and interactive work, high levels of autonomy and a great deal of shared support of different kinds. In other words there is a lot of every kind of office activity.

Consequently clubs tend to be rich and diverse in the variety of work settings they provide. However, the one essential and overriding characteristic of the club office is that advantage is taken of the mobility of the work force, and consequent intermittent occupancy, to intensify space use by sharing workstations and other resources over extended working days. Indeed, it is only through time-sharing that the relatively elaborate work settings inherent in the idea of the club can be afforded.

Digital, in Sweden, and IBM (UK) were among the pioneers of club offices, in very different ways. Digital's response was quick, intuitive, low-cost, and bottom-up, invented by the workers themselves. IBM's version of the same basic idea was much more carefully structured and studied. The results are startlingly different. Digital's offices have a crude, folksy immediacy which may not stand the test of time. On the other hand, IBM's more considered, more timeless club interiors at Bedfont Lakes are almost indistinguishable, at first sight, from a conventional office of a somewhat old-fashioned corporate kind. It is only when one examines the statistics of use that the true extent of their originality emerges.

British Telecom's offices at Stockley Park and Benevia's in Chicago represent a second generation of space-sharing in club-type offices. Both show considerable confidence in finding appropriate and supportive information technology, as well as in establishing practical routines for ensuring access to shared resources. In both examples, there is a discrepancy between the novelty of the club idea and the predictability of the furniture layout. BT is saved from banality by its elegance and by the wonderful Foster building that houses it, Benevia by the big-boned structure of its context – the raw space of the Chicago Merchandise Mart. Operationally both seem to be successful – by all accounts, new ways of working are being quickly taken for granted.

Rijksgebouwendienst and Chiat/Day are also second-generation experimenters. In different ways they are more original, both in appearance and in organizational invention, than the other clubs. The Dutch example, a prototype for other government offices, is particularly ingenious and well worked out, both in the design of the details of the layout and the protocols of the shared working environment. Chiat/Day in New York is largely concerned with exploring appropriate imagery for the future office. Not only is this done with great élan – rather too much, less flamboyant organizations might think – but this club also shows a more serious underlying willingness to question and subvert the old, established conventions of office work as well as of office design. Despite the occasional silliness, this kind of design energy and design rhetoric is necessary to escape from the enormous weight of the past. Tremendous organizational imagination, as well as the freshest design invention, is necessary to create new office cultures.

'The project was about creating a cohesive social environment as well as a workplace,' says Peter Wingrave of IBM (UK). 'It was designed to provide good working conditions for a highly dedicated team. We had to achieve change, but also keep people happy.' At the same time, there was a perceived need at IBM to be 'commercially realistic'. 'We had to cater for the eventuality that some of our buildings might be sublet in the future. Some of the schemes we'd done in the past were seen as too specific, too esoteric.' In this respect, the project was, to a significant degree, 'property led'.

In 1989 when IBM (UK), the British arm of the business machines giant, began to explore ways of housing its sales staff more effectively – marketing operations were spread across four sites in west London – it quickly recognized the need for radical changes. In the course of that decade, the company's corporate agenda – and its approach to commissioning buildings – had changed markedly under the pressure of stiff international competition. Now buildings, as well as people, had to justify their place in the organization and here too the key criterion was effective performance.

IBM had been the international leader in managing corporate real estate between the 1960s and the late 1980s. The origins of the Bedfont Lakes project were indicative of major changes that were to come, and lay in IBM's conviction that speculative, rather than specific, buildings would provide a way to cut costs and tie in with a general campaign towards downsizing, high efficiency and time management. This trend towards cutting waste extended to other matters besides

IBM (UK) – Bedfont Lakes

West London, UK

real estate. In 1989 the SMART programme, a series of pioneering, interdisciplinary studies into all aspects of IBM working practices – for which architects/space-planners DEGW invented new techniques of measuring space utilization – found what had long been suspected was true: that the marketing offices were, on average, two-thirds empty. Meanwhile, information technology was developing rapidly, making new working processes possible – indeed inevitable. No longer would it be necessary to accommodate everyone at individual desks from nine to five, five days a week. To salespeople, customer contact time and having access to the best technology, was more important than 'owning' their own desks. The operational and economic case for a system of sharing expensive office space was strong. So when IBM decided to relocate a major part of its sales staff to Bedfont Lakes it made sense not only to experiment with one of the earliest – and certainly the one of the best-researched – programmes of intensifying space use, but also to collaborate with a major office property developer, in this case MEPC, to reduce the commercial risk inherent in such a project.

The site at Bedfont Lakes, near Heathrow Airport, was eventually identified as a suitable location. It was developed to a master plan by Michael Hopkins & Partners, but with half of the buildings (those intended for commercial renting) designed by Edward Cullinan Architects. MEPC were project managers, supported by a small management team containing representatives of both IBM and MEPC. The aim on IBM's

> *Few big companies have a more distinguished past record of building procurement, property management, and, indeed, architectural patronage than IBM and the buildings at Bedfont Lakes, completed in 1992, can justly be counted as part of a fine tradition.*

DEN	CLUB
HIVE	CELL

BUILDING STATISTICS

CLIENT: IBM (UK) Limited		**FUNCTION:** Sales and marketing division of electronics company		
TOTAL FLOOR AREA: 16,822 sq. m / 180,000 sq. ft		**TOTAL POPULATION:** 1500	**OVERALL DENSITY:** 11.2 sq. m per person / 120 sq. ft per person	
SAMPLE PLAN AREA (less core): 3,305 sq. m / 35,000 sq. ft	**Circulation:** 17.8%	**Support:** 45.0%	**Cellular:** 19.0%	**Open plan:** 18.0%
CONSULTANTS: *Architect and Interior Design* Michael Hopkins & Partners				

Above **The exteriors of the three IBM buildings are uniform: highly disciplined, even austere, but with a strong element of transparency. The setting is a landscaped park close to Heathrow airport.**

Left **The atrium of each building is its true heart and provides space for the socializing and networking that is vital for staff who do not work on a traditional nine-to-five schedule.**

part was to secure high-quality new offices at the best possible price and to profit from a stake in a speculative scheme on the remainder of the Bedfont site.

For IBM, a company with a tradition of a 'democratic' inclination to seek consensus before embarking on major changes in policy affecting employees, the process of transition was all the more sensitive. The views of staff were sought at regular departmental meetings. They were unhappy at the prospect of quitting offices in town centres for what sounded like a bleak outpost on the edge of an airport. Wingrave recalls that, 'Though the meetings could be uncomfortable on occasions, they began to convince people that what we were offering was a superior work environment.'

'The design of the office buildings developed in tandem as a speculative standard and an IBM standard,' says Peter Romaniuk of Michael Hopkins & Partners. The Bedfont Lakes project takes the form of seven three-storey buildings – three by Michael Hopkins – around a central square which covers extensive underground car-parking. Hopkins' disciplined façades contrast with the more expressive style of the Edward Cullinan buildings – the contrast was probably deliberate, providing IBM, as the chief

Below **One of the three buildings occupied by IBM. The complex is attractively landscaped but its location was initially controversial with staff.**

covenantor of the project, with buildings with a distinctive look. Romaniuk feels that the project worked to the benefit of both development partners though, as architects working in effect for two clients, IBM as tenant and MEPC as developer, they had to erect 'Chinese walls' to separate their work on the base buildings from the fit-out designed specifically for IBM. Typically, landlords and tenants have quite different, and potentially conflicting, commercial motivations which affect design priorities.

Initially, the IBM buildings were intended to house 900 sales and marketing staff. As a result of the SMART programme, which recommended more shared workplaces, it now provides accommodation for 1500. 'After occupation, we did a further detailed space study,' Wingrave explains. 'There was still a lot of slack and great scope for intensifying use. In effect, we re-evaluated the whole space.' There were some unanticipated problems. The large areas of shared-desk space proved to be intimidating for sales people used to more intimate working environments in older buildings. There were complaints, too, about loss of privacy. Differences in emphasis of use emerged. For example, originally a number of common rooms had been provided as bolt holes on each floor, places to chat over a cup of coffee. But these were little used and were eventually closed. Instead, people gravitated to the café in the atrium. For staff who may be in the building for only a day of their working week, it's a place to catch up with colleagues and news.

IBM at Bedfont Lakes was one of the first attempts to reconceptualize the office as a club, and it was designed to take advantage of extensive sharing of common and support amenities, as well as of workstations. Operationally the project is a clear success. The chief disappointment, however, lies in the design of the shared workplaces themselves. Neatly arranged as they are, they take up a high proportion of the usable area and are, to the naked eye, practically indistinguishable from the better kind of

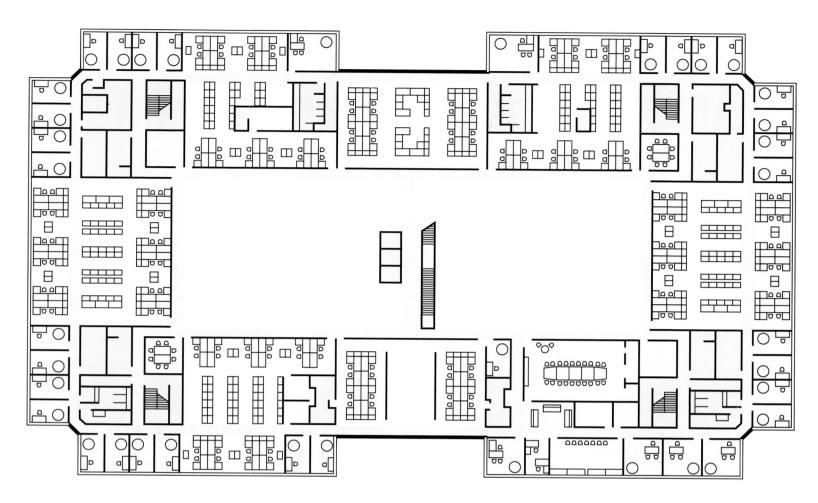

corporate office layouts of the old sort, even though their pattern of use, their operational significance and their financial impact on IBM's business are all quite extraordinary.

This is a real pity. Historically the move to Bedfont Lakes was a landmark event, not just for IBM (UK) but for office design internationally – the company's commitment to space sharing influenced many other organizations to pursue this approach. The completed building, and particularly the interiors, simply do not express the excitement and novelty of the project as first conceived. Only the well-used atrium has real dynamism. It isn't easy for architecture to reflect organizational change, but Hopkins' dignified, somewhat cold interiors have a distinctly traditional 'corporate' look, with little sense of excitement. Peter Wingrave feels that the building 'looks well and generally works well.' Drawbacks which have emerged include a relatively high maintenance budget (the result of having large areas of glass) and a severe lack of storage space. 'But this has led us to crack down on paper,' Wingrave adds, 'which we badly needed to do, anyway.'

Many of the customs now general in the company, such as flexible hours, project-working, and desk-sharing, were in their infancy in 1989. The Bedfont Lakes project effectively acted as a spur to new ways of working. These have since advanced markedly in IBM though the company, as it entered the most turbulent period of its history, was not, it appears, able to embrace and take full advantage of the office design potential of these dramatic changes. Subsequent IBM projects in the USA, based on similar principles of intensifying space-use, have been an aesthetic disgrace. Well researched, 'property led', and focused on the most intelligent and effective use of office space, the Bedfont Lakes project could have changed not only people's habits but the look of the office for ever. In a global industry characterized by the accelerating pace of experiments in the workplace, Bedfont Lakes, the turning point, stands out ironically enough as a visual reminder of more conservative days.

IBM (UK) – Bedfont Lakes
Sample plan area

☐ Cellular		☐ Open-plan/Hot desk
☐ Support		☐ Primary circulation
☐ Core		☐ Secondary circulation

0	5	10	15	20

meters

Above **The first-floor plan of the central building shows how the big internal atrium provides a focus for the whole office. Time-shared cellular offices line the external walls, while most of the open-plan, but formally laid out, time-shared workstations overlook the atrium, which contains the elevators and stairs that give the main access to all the floors.**

Chiat/Day

New York City, USA

Chiat/Day was never anything if not innovative, and the company's approach to its business is mirrored in its approach to the design and use of work spaces in the buildings it occupies. For Chiat/Day, using a building fully as a resource implies turning over the whole space to collaboration so as to 'harvest and build a collective intelligence.' Described as 'resource architecture' by Laurie Coots, the advertising agency's director of administration and business development, it is a strategy based on a fusion of architecture and liberating technology – freeing staff to work when and where they choose to but giving them a working base designed to maximize creativity. It has been wholeheartedly adopted by Chiat/Day in their ground-breaking offices in Venice, California, and in New York. Both were conceived as part of the same process of physical and psychological transformation.

Chiat/Day made its name in the late 1970s, working from a former hotel in downtown Los Angeles, and by the mid-1980s had become one of the advertising industry's pacesetters. In 1995 it joined forces with the even larger TBWA agency to form TBWA Chiat/Day (with 58 offices in 40 countries). The company's office in Venice, California, is a spectacular image-maker, with architecture by Frank Gehry and applied art (in the form of a gigantic pair of binoculars forming an entrance portico) by Claes Oldenburg. Before it occupied this, in 1994, Chiat/Day operated from a converted warehouse nearby, complete with an extraordinary fit-out which included a conference room in the shape of a fish. The agency abolished conventional office spaces 20 years ago in favour of standard-size, non-hierarchical cubicles. Chiat/Day's move to the Gehry building coincided with a period of even more radical change. The idea, according to founder Jay Chiat, was to 'transcend traditional behaviour patterns. This isn't about creating structure and predictability: it's about people working together in the most efficient way possible.' Chiat/Day had moved into the age of the virtual office with 'team architecture' providing communal space for activities and teamwork, rather than individual work spaces, the whole enterprise backed by a total commitment to new office technology. Laurie Coots sees the process as one of liberation for the employees: an office is a resource to be used when needed, not a place you have to go to for set hours. It is the end product that matters. Coots defines the five qualities that any company must possess to succeed in the future: first, a positive approach to change; second, a strategic use of technology; third, an ability to turn information into intelligence; fourth, a willingness to invest in relationships; and fifth, strong teamwork.

Chiat/Day began on the West Coast but it inevitably moved into the New York scene, opening an office, initially in the Midtown area, in 1981. The office moved twice before settling in Lower Manhattan, close to South Street Seaport. The firm's present New York office (opened in June 1994 and designed by the architect/designer Gaetano Pesce) is located not in a custom-made building, nor even in an 'interesting' old structure, but in a typically bland 1980s rented slab in the

> 'We never actually referred to the virtual office – our concern was to have completely fluid movement. This was to be the office as club,' says Laurie Coots of Chiat/Day. 'The conventional way of getting things done is no longer good enough,' says Jay Chiat, founder of the company. 'Today change isn't a good idea – it's a necessity.'

DEN	CLUB
HIVE	CELL

BUILDING STATISTICS					
CLIENT: TBWA Chiat / Day			**FUNCTION:** Advertising agency		
TOTAL FLOOR AREA: 4,500 sq. m / 50,000 sq. ft		**TOTAL POPULATION:** 150	**OVERALL DENSITY:** 30 sq. m per person / 333 sq. ft per person		
SAMPLE PLAN AREA (less core): 2,008 sq. m / 21,500 sq. ft		**Circulation:** 29.0%	**Support:** 50.0%	**Cellular:** 3.0%	**Open plan:** 17.3%
CONSULTANTS: *Interior Design* Gaetano Pesce / Pesce, Ltd.					

Above **Chiat/Day's New York office is an open-space club, where staff are seen as visitors, who use it as a base but not a full-time home. Places to work have to be reserved – as in a restaurant.**

Left **Laptop computers are collected from a central store, via a huge pair of red lips. Lockers are provided for personal belongings or papers.**

Wall Street area. It occupies space on one floor – less than a third of the area it had before the move. (Since the TBWA merger, operations have expanded into another floor of the same building without obvious problems.)

As in California, Chiat/Day has abandoned private offices and conventional meeting rooms along with the traditional working day. Instead it has given its 150 employees not so much a *tabula rasa* on which to build their own work spaces, but a highly stylized environment which reflects Jay Chiat's theories of 'architectural management'. At least half the New York office (as opened in 1994) was open space, demarcated only as activity areas, such as 'the Piazza' and 'the Club House'. Cellular spaces, in so far as they existed, were allocated not to people but to projects and clients: there might be a 'Nissan room' or an 'Absolut Vodka room'. There are small studies for people who need to work alone, but they must be reserved in

Below **Image and immediacy are important in creating a strong impact. This is the exterior of one of the private meeting rooms that are set aside for specific jobs or clients and used for intensive brainstorming sessions.**

advance. The library, print room and other specialized functions are also partitioned off, but the rest of the office is, in the words of one of its critics, 'an adult play-pen, a thirty-eighth floor tree-house … boisterously communal and aggressively fun ….' There is no private space, except for the small lockers where staff keep their personal effects. Laptop computers (in general use) are collected daily from a central base (through an opening strikingly, if somewhat incongruously, contrived as a huge pair of red lips). Everything is brightly, even garishly, coloured and visual conceits are thickly scattered: a meeting room in the form of a giant dog kennel, a door opening shaped like a bottle, an enigmatic question mark cut out of a wall. All these artefacts were made in Pesce's own workshop.

It is all very memorable, but what were the business objectives behind the project – and have they been met? One thing that it was not about was gaining more space – the office contracted from three floors to one. It was entirely a matter of enhancing the quality of the space. An open space

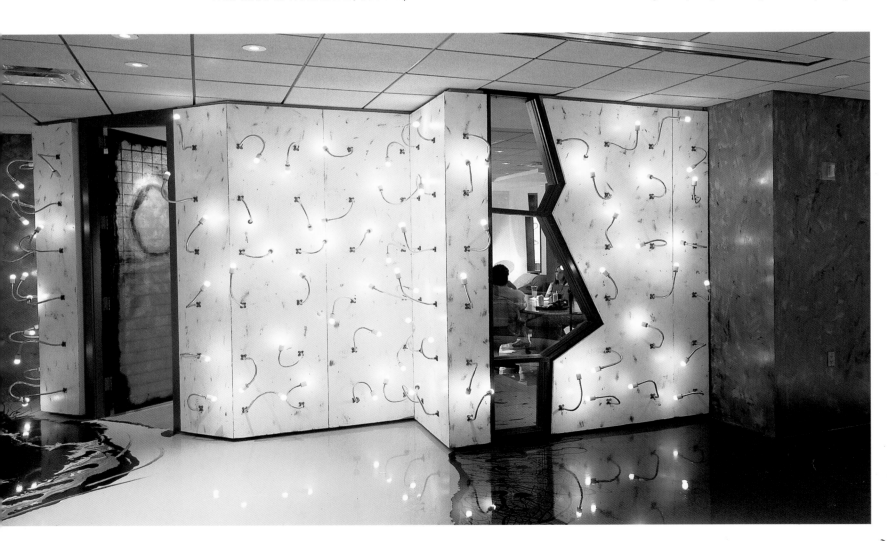

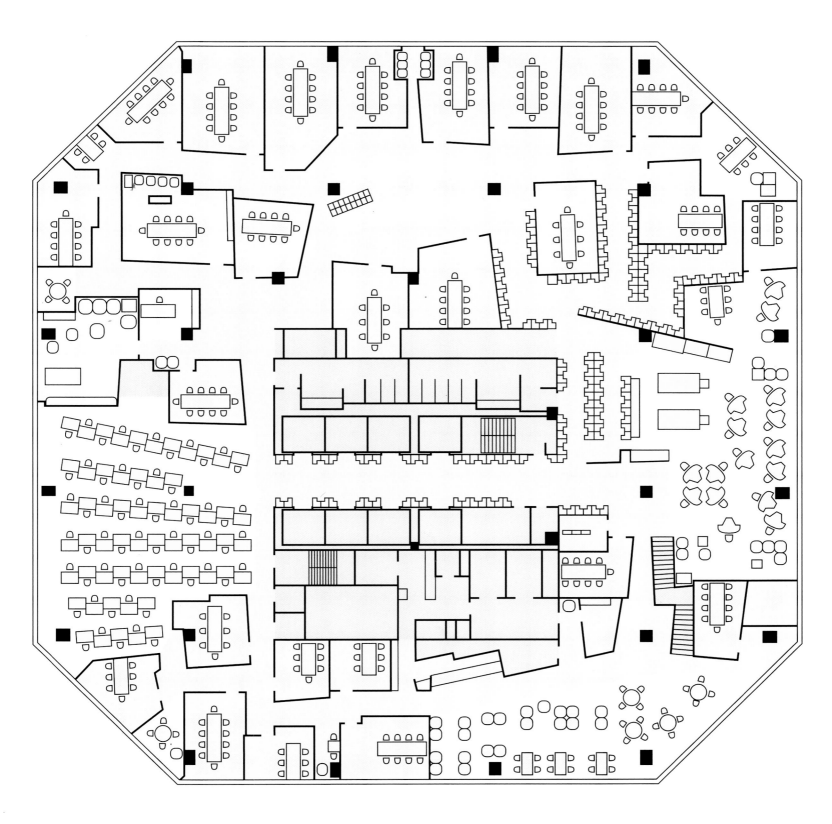

was required, entirely dedicated to collaborative working. Suggestions that the new office was simply an economy measure are rejected: the move was about new ways of working and a new view of the company. It is seen as an enabler, serving the staff. Too often, the priority is reversed: issues of space and finance dominate and staff have to adjust to prescriptive design.

Chiat/Day
Sample plan area

☐ Cellular   ☐ Open-plan/Hot desk
☐ Support   ☐ Primary circulation
☐ Core   ☐ Secondary circulation

0   3   6   9   12
meters

Above **The inventive and free-form scatter of activity areas on this floor plan reflects the fluid way in which the company operates. A very high proportion of space is given over to to presentation rooms and support activities. Chiat/Day has made a standard office building completely their own.**

195

Above **Workstations are portable, time-shared, and often highly individual in design. A concern for high style is to the fore – the textured screen is probably more of an artistic gesture than a practical soundproofing device.**

It is clear that Jay Chiat put his personal stamp on the New York office, building on the perceived success of the California one. When the latter was being planned, there was a very open system of consultation and comment. Staff were free to make suggestions and criticize the management's proposals. There was a good deal less consultation in the case of the New York project – 'Jay Chiat was very much the leader,' says Laurie Coots. Coots sees the agency's staff as 'explorers – great innovators, wonderful to work with.' She has been closely involved in Chiat/Day's (latterly TBWA Chiat/Day's) office revolution and the problems, as she sees them, are about human beings rather than technology.

The positive benefits of the New York project are many, according to Coots: very intensive, cost-effective use of technology via the 'communal lodge', i.e. the bank of laptops, plenty of choice for staff, who can work when and where they like, excellent, well-used communal facilities (like the Club House and library) and optimum use of people's talents in a new age of self-determination. The project is seen as the summation of a long process of planned change, designed to ensure that the company continues to grow and innovate as it has done in the past.

Laurie Coots sees the culture of the company as 'about hunting and gathering', working 'on the hoof', about spontaneity, quick thinking, the ability to adapt rapidly and seize opportunities as they arise. The new physical context of the business reflects a total commitment to those values. This is certainly the office-as-club – with a vengeance. Now, however, something of a new mood is beginning to emerge. 'We assumed that people, given a choice, would opt to work more out of the office than in,' says Coots, 'merely checking in a few times a week. In fact, most come in for periods every day.' Many, it appears, find the total absence of territorial space something of a trial. 'It's rather as if the only place you have to work is an airport business lounge – comfortable and acceptable, but far from ideal and nothing to do with you.' Coots foresees significant changes in the way the office is

used. 'Nobody wants to go back to conventional spaces,' she says, 'but 100 per cent non-territorial space is a problem. We need to look more closely at the human factor and get more of a sense of community.'

The future, Coots believes, lies in the 'village' rather than the 'club'. A more recent office opened by the company in Canada is seen as a pointer in this direction, less prescriptive, more inviting, more conducive to 'bonding'. Every office project is seen as an experiment, a step towards an ideal. 'New York wasn't perfect,' says Coots, 'but it has been a considerable success and has reinforced our collaborative work culture.' Coots compares the culture of an office to the culture of a city. Manhattan is a vibrant place because of the interaction of East Side and West Side, uptown and downtown, Chinatown and Little Italy, Chelsea and Soho, the sub-cultures of the city. 'We need to provide space for office sub-cultures to which people relate,' says Coots. 'We've got to embrace diversity and individual taste and realize the benefits.' The ideal lies somewhere between old-style, hierarchical, prescriptive 'corporate' culture and total, anarchic individualism. Chiat/Day is striving to identify this optimum point. The experience of

some staff, who find the office disorienting and comfortless, has to be tackled, not dismissed. There are limits, it seems, to the virtual office.

Perhaps people are experiencing 'the weight of too much freedom'. Work is a discipline and a definer of a way of life, not just a means of earning money. TBWA Chiat/ Day evidently understands the impact of work on the totality of people's lives and is prepared to take a holistic view of the work place.

The company is entering a further period of physical change. The Gehry office building in Venice is due for relocation in 1998. Gaetano Pesce's New York interior, which is 'maybe a little over-stimulating' according to Laurie Coots, could also face radical changes. By its very nature, it is restless and ephemeral – not made to last. As a company TBWA Chiat/Day embraces the theory of 'creative unrest' – nothing must remain unchanged for too long.

The successes and weaknesses of the office are now becoming apparent. Perhaps its gravest weakness is that it is a place where 'play' is enforced on everyone, all the time. It isn't hard to tire of its relentless quirkiness, its rejection of calm and conventional order. But it stands, for the moment, as a monument to a strongly expressed vision of the future of the office as club – or playpen.

Left **Architect Gaetano Pesce sought to break down old corporate ideas by turning office furnishings into unique, specially-made works of art. This design is for the portable workstations seen opposite.**

Below **The individual look extends to the meeting rooms, which may be styled to reflect a particular media campaign and then redecorated.**

Digital Equipment

Stockholm, Sweden

'Creating an open, flexible organization in an open, flexible workplace – better for staff, customers, and the company.' This was the stated aim behind Digital Equipment's radical (and widely acclaimed) revamp of its Stockholm office. **According to Bertil Arnius,** property manager of Digital Equipment AB (Sweden), the objective behind the project was 'a new way of working in a living office which works for people.'

Digital has been a consistently interesting player on the global information technology scene – and in office design – for over 30 years. From its roots in Massachusetts the company has advanced internationally, and its commitment to redefining the workplace and challenging established ways of working is now central to its business strategy for the future. Christopher Hood, Digital's US-based principal projects manager, has been spearheading organizational change in the company since 1991. During the 1980s, Digital was growing at 30 per cent a year, taking on staff and acquiring more space for manufacturing, research, marketing, and administration. By the late 1980s, Hood explains, 'we were starting to take a fundamental look at how work was being performed and, indeed, what quality of work was being performed – better performance was the aim. It was about business, not interior design.'

The impact on Digital of an increasingly competitive world market had been reflected in heavy cost-cutting during the early 1990s: sales and management staff numbers were reduced and offices closed worldwide in an attempt to slash overheads radically. 'In that period the emphasis was on cutting everything, including space, and squeezing operations into smaller spaces,' says Hood. But the advent of mobile technology and communications ameliorated the financial impact of change – people could now work away from the office, in their homes or with customers. For the vital sales and marketing staff, around 10,000 of them out of a total Digital work force (1997) of 55,000, this meant being able to spend more time actually selling. 'But most people's jobs do need an office-based element,' says Hood. 'We had to find out what sort of facility they needed.' Studies revealed that at any one time no more than 35 per cent of workstation spaces at Digital were actually being used. The obvious conclusion was that dedicated workstations should be restricted to staff who spent all or most of their day in the office and that most staff would be better served by flexible, touchdown space. The priority, Hood concluded, was not simply a matter of saving space or even saving money, but increasing productivity, encouraging new ways of working and getting the best possible performance from a highly motivated work force. Carefully targeted investment should address these goals. Standardization of furnishings, for example, would produce clear economies – though there was a danger that standardized interiors would undermine the identity of individual offices within an organization that operated globally.

Digital's current stress on 'activity-based design' indicates a new determination to relate office space to the work that is done within that space. Each work setting should be

> *Bertil Arnius, property manager of Digital Equipment in Sweden, typifies the new regime there. 'Although I come from the property arm of the company, my starting point on the project was to talk to our sales force, those who actually sell our products and use the office, to discover what they needed to do their job better.'*

DEN	CLUB
HIVE	CELL

BUILDING STATISTICS						
CLIENT: Digital Equipment AB			**FUNCTION:** Computer sales and marketing base of electronics company			
TOTAL FLOOR AREA: 3,300 sq. m / 35,300 sq. ft		**TOTAL POPULATION:** 240		**OVERALL DENSITY:** 13.75 sq. m per person / 147 sq. ft per person		
SAMPLE PLAN AREA (less core): 227 sq. m / 2,428 sq. ft			**Circulation:** 33.8%	**Support:** 30.6%	**Cellular:** 0%	**Open plan:** 35.5%
CONSULTANTS: In-house design						

directly related to what people do in it: conferencing or networking or concentrated writing. But most jobs contain many
elements, so Digital offices should always be designed to
provide diverse settings to accommodate a wide range of
experiences. Involving employees and meeting their requirements for the surroundings they work in has equally been a
fundamental element in Digital's new work environment programme of the 1990s and is seen as an adjunct to the drive
for greater productivity and synergy in the organization. The
new approach found a particularly vivid expression in Digital's
Stockholm office project, completed in 1993.

Like the earlier – and perhaps better known – experimental Digital office in Helsinki, the new one in Stockholm is
a sales office. It is located in an undistinguished, suburban
former cable factory, known as the Sundbyberg building, built
c.1900 and converted to offices by a developer in the early
1980s. Around 240 Digital sales and management staff

Top and above **The office interior has an idiosyncratic, folksy, specifically
Scandinavian character. In the highly flexible central space, workstations can
be pulled down from the boughs of a decorative tree; papers are stored in
rolling cabinets, seen in the top photograph.**

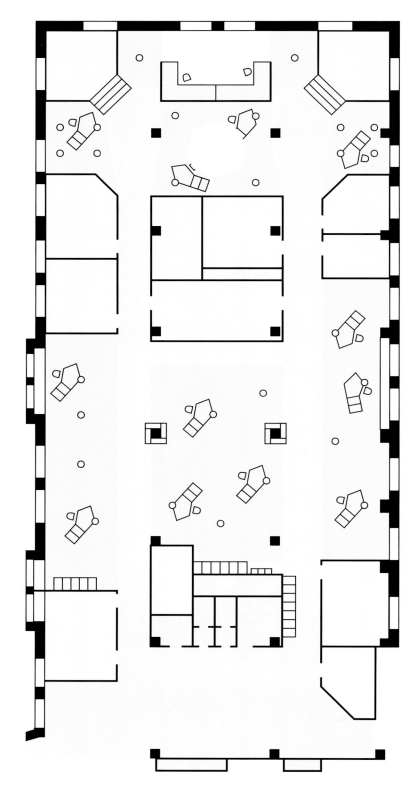

Above **The floor plan reveals a layout like no other. This is because nearly all the workstations are mobile. They can be connected for power and data either to 'hitching posts' that distribute services at desk height at a variety of points, or to equipment that is stored at ceiling height, for example in the 'tree' at the top of the plan.**

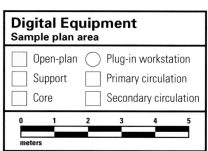

Digital Equipment
Sample plan area

☐ Open-plan	◯ Plug-in workstation
☐ Support	☐ Primary circulation
☐ Core	☐ Secondary circulation

0   1   2   3   4   5

meters

occupy one of the four large floors in the building, which it shares with other companies. As at Helsinki, the northern European tradition of consultation and worker empowerment underpins the Stockholm project. Some 30 staff members represented their colleagues as it took shape and were closely involved in all the stages. It could be said that they designed their new offices to support the way they wanted to work: they knew what they were selling, and thus had a direct interest in the new technology that was making possible new, mobile, more economical ways of working.

The basic space strategy was to mix open-plan office areas with non-allocated workstations – some of them conveniently formed around the steel columns of the old factory building – and with conference and meeting areas, some of them enclosed. No private offices were provided, except one for a finance manager (almost always in the office), though there are small enclosed spaces for concentrated work. Staff are given rolling cabinets for paper files, incorporating fold-down worktops. These are stored centrally, as are the mobile phones that permit an unprecedented mobility within the office and allow any space to be occupied for any purpose. A central 'library' is provided for shared books and technical files, thus getting rid of a great deal of the redundant hoarding of multiple copies of files and manuals that used to be typical of all electronic companies' sales offices.

Getting the project done, says Bertil Arnius, was 'a very tight thing – just six months from start to finish, including time for consultation,' especially when the technological context within Digital was changing at the same time. A clear chain of command inside the company, with the implicit support of top management, helped. Arnius believes that the project has been a marked success. In Sweden, it has been seen as a marker in new office design and internationally it has presented a positive image for Digital. Since it was completed in August 1993, staff numbers have fluctuated considerably, but the office has coped with change. 'It has increased our productivity,' says Arnius. 'That is quantifiable. Of course, the project coincided with other changes, for example, new information technology, but it was designed to accommodate them and to capitalize on their benefits for us. It seems to be a healthier place – fewer staff call in sick now. We're sure that the building has worked.'

Left **The office is housed in a converted factory building – generous spaces provide the flexibility sought by Digital in all its new projects.**

It helped that some key new Digital technology. of which the project makes full use, was coming on stream when the project was launched in 1993 – cordless phones, personal computers, and subsequently, laptops and voicemail. These were all quite new to the company at this time but their advent, and the commercial reality that the salespeople were selling them, helped to smooth the path of change. The changeover in computer hardware was 'a great step forward' says Arnius, allowing greater flexibility and mobility.

Left **Meeting spaces are often free standing in the open-plan of the interior. Some are decorated to provide surroundings that have an echo of favourite country scenes.**

He concludes that the Stockholm project has been 'a considerable success', not least for its ability to accommodate change. 'The basic idea has worked very well,' he says. 'The essence of it is the integration of IT with business objectives – the element of building design and property management is only secondary.' Advances in information technology are certain to alter the way in which the office works still further.

The building has an underlying strength characteristic of industrial structures. Its austerity has been softened by the use of colour and eye-catching, even fanciful, furnishings, intended to foster a folksy and quasi-domestic, quasi-rural Scandinavian ambience utterly unlike standard North American corporate imagery. The company embraced the ideas of the users in this respect, who wanted the office to be like the places where they had their best ideas – by the lake, at the country cottage, on Sunday afternoon. The strikingly redesigned interior has attracted a lot of attention but, as Arnius insists, the populist imagery is a serious business proposition, not an exercise in interior design. And it has worked. It really is popular with Digital's highly motivated and mobile sales personnel.

In Sweden, Digital acted on the evidence of research into what people did and how they did it and achieved results which demonstrate that new ways of working can address the needs of individuals as well as corporations. Under the umbrella of a multinational organization, scope is offered for individual identity and a sense of belonging.

Revolutionary within its context of government offices, this pilot study for change has had a strong influence on other Dutch government building projects. The architecture of government ministries and

Rijksgebouwendienst

Haarlem, The Netherlands

public agencies ought to be an inspiration to private-sector clients, but rarely is. Where the design of workplaces is concerned, the public sector is often ultra-conservative, even reactionary, as if fearing the stimulus of new ways of working. The new regional offices of the Rijksgebouwendienst (RGD, the Dutch building ministry), located on the fourth floor of a stock modern commercial block in Haarlem, reflect an enlightened awareness of the need for change in the way that government offices are organized which is symptomatic of a more forward-looking approach in the Netherlands generally.

The move to the new offices, which was completed in 1994, was planned by a team of three RGD staff members, led by Marcel Maasen who acknowledges the influence of Scandinavia on his thinking when he was planning the new, more collaborative base for the agency. Staff were intensively consulted. 'We actively looked for ideas and there was a great deal of discussion,' says Maasen. 'It took a solid year, but it was worth the effort.' In the former offices, staff (12 area managers, plus secretarial and administrative assistants, and currently totalling 27) were frequently away from their desks on site visits or at external meetings; the area managers were found to be in the office on an average of only two days a week. The flexitime system under which the office operates also meant staggered working hours. The result, they discovered, was that at any one moment only 30 per cent of desk spaces were occupied.

There was an obvious need to make more efficient use of space. There was also, however, a perceived need for space for more interactive work. Indeed, at the heart of the project was a much greater stress on shared space. Previously, people had worked two or three to a room, in close contact with their 'room mates' but detached from other staff. A central meeting area, where team discussions and collaborative work could take place, was considered vital. It was felt that separate, individual offices would continue to be necessary but that these should be small, and time-shared by a number of users rather than allocated to an individual, with files generally kept in a central location. All this amounts to the extremely unusual decision by a government office to reconstitute itself in the form of the club.

The physical solution was a club-like development of the basic idea of the combi-office and, as built, includes four small so-called 'coupé' work spaces, each measuring 2 x 1.7 m/ 6½ x 5½ ft, which can be reserved for private work by area managers, a group room for secretarial staff, and two two-person offices for finance and accounting staff. (There was also a larger office for the head of the group, which doubled up as a meeting room, but this is now no longer used as part of the project.) They are all located around a large shared space which includes several meeting areas – which can also be used for private or concentrated work – as well as an

> *'It's a new sort of workplace for a very special sort of worker,' says Marcel Maasen, who led the planning team of staff members. 'This project was a test-bed for us, a pilot study for the new ways of working we hope to introduce throughout the organization.'*

DEN	CLUB
HIVE	CELL

BUILDING STATISTICS					
CLIENT: Rijksgebouwendienst			**FUNCTION:** Regional government office		
TOTAL FLOOR AREA: 199 sq. m / 2,129 sq. ft		**TOTAL POPULATION:** 27	**OVERALL DENSITY:** 7 sq. m per person / 79 sq. ft per person		
SAMPLE PLAN AREA (less core): 199 sq. m / 2,129 sq. ft		**Circulation:** 22.5%	**Support:** 47.7%	**Cellular:** 22.5%	**Open plan:** 7.2%
CONSULTANTS: *Interior Design* Rijksgebouwendienst staff					

Above **Though located in a standard modern commercial building, the new offices mix open-plan and cellular space to provide a highly innovative and extremely flexible working environment. Quiet, enclosed spaces contrast with group areas and allow scope for private as well as teamwork.**

Left **Small cellular offices, which can be reserved for individual use, are an essential element in the scheme. Sliding walls provide multiple options for privacy and contact.**

enclosed meeting room with partly glazed walls which sits in the space somewhat like a free-standing cabin. A secretary has been given the task of allocating the work spaces and no more than a day can be reserved at one time, except in special and specific circumstances. There has to be a discipline for this way of working – like the rules of any club. Non-smokers, for example, object to using a room where someone has been smoking. 'There had to be a general non-smoking policy,' says Maasen, 'but there is a room for

Below **Designed as a group space for the staff who are based permanently in the office, these workplaces are also close to the majority of other work settings that are used by more transient staff.**

smokers – we want to allow maximum choice.' A rigorous clean-desk policy is also necessary if the desk is to be used by a succession of people. Managers found the initial strictures of completely centralized filing difficult and now keep individual files in the central bank of filing and shared equipment. Mobility is naturally a priority in a changing government organization. Mobile pedestals, designed to be used as temporary worktops with even a place for a cup of coffee, have been provided for nomadic

staff. The first prototypes for these were not popular – moving one was likened to 'pushing a supermarket trolley or a pram around', but a more compact, lighter version was subsequently introduced. The 'nomads' are parked centrally in the secretarial area when not needed. Cordless phones, standard for the nomads, are also lodged up at the central bank. Computers are all programmed for shared use. Each nomad has its own laptop, and every desk is equipped with a duodock and a big screen. Printers are provided at a number of locations. E-mail is widely used and has helped to reduce the use of paper in the office.

Maasen and his team handled the whole process of the move, including construction work and the installation of the information technology. Sub-contractors were brought in for specific elements; and furniture manufacturers Gispen played a supporting role. Maasen feels that the project has, on the whole, worked very well in terms of the organization as well as for the staff. The feedback from user surveys has been generally positive. Teamworking has become a reality. The office is generally considered comfortable and convenient

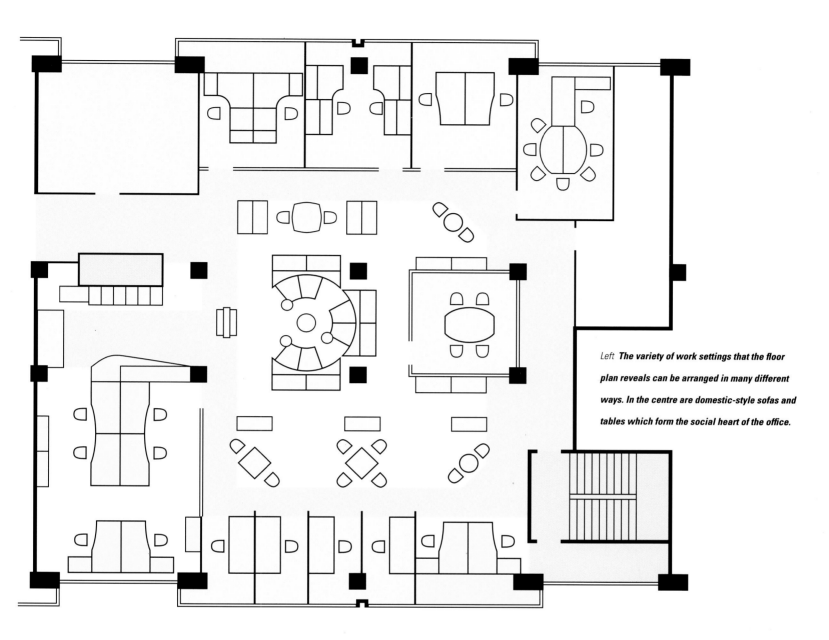

Left ***The variety of work settings that the floor plan reveals can be arranged in many different ways. In the centre are domestic-style sofas and tables which form the social heart of the office.***

and its club-like qualities are appreciated. The variety of work spaces is much appreciated, but some are seen as more comfortable than others. The drawbacks are largely the consequence of the RGD's location in an inferior building, and the project's status as a pilot study. The office suffers from problems common to many retro-fits. The environmental systems, for example, were not redesigned to suit the new spaces and excessive summer heat is a common complaint. In the coupé offices, only half of the windows can be opened and there is only limited individual control of light levels, though the central, shared space is air-conditioned.

The RGD project is relatively small in scale. It was planned specifically for an established team who had a say in its planning and who therefore have an interest in adapting to that particular space as effectively as possible. It was never envisaged that the partitions between the spaces would need to be moved. Soon, however, this facility will form part of a larger office with 260 staff sharing 170 desk spaces. The impending move will build on what has been achieved. 'We'll be doing roughly the same thing, but in a different place,' says Maasen, 'and developing what we've learned so far.' There will be a much more sophisticated approach to environmental control and common-sense measures, like locating the coupé offices on the shady rather than the sun-facing side of the building. The RGD project, a bold experiment in its own milieu, has been a success in its own terms; the implications it has on future developments are considerable.

Rijksgebouwendienst
Sample plan area

☐ Cellular	☐ Open-plan/Hot desk
☐ Support	☐ Primary circulation
☐ Core	☐ Secondary circulation

0   1   2   3   4
meters

British Telecom – Stockley Park

West London, UK

Seen by the company as 'a hub or a club' for staff who spend no more than three days a week there, British Telecom's new offices are based on the company's belief that the future lies in project-based teamwork achieved by highly mobile, highly motivated people working at home or in one of a number of offices, located on urban fringes, where they network and socialize, and, on occasion, find a quiet corner for concentrated work.

BT is one of Britain's largest companies and a world leader in its field. The newly privatized (and rapidly developing) organization inherited attitudes, ways of working, workplaces, and a work force, as well as a telecommunications system, from its public-sector predecessor. It is in the middle of a process of transformation, the Workstyle 2000 programme, which affects every member of its 60,000-strong office work force (downsized from 150,000 in five years). This takes a radical approach to the company's property portfolio – not only to the locations and buildings, but also to the office space within them. Workstyle 2000 provides for the closure of the majority of existing offices and redeployment to a series of regional hubs in areas with good transport links. Though the need for costly inner city office space is rightly questioned, this is not just about saving money. BT's inherited stock of office buildings was dangerously anachronistic in location, function, and appearance. Ways of working must change if the copmpany is to succeed in the highly competitive world of global telecommunications. Many staff no longer work in a single office in the way they did in the past, but work from more than one, travelling the country and needing a home base on some days but not others. Conventional offices are clearly a costly irrelevance in the circumstances. The prototype for Workstyle 2000 in the London area was the Westside project (designed by Aukett Associates) at Apsley, near Hemel Hempstead. Launched in 1993 as 'the physical manifestation of a transformed business', Westside was intended to maximize the potential of people and of technology in the interests of greater productivity. It accorded with guidelines laid down for Workstyle 2000. These stipulated that suitable buildings would be at least 30,000 sq. m/320,300 sq. ft in area, with floor plates of at least 450 sq. m/4,800 sq. ft. Open-plan layouts, air conditioning, and the ability to house state-of-the-art communications and information technology were regarded as vital. The new generation of BT offices would be primarily designed for teamworking, with plenty of scope for hot desking. They should provide excellent working environments, with better than average staff facilities, and present a positive image for the company, inside and out. Interiors would be of a standard that they would be a showcase to which visitors and customers could be welcomed.

BT's offices at Stockley Park were seen as a logical next step after the successful initiative at Westside and were intended as the base for 1500 staff – basically managers, dealing with projects both in Britain and globally. Most staff spend no more than three days a week in the office, working at home or with clients on other days. Stockley Park, on the

> *'People do meet here and network,' claims Neil McLocklin of BT. 'There is a dynamic mood and people have responded to the new ways of working, being more flexible and responsible.'*

DEN	CLUB
HIVE	CELL

BUILDING STATISTICS

CLIENT: British Telecom			**FUNCTION:** Sales and marketing base of telecommunications company	
TOTAL FLOOR AREA: 16,808 sq. m / 180,900 sq. ft		**TOTAL POPULATION:** 1500	**OVERALL DENSITY:** 11.2 sq. m per person / 119 sq. ft per person	
SAMPLE PLAN AREA (less core): 3,127 sq. m / 33,700 sq. ft	**Circulation:** 15.8%	**Support:** 28%	**Cellular:** 4.8%	**Open plan:** 51.4%
CONSULTANTS: *Architect* Foster & Partners (building 5), Arup Associates (building 4) ***Interior Design*** DEGW London Limited				

Above **Most of the space in the British Telecom buildings, at Stockley Park, near Heathrow Airport, is open-plan, with views out to the surrounding landscape and lakes.**

Left **The main entrance to the building by Foster & Partners, one of the two buildings occupied by BT, at Stockley Park. Elegant and strikingly transparent, the building is a flagship for the company's Workstyle 2000 project, which involved the relocation of large numbers of staff from city centres to urban fringes.**

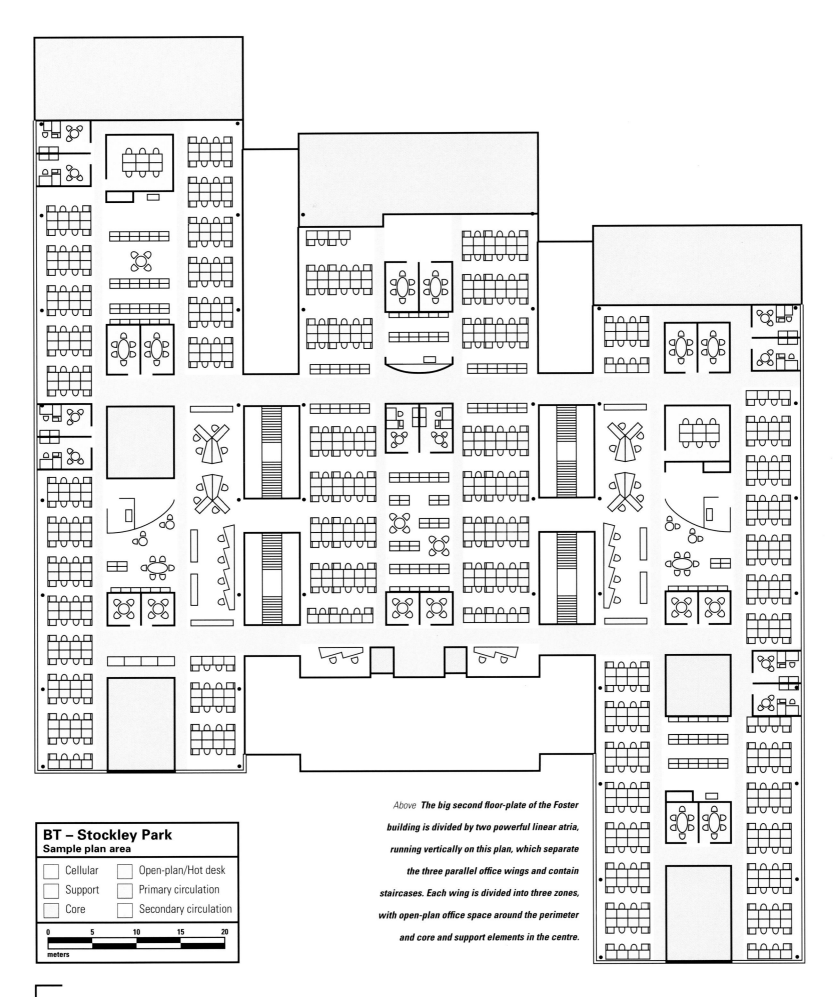

BT – Stockley Park
Sample plan area

- ☐ Cellular
- ☐ Support
- ☐ Core
- ☐ Open-plan/Hot desk
- ☐ Primary circulation
- ☐ Secondary circulation

0   5   10   15   20
meters

Above **The big second floor-plate of the Foster building is divided by two powerful linear atria, running vertically on this plan, which separate the three parallel office wings and contain staircases. Each wing is divided into three zones, with open-plan office space around the perimeter and core and support elements in the centre.**

M25 motorway around London near Heathrow Airport, had been formally opened in 1986 and was one of the great development success stories of the 1980s, an international model for other 'business parks'. The development of the site, which had been a huge garbage dump, was master-planned by Arup Associates with space-planners DEGW providing strategic and research briefing. It featured lavish planting and high-quality architectural design, and many 'high-tech' tenants, particularly in electronics, telecoms and pharmaceuticals, were attracted there. When BP (British Petroleum) vacated Buildings 4 and 5, these came to the attention of DEGW, who had been commissioned by BT to assess sites for new offices. Building 4 was one of a number designed by Arup Associates, while its neighbour was the work of Foster Associates (now Foster & Partners) and was one of the most striking buildings on the site, dramatic in form both externally and internally. The two buildings were occupied by BT early in 1996, after a 19-week design-and-build contract.

The speed of the project was remarkable. Neil McLocklin was effectively project leader for BT, working with Tony Wilson of BT's construction group and with DEGW. Design work, says David Sadeghi of DEGW, had to be completed in only six weeks. Based on Workstyle 2000, the client brief was developed in collaboration with DEGW, who finalized the construction programme with the appointed contractor for the refit: Interior PLC. There were a number of distinct client groups within BT to be dealt with, but the coordination of their various interests was well handled, says Sadeghi. McLocklin stresses that staff were fully consulted, by means of workshops and an exhibition of proposals. Future users were bussed out to visit the site. David Sadeghi says that the speed of the

Stockley project implied that consultation with future users could not be very extensive: 'It was a very unusual way for us to work – as a practice, normally we're very user-oriented.' When the project started, there were in fact no clearly identified users. When it got under way, the momentum was such that there was little scope for making changes. However, the project ran smoothly: 'There were no communications problems,' says Sadeghi, and a more than satisfactory working relationship with the various contractors

Below **BT's interior plan contains a large number of touch-down desks that are reserved for a time, rather than 'owned'. The many other facilities needed by peripatetic workers include a variety of meeting spaces and the well-used cafeteria.**

was soon established, and the project was completed well within the allotted time.

Before the staff moved in, a family day was held, complete with children's games, a barbecue, and music, to acquaint people with the site. 'Unfortunately, it was just about the wettest day of the summer,' recalls McLocklin, 'but it

Above **A small proportion of workstations are permanently allocated to full-time staff and are located on the outer edge of the building. The inner areas are devoted to support space – here a coffee point secluded by a curved wall.**

helped answer questions and reassure the sceptics.' There is a perception – not entirely unfounded – that Stockley Park is remote and insulated from the outside world, and devoid of the amenities found in central London. Even the existence of agreeable staff catering does not entirely compensate for the absence of places to eat in the area – to

escape from the office. There is effectively no public transportation available, so that everyone who works there must drive. Yet for many of the BT staff, whose jobs involve a great deal of travelling, this is hardly an inconvenience and in any case has to be balanced against the time-consuming chore of driving in central London.

The users of Stockley need a very efficient base – effectively a club – where they may spend a day or just an hour or two with access to a computer. Managing information technology comes easily to BT, though the use of laptops has, in fact, advanced rapidly only since the Stockley offices opened: around 50 per cent of staff there are now users. 'What we have had to learn is the management of human resources,' says McLocklin. 'BT has not been very good in that area in the past.' The image of the company, even a few years ago, was of hierarchical structures, of a closed world where cellular offices signified a very compartmented pattern of work that provided little scope for initiative and self-motivation.

BT is changing rapidly and the Stockley offices reflect the accelerating pace of change and the inexorable move towards the paper-free and virtual office – the company sees itself as a natural leader in this process and wants to be seen as such. Perhaps the speed of the project undermined its total success. David Sadeghi describes as 'unfortunate' the intervention by BT's procurement department which led to the cancellation (presumably on cost grounds) of the proposed workstation layout – designed for very flexible information technology provision and the extensive use of laptops. Neil McLocklin concedes that 'the way that furniture and cable management were handled wasn't good.' In the event, a further refit of workstations has been necessary, leading to inconvenience and added costs – the economies made turned out to be false ones.

Nonetheless, BT Stockley Park is a clear statement of intent. Some staff found it hard to adjust to the rate of change – moving from a cellular office in the heart of London's West End to an open-plan, high-tech shed in a business park, with no fixed place to work, is bound to cause culture shock. The minimalist workstations and rigid layout probably didn't help; nor did the operational divorce of physical design from BT's programme of change management. The Stockley Park offices manage to look a lot more like a hive than the club that they are intended to be. Nevertheless Neil McLocklin

sees the Stockley project as a considerable success and a marker in BT's process of transformation. Productivity is up – reflecting the substantial improvement on former accommodation as well as new ways of working. In many respects he would have preferred to have had a new building, but this was never on the agenda. Adapting the existing two buildings, and accepting that operations would be divided between them, was a compromise. The possibility of constructing a physical link between the buildings was explored – and would have been countenanced by the landlords – but not proceeded with. If anything, the Foster building, despite its undoubted architectural excellence, is the less successful of the two – sheer size is its main drawback. 'People find it very hard to relate to it or to feel at home there,' says McLocklin, who finds it elegant but 'very big and a bit daunting' and so open and minimal as to be rather anonymous. An attempt is being made to address this perceived failing by improving the signage and hanging colourful banners, to denote more clearly the boundaries of various departments and to give staff and visitors a more obvious sense of arrival. In business terms, Stockley Park is seen as a clear success by BT. Users benefit from highly flexible facilities which address the needs of a very mobile work force. For many staff the move meant a change of lifestyle – tackling the associated problems has been a prime concern of the in-house facilities management team – and some are still dissatisfied with working conditions. Combining a radical and rapid transformation in ways of working with a complete change of locale was an entirely logical operation as well as a considerable logistical achievement – but it also meant throwing staff in at the deep end. The consequences, in human terms, of the success of this handsome project are currently being carefully studied by BT.

Above **Because the Foster building is very large, its social focus – the café on the ground floor – is important. Here architecture and amenities come together: it is a place to work and to socialize.**

Below **The impact of the concentration of vertical movement in the two highly visible atria is made clear in the cross-section of the Foster building.**

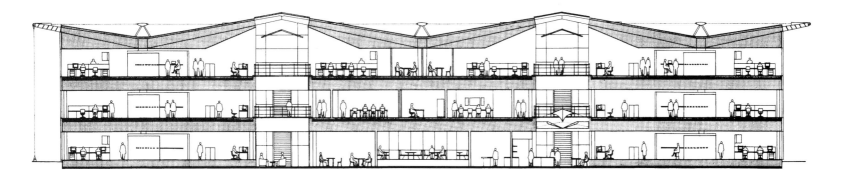

Benevia

Chicago, USA

'Our reasons for moving were cultural rather than economic. We wanted a new stimulus, a place to inspire collaboration and creativity,' says Nancy Nevin, director of communications for Benevia, a company which has rediscov-

ered the city, in this case downtown Chicago. The mood in the company was optimistic, one of growth and diversification – a new work setting was seen as vital.

Benevia, part of the giant Monsanto empire, was created in 1995. It was formerly the Nutrasweet consumer products division. As Nancy Nevin explains, the name itself is significant, intended to express an idea of healthy living. Benevia markets 'on the table' products, as opposed to Nutrasweet Kelco, which sells ingredients to the food industry. The change of name was deliberately intended to presage a change in attitudes. Not only this, the company was finding its suburban location increasingly inconvenient. Business contacts, advertising agencies, and marketing and other companies with which Benevia worked tended to be downtown. The search for a new location began late in 1995. A competition for the – essentially conceptual – design of the offices was won by The Environments Group, an architectural practice led by Rod Vickroy. At this stage, no decision had been taken on the new home of the company. Real estate advisers, The Buck Company, had drawn up a relocation brief, specifying the amount and type of space needed, and on this basis, Vickroy and his colleagues produced a concept. One major consideration was cost. Benevia didn't want a 'corporate' look or a luxurious building. They effectively ruled out top-of-the-market high-rises and there was talk of 'loft' type accommodation. The idea that the company should move into the city centre was widely welcomed. (And the continuing resilience and attraction of a traditional urban heartland like that of Chicago is reassuring.) 'The city is diverse and full of interest,' says Nancy Nevin. A number of buildings were looked at, including the Civic Opera building and the Merchandise Mart. Among Chicago's many landmarks, the latter is hard to miss. The huge 1930s Art Deco building on the Chicago River close to the Loop, designed by Graham, Anderson, Probst & White as a warehouse for Marshall Field and later converted into a wholesale mart, is one of the largest buildings in the world. The Benevia company's recent move into it underlines its abiding strengths. The Mart was chosen not simply because its owners made a very good offer, but because of its very generous spatial qualities. Its big-boned structure and high ceilings appealed to the architects, who convinced the clients of its merits.

Rod Vickroy says that the progress of the project was 'exceptionally smooth', with a very clear vision on the client's side of what was wanted. Unlike many more conventional organizations, only a quarter of Benevia's staff spend all their time in the office. As many are almost permanently on the move, using the office as a base, while 50 per cent of the total divide their time. 'They are a highly able, very close bunch of people,' says Vickroy. Meetings with heads of departments, focus groups and a steering committee – the germ of the group within Benevia which eventually managed

> *'We wanted a new operating culture,' says Nancy Nevin of Benevia, 'a more cooperative way of working, embracing new technology.'*

DEN	CLUB
HIVE	CELL

BUILDING STATISTICS

CLIENT: Benevia			**FUNCTION:** Sales and marketing division of food manufacturer		
TOTAL FLOOR AREA: 3,240 sq. m / 35,000 sq. ft		**TOTAL POPULATION:** 120 (stage 1)	**OVERALL DENSITY:** 27 sq. m per person / 291 sq. ft per person		
SAMPLE PLAN AREA (less core): 3240 sq. m / 35,000 sq. ft		**Circulation:** 29.8%	**Support:** 38.6%	**Cellular:** 0%	**Open plan:** 31.5%
CONSULTANTS: *Programming and Interior Design* The Environments Group					

Above **The transformation of a big-boned industrial space has created an interior which is loft-like and far removed from the typical corporate look.**

Left **Many of the furnishings – these mobile storage trolleys are an example – are chosen for their flexibility and portability.**

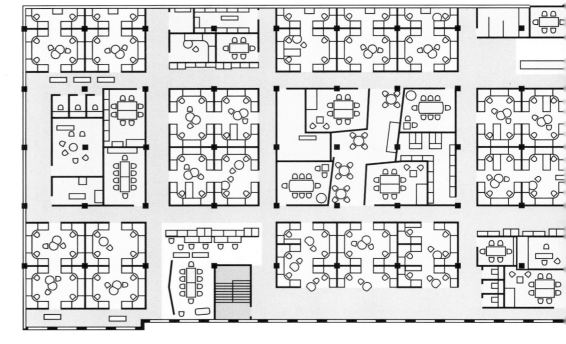

Benevia
Sample plan area

☐ Cellular	☐ Open-plan/Hot desk
☐ Support	☐ Primary circulation
☐ Core	☐ Secondary circulation

0   5   10   15
meters

the move – established innovatory guidelines for the kind of interior design required to accommodate a changing organization. 'We spent a great deal of time there,' says Vickroy, 'finding out what they did and how they did it.' The steering committee worked closely with the architects to define space requirements in detail. There were constraints – notably, the Merchandise Mart's own structural format with columns at 6.4 m/21 ft intervals imposed a certain obvious discipline – if not rigidity – on the layout of the workstations. But there were also plenty of opportunities to challenge the formality of the interior through creating irregularly shaped conference spaces, some of them also 'creatively' named (for example, the 'Bored Room'), through exploiting the height of the space, through a bold use of colours and textures, and through introducing such non-corporate work settings as a pool table, located in the 'recreation bay' at one corner of the building. The most important innovation is that nobody in this highly interactive and highly autonomous, club-like organization 'owns' an individual work space. All workstations ('power pods') are the same basic size and so interchangeable. The layout of the screened workstations is, in consequence, somewhat dull and uniform – reminiscent of the cookie-cutter monotony of

Right **The basic character of the Mart has been retained in the conversion, which provides a den-like working environment for a highly mobile work force, most of whom need to use meeting spaces and touch-down desks when they are in the building.**

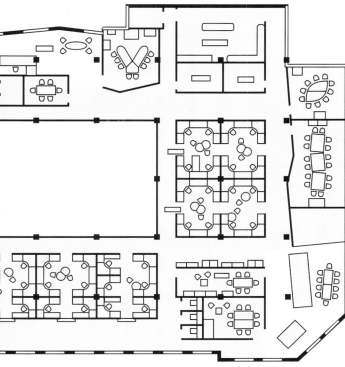

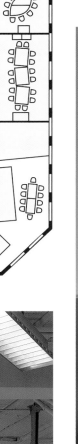

Left **Standard clusters of screened workstations, some of which are time-shared, alternate with very large amounts of meeeting rooms and other support space. A major circulation route follows the perimeter.**

so many conventional North American offices. However, what makes the big floor layout more interesting than usual is Benevia's insistence on shared amenities. Since work places are not specifically allocated to individuals, there have to be plenty of places for informal and chance meetings, for example, in the passageway which runs along the riverfront of the offices. A 'research bay' combines the functions of a traditional library and an electronic resource base. 'Plug in and play' facilities make it

Above **A clear perimeter route has been maintained around the central work space, to encourage easy movement and interaction, and informal meeting points are provided there. Because it is on the outside of the building, this space is well lit and particularly pleasant to be in.**

Right **Office tensions can be released in a game of pool in one of the many meeting spaces. These are mostly situated on the perimeter in space that would once have been given over to enclosed offices for senior staff.**

possible to use laptop computers everywhere around the building. This overall desire for greater fluidity and enhanced interaction led to the look of the interiors being made deliberately ad hoc rather than sleek – they were intended to form something of a *tabula rasa* on which new ideas could be imposed. Benevia moved into the Mart in July 1996, after a fast-track fit-out.

Nancy Nevin defines the character of the offices as 'comfortable, colourful, informal, maybe just a little whimsical.' She points to the abundance of natural light and views out to the river and Loop as widely appreciated attractions of the new headquarters. 'It's generally a popular place', she claims, and is convinced that the move has worked. The company is doing well and the spirit of integration and participation it was seeking is being fostered. Staff enjoy the facilities available in the city centre, though there are still complaints about the chore of commuting; in Deerfield, everybody drove to work, now most use trains. Rod Vickroy notes that there is 'some continuing resistance' to the loss of privacy in the new offices and complaints too about the supposedly high level of noise – steps are being taken to soften the acoustic of the building. Some keen criticism of any changes was inevitable. However, a post-occupancy survey found a more positive reaction to the new site than had been anticipated.

The new Benevia office is a typical city-centre club for a very diverse group of people who need to be in contact, despite their very divergent job profiles. In business terms, it is seen as a success, though integration is still taking place: 'It will come,' says Nevin. The project is too new to have needed major changes, though these are envisaged. Asked

neighbourhoods, an issue which The Environments Group is considering. 'It is a very large building and there is a danger of people feeling very disoriented,' says Vickroy.

Benevia is an example of how a determined company approaches the issue of changing its culture and habits as well as its habitat. Because the company's sales and marketing staff are so highly mobile, they need a highly efficient, integrating, distinctive and welcoming home base – a downtown club in all but name. The marketing arm of a manufacturing organization would normally be somewhat removed from the lifestyle of media and advertising companies, yet these new Chicago city-centre offices have obviously taken part of their cue from the vividly alternative and expressive workplaces of the media world, as well as from the counter-culture of the urban loft.

Below **Glazed meeting rooms provide places for quiet internal discussions.**

if Benevia would do the same again, Nancy Nevin replies: 'We already are.' The other half of the company is soon to move into the Merchandise Mart, extending into the same floor and so increasing the total of staff there from 120 to 270. As a result, there is a recognized need to instil a greater sense of identity into what could be somewhat anonymous

the implications for business

There is a direct correspondence between the rigour and simplicity of Sir Norman Foster's own office, in London, and the controlled, ruthlessly contemporary, high-quality design work produced within it. A very different kind of message, but one that also makes a clear link between the office environment and its product, is projected by the richly natural, hall-like interior of the Oketo National District Forest Office in Japan. Designed by Tetsuro Kurokawa, it is especially unusual in the context of Japanese offices, which tend to be conventional and corporate in style.

What is most characteristic of, and absolutely essential to, modern business is measurement – relating, by whatever means, cause and effect. Unless the impact of the office working environment on business performance is made manifest, the contribution – as well as the costs – of environmental design to business will never be properly valued. Fortunately the analytical and data-processing power of the same information technology that has made new thinking in both office and organizational design so urgently necessary is now making it possible to measure the ways in which the physical office environment contributes to business performance.

Even five years ago this would have been just an aspiration. Happily, there are now more and more cases where the use of business-like metrics in procuring, designing, and managing office design is being taken for granted. But it has taken too long for the penny to drop. The reasons are various, but stem from prolonged and continuing failures of communication between the users of office space and those whose job it is to supply that space, including architects and developers, space planners, and furniture manufacturers. Consumers of the space are partly to blame. They have allowed themselves to be persuaded that the physical environment is of no significance for serious business purposes. But the suppliers of office space must take most of the responsibility – partly through the adverse consequences of the driving need to keep fees competitive, partly through laziness, and partly through lack of intellectual firepower. In a business world increasingly characterized by innovation, most designers of office space have become content to deliver what they are supposed to like to deliver. They certainly no longer hold the position that the best architects often used to enjoy – that of being the client's clear-eyed, truthful, and trusted friend.

The same failure of communication between managers and designers has been responsible for the slow translation of advanced managerial ideas into challenging and innovative architecture and interior design. The successful examples that are explored in the case studies in this book have all occurred, for one pressing business reason or another, because the barriers preventing communication between

demand and supply, between users and designers, have been breached. The chief objective of this book is to accelerate this slow progress, for the benefit of both clients and architects. The most rapid way of achieving and sustaining the serial breakthroughs that business and architecture so badly need would be the general acceptance and customary application of measures linking organizational performance and the physical environment of the office.

Why is it that the impact of office accommodation on organizational performance has been so difficult to establish? Perhaps the costs of office space are so small that they are not worth management time? However, in many businesses, and especially in labour-intensive organizations in the service sector, occupancy costs, i.e. the annual cost of accommodating staff in office space, is second only to the cost of labour. Even the annual cost of installing and running information technology is still generally less than the cost per head of providing office accommodation. Ten per cent of turnover, which is what occupancy costs often represent, is quite enough,

*Left **The power that architecture has to express organizational priorities is clear in the Ark Building – now occupied by Seagrams – in London, designed by the Anglo-Swedish architect Ralph Erskine. The atrium with its sailing roof and all-round visibility says volumes about the importance of organizational unity. The relatively modest entrance, closely associated with club-like common facilities, is eloquent about the importance of the individual workers as opposed to the big corporation.***

coming straight off the bottom line as it does, to make all the difference to profitability. In fact, as many firms discovered during the recent recession, it is quite enough to put you out of business for ever.

Perhaps the explanation lies in the inherent intellectual and practical difficulties of charting the relationship between the physical environment and organizational performance. From the point of view of conventional social science, many of the problems are caused by the number of variables that lie between the effect of any single physical element – a particular colour range, a certain level of humidity, a particularly convenient pattern of layout, for example – and any social or behavioural consequences. How does one control such factors as the motivation of the respondents, their economic circumstances, or their cultural backgrounds?

Much damage was done to the development of the measures connecting environmental and organizational performance in the late 1920s as a result of a series of investigations, carried out by Elton Mayo and his colleagues at the

Above **The Lloyd's of London building (see also page 32) is not only an architectural tour de force. It also reflects a profound understanding of how to use architectural resources to project, both externally and internally, a complex, historic organization's search for modernization.**

Hawthorne plant of the General Electric Company. The objective was to investigate, among other matters, the relationship between the physical environment and productivity. However, it proved so difficult to isolate environmental matters from other factors affecting production – such as the presence of the investigators themselves in the factory, not to mention the economic effects of the beginning of the great recession – that even such a simple variable as lighting levels, which had been assumed to be directly related to manipulative skills at the

work place, was found to be overlaid by other, wider issues of human relations. From the confident, late nineteenth-century belief that a purer environment would automatically guarantee better health and better performance, the most that Mayo and his colleagues came to expect of the physical environment was that it would not cause any friction that would detract from productivity. Hygiene was all that it seemed able to offer employers. In fact, in the special and highly artificial circumstances created by the design and conduct of the Hawthorne experiments, it did not seem to matter to the respondents how much or how little light was shed upon their workbenches. What actually affected the

temperature, one level of lighting, as the key to determining any single aspect of business success. In every case, whether consciously or not, many design and managerial variables were addressed simultaneously in order to achieve improvement of performance in both. This new, more appropriate approach, which has its origins in the study of what are called 'open socio-technical systems', sets out to explore all the factors at work within a situation – as well, of course, as the difference that is made to the situation by the changing context that surrounds it. This kind of analysis depends for success upon motivating and involving everyone concerned. As such it resembles the cut and thrust of real-life management – not to mention real life itself – more than any highly controlled experiment in a clinic or laboratory.

How do we know what kind of an office an organization really wants? How do we know what type of office accommodation would suit it best? And, once we have discovered the answers, how can we best implement them? New techniques have been developed as a direct result of financial pressures caused by the failures in communication and the disappointing design performance described at the start of this chapter. Many of these techniques would not be possible without the data-processing power of information technology. Some are strategic, in that they are designed to relate the planning and the use of office space to long-term business goals. Others are tactical, in that they help office workers to use space, furniture, and equipment to respond to urgent, practical, daily business requirements. While each technique and each measurement links some aspect of the environment to an organizational issue, for best effect they must all be used together. Used separately, these techniques tell only fragments of the whole story. Used together, dealing with big, long-term issues first and then moving on to short-term detail, they build up a well-rounded picture of the ways in which office space can be driven harder to achieve better business performance. The techniques that are described on the following pages have all been designed to link organizational and physical variables, that is, people and space. Needless to say, to be successful, they depend upon willing, close, and intelligent collaboration between clients and users on the one hand, and architects and designers on the other.

The sources for this new methodology are listed at the end of the book, in Chapter 6.

productivity of the women in the teams being studied was not so much the lighting levels as the unprecedented experience of being set apart and given the attention of sophisticated researchers, in other words, being told implicitly that they were special and that they mattered. In this way the so-called 'Hawthorne effect' was identified and, as one out of many consequences, the bottom dropped out of serious research into the relationship between environmental variables and productivity for decades.

What is clear from the case studies in this book is that in none was there any such attempt to isolate one single environmental variable, such as a particular colour, a certain

New measurement techniques

Generally in office design it is best to start from the big and the long-term and then move into short-term detail. At the bigger end of this scale comes the categorization of organizational types and the correlation of these with typical office shells and layouts – as was discussed in Chapter 2. Other more detailed techniques measure how time and space are used in the office; the often surprising evidence that comes from these observations is leading to the development of new kinds of space budgeting. Yet other techniques are concerned with opening up and accelerating briefing, so that many more office workers can contribute their views and experience to the space-planning process. Other techniques have been developed to ensure that user requirements can be accommodated by particular buildings and layouts, while systematic procedures are now used to monitor how well offices are performing through time. Such 'post-occupancy evaluation' is invaluable not just in providing feedback for planning new buildings, but also in making the best use of existing space.

Building Appraisal

Choosing the right building is a task that all office clients must address sooner rather than later in the design process. Designing buildings that suit different kinds of client is ultimately a task that architects, developers, and even the institutions that finance office buildings cannot avoid. Until relatively recently there was very little comparative data and even less system, in the ways in which these two complementary problems were handled.

Building Appraisal was invented in the context of two big British office developments of the mid 1980s – Broadgate in the City of London and Stockley Park near Heathrow Airport – in order to fill what was certainly in the British context a yawning gap between potential tenants and building owners. The technique is simply to test whether the spatial needs of particular types of office users could be met by typical floors of proposed – or real – office buildings. Key physical variables, including such features as image to outsiders, the

Right **The novel, boat-like shape of this building, specifically designed for the advertising agency CLM/BBDO by Jean Nouvel, is justified in terms of Building Appraisal because it links group spaces around the perimeter with a dramatic common central space used for display (see also page 69).**

capacity of the floors to accommodate high or low proportions of cellular offices, the ease with which support spaces can be accommodated, and the capacity of the building services to absorb and distribute information technology, are measured and then related to the priority given to each feature by different user organizations.

Building Appraisal is based on tenant preferences expressed as 'User Profiles'. For example, to guide Broadgate's developers and their architects, the space needs and preferences of seven sectors of business in the City of London, such as banking, accountancy, and law, were systematically studied and charted. It was the task of space planners DEGW to identify these User Profiles; to establish how consistent they were and what each meant for the design specification of each building on the huge site; to convey these preferences to the two design teams (Skidmore, Owings & Merrill, and Arup Associates) working on Broadgate in its various phases; and to demonstrate through test layouts to potential tenants from all seven sectors how they could fit into the emerging designs. As DEGW had predicted, some building forms turned out to be

particularly good at accommodating certain types of organization, and very few, if any, were equally good for all types.

Building Appraisal is a practical and powerful technique for improving office design. Essentially it helps users because it brings them closer to designers through the consumerist process of quantifying and demystifying choices between options. Cumulatively, however, Building Appraisal has greater significance for architects because it revolutionizes the design process: it makes possible the collection of large amounts of consistent data about building capacity and about changing profiles

Above **Building Appraisal involves more than just measuring the potential use of floor plans. The big floor-plates of this 1960s building were brought back to useful life in the 1990s through winning extra space for cable distribution by installing a slim-line, cooled ceiling throughout the entire building. Department of Trade and Industry, London. Architect: DEGW.**

of user requirements, sector by sector, building type by building type. Just as information technology generates and accelerates change in user requirements so IT itself, with its enormous capacity for handling data, is making possible the management of change by allowing the relationship between supply and demand in the field of office design to be studied and matched more thoroughly than ever before.

Categorizing organizations and matching them to layout and building types

Once the building is chosen, it is very important for architects and designers to be able to distinguish between the different space-planning requirements of the various types of organizational structures within a company. Nothing is less productive than attempting to impose homogeneous layouts or design solutions upon heterogeneous organizations. Obviously it makes a lot of sense to determine which types of layout best suit the working patterns of different departments, but it is also critical to anticipate how the layouts – and buildings – will change through time because patterns of use are likely to develop within them

A powerful way of doing this is to categorize the organizational types through the Interaction/ Autonomy model described in Chapter 2 (see page 61). Degrees of both interaction and autonomy are quantifiable on information derived from user interviews and focus groups. Respondents are asked to rate, on standard nine-point scales, whether, for example, their organization is now, or is likely to become, traditional or experimental, formal or informal, whether characterized by low or high interaction, and whether interaction is mostly within departments or across group boundaries. The aggregation of this data allows organizations

– or, more importantly, business units or functional divisions within them – to categorize themselves and decide which type of layout makes most sense. For example, if the score is low in interaction but high in autonomy, cell-type layouts would be most suitable, if it is high in interaction and lower in autonomy, den layouts are preferable.

Workplace Envisioning (WE)

Involving users in the design process substantially increases the chances of success in office design. This is not just because more accurate information about what they want can be collected in this way. It also seems that the very act of consulting users usually leads to far greater commitment to the environment that is being planned. However, involving large numbers of them was, until recently, cumbersome and labour-intensive.

Workplace Envisioning was invented to ease and accelerate this process. Envisioning is a computer-aided means of encouraging management and staff to investigate both better ways of working and the best possible organizational structure. The process, developed by Steelcase with support from DEGW, takes the form of three computer-aided workshops. The first, for senior management, is focused on strategic managerial issues and their spatial consequences. The second, for operational staff, is concerned with specifying the best environment for accommodating particular individuals and groups. This second workshop acts as a reality check on the longer term managerial views expressed earlier because the same questions are asked and the results of both can be compared. The third workshop, again for senior management, is devised to reconcile managerial and operational views about what kind of office environment is most appropriate for the future within a realistic financial framework. The output is, in effect, the brief for a project.

Workplace Envisioning helps users to express their priorities in a quantitative way. These insights help designers to support particular organizations or organizational units. Of course, skilled design judgment is necessary to turn insights into effective layout proposals. However, the principal benefit of Workplace Envisioning is not only that it accelerates briefing but also that it provides an excellent means of coordinating what are often conflicting points of view about organizational futures and the utility of design.

Opposite **Typical read-outs of the computer-aided process of observing how space and time are used in the office. The vertical axis represents the proportion of spaces actually occupied. The horizontal axis represents the hours of the working day. The colours represent typical office activities. Observations are taken at fixed points over a two-week period, making sure that all workstations and meeting areas are noted at frequent intervals.**

The middle graph shows that a significant proportion of enclosed office space is not occupied. Both the top and the middle graphs record another kind of vacancy: the phenomenon of workplaces that are 'temporarily unoccupied' – evidence that staff are in the office but absent from their individual work places. Often a third of the available time is spent thus – probably

because people spend a lot of time in very small, spontaneous, intermittent 'meetings'. This observation has led space planners to question the predominant importance that has been conventionally given to individual work place design and to explore, instead, alternative or parallel office environments that are good at fostering interactive behaviour.

The lowest graph records observations of meeting-room use. Although people often complain about the scarcity of such rooms, actual meeting room occupancy is typically very low. This paradox is explained by the great preponderance of very small, unscheduled meetings which conventional twelve-or-sixteen-person meeting rooms do not accommodate well – another example of the mismatch between conventional office design and observed reality.

Time Utilization Studies (TUS)

Conventional space-planning techniques are very rigid and simplistic, rarely going beyond head-count, hierarchical space standards, estimating filing space, and the crude prioritization of adjacencies. A thorough examination of the way in which office work could be done better is now being attempted.

Computer-aided techniques are now available to measure how effectively time and space are being used in the office. Hand-held computers, operated by trained staff, can be used to observe what is really happening. At each workstation, on a standard, predetermined route around the office, observations are recorded, usually about once an hour, over the entire diurnal cycle. These show whether work places are occupied, temporarily unoccupied, or entirely empty. If the work place is occupied a note is made of the activity – for example, computer work, reading, or meeting – currently being carried out there. It is essential that observations are made every working day over a two-week period to ensure reliability.

Read-outs, such as those seen on the right, take the form of colour-coded graphs showing cumulative occupancy for all work places or of histograms for particular subcategories of office worker. They are almost always very revealing. There are often big differences in the patterns of occupancy of different kinds of staff that are helpful in determining which physical conditions are appropriate. However, there is great consistency in the findings on levels of occupancy: individual workstations are generally not very intensively occupied – even at peak times they are often two-thirds empty. In contrast, observations in many types of organization indicate that often not enough space is available for smaller meetings and for casual interaction.

TUS can be used to help determine, on an empirical basis, whether there is any case for space-use intensification, such as the time-sharing of desks or hotelling. They also help to decide how much space should be provided for supplementary support and meeting spaces.

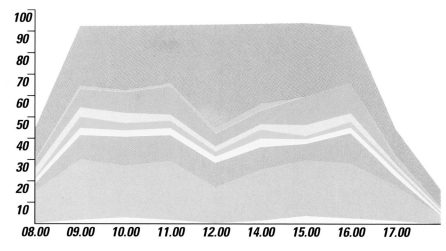

Occupancy of open-plan offices

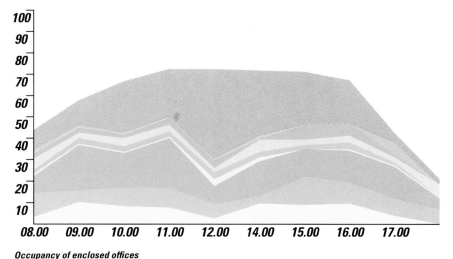

Occupancy of enclosed offices

Occupancy of meeting rooms

KEY TO GRAPHS			
• *Horizontal axis = time of day*	Pausing		Talking
• *Vertical axis = percentage of*	Paper handling		Telephone
occupancy	Reading		Computer
Temporarily unoccupied	Writing		Meeting

Finding out what happens after moving in is an extremely important way of gathering the feedback that is essential if office design is to be improved. Curiously, there is still strong resistance among some architects and more users to post-occupancy studies. It seems to be difficult for clients to justify the funding for such work and sometimes projects are so fraught that it is emotionally almost impossible for architects to revisit the scene of so much worry and strife.

However, when POE is is carried out the results are always beneficial to all concerned. Clients and users learn how to get more out of their individual projects; architects and designers benefit by building up a body of knowledge not only about the failure or success of various design features, but also about the more subtle dimension of how building performance changes through time. Guidelines for conducting POEs include the necessity to be comprehensive, i.e. looking at the widest practical range of design features – not just construction on its own, for example, but in relation to environmental and space-planning matters. Equally important is using POEs to make contact with a wide range of user constituencies, drawn from the constituent parts of the user organization, so that an overall picture of performance can be achieved. Techniques of conducting POEs range from detailed physical and environmental measurements to extensive questionnaire surveys of user opinion, from carefully conducted interviews with key personnel to simply walking about, using the study team's collective eyes to observe signs of satisfaction or symptoms of pressure or under-use.

What must be stressed is that the long-term value of POEs, and indeed of all the new measurement techniques listed above, is not just the value of learning from what happened on any single project; it is also the gradual accumulation of a body of knowledge, shared among architects and clients, about the performance of whole classes of buildings in relation to whole classes of use.

Workplace Performance Survey (WPS)

This is a way to find out what office workers' priorities are as well what they consider to be the benefits and shortcomings of the accommodation they are currently occupying. The WPS asks office staff for their perception of both the importance and the effectiveness of their accommodation – especially in terms of how well it supports the particular work they are doing.

*Above **What people actually do in the office often differs from what they were expected to do. An impromptu meeting is taking place here at an individual workstation, leaving others temporarily unoccupied. Offices for Classic FM, a radio station in London.***

Output is in the form of bar charts that show, by department or by work group, the average performance and the relative importance of 50 to 60 aspects of the office environment such as lighting and heating levels. The ratings reveal which particular environmental items perform best and worst from the point of view of the users.

WPSs carried out systematically over a period of time quickly show changes in employee attitudes and pinpoint emerging problems. In this way the technique is a cumulative measure of building performance and is an indicator of the organizational and environmental issues to which management and designers should pay most attention.

From technique into business

Important as these new techniques are for improving the quality of the design of the working environment – they are already making an enormous difference to space planning – they have to be translated into the language of business. As has already been stressed several times in this book, the precious resource of office space only makes business sense if it is constantly related to organizational goals and to human and technological resources.

There are only two ways to achieve better organizational performance from office space: through greater efficiency by 'doing things right', i.e. as economically and elegantly as possible; and through greater effectiveness by 'doing the right thing', i.e. by adding value to the enterprise in every possible way, not least through imaginative and open-ended design.

Efficiency and effectiveness

Efficiency and effectiveness must be taken together in order to maximize the cumulative impact of both. The pie diagram shown here represents the total annual cost of employing one office worker including all elements of salary, pensions insurances, information technology, and, of course, occupancy costs. Occupancy costs, i.e. all the costs associated with office accommodation such as rent, taxes, energy, amortization of fit-out costs, etc., usually amount to somewhat less than 10 per cent of the total.

The major point about this ratio is that the efficiency measures listed overleaf relate only to this 10 per cent tranche of each office worker's total employment costs. The benefits – direct, real, and important as they are – that more efficient use of office space can bring are unlikely to be more than one-third of that 10 per cent.

Much greater potential lies within the remaining 90 per cent of employment costs. Achieving greater efficiency, as shown overleaf, has much to do with the direct application of the skills of the architect and space planner – although even such gains are likely to be short term, and even pointless and illusory,

without the willing cooperation of both office management and office workers. Achieving greater effectiveness, on the other hand, can only be done in ways that are relatively indirect as far as the designer is concerned, because success depends upon the close collaboration of management and workers. What the architect can do is add potential to the working environment, much in the same way that features can be added to a personal computer. To be able to invent and install such features requires, on the part of the designer, an intelligent understanding of what user needs are – and, perhaps more importantly, how they are developing. On the part of the user, this requires an understanding of what the designer has made possible and a willingness to use it. As in personal computer applications – the new software package shining in its box – the potential leverage is terrific, but the rewards are not guaranteed unless the new toy is taken out of its box and put intelligently to use.

Below **The fraction of the annual costs of employing each office worker that is taken up by occupancy costs, i.e. rent, taxes, heating, lighting, and service charges, is small – usually well below 10 per cent. This has led to the conclusion that they are too insignificant to deserve much management attention. But occupancy costs are often second only to the direct costs of staff salaries and benefits, and often higher than those of information technology. All too often, wasteful expenditure on office space comes straight off the bottom line. But however much can be cut directly from occupancy costs by greater planning efficiency, the potential of the 90 per cent of employment costs is obviously far greater.**

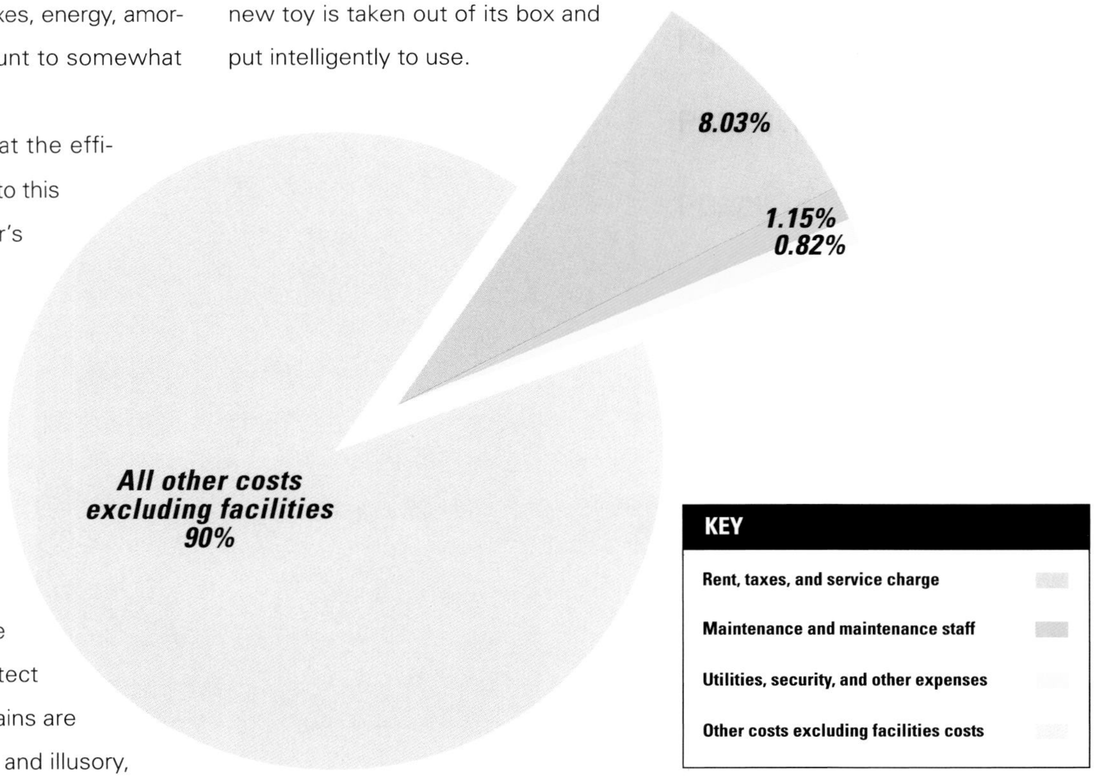

8.03%

1.15%
0.82%

**All other costs
excluding facilities
90%**

KEY	
Rent, taxes, and service charge	
Maintenance and maintenance staff	
Utilities, security, and other expenses	
Other costs excluding facilities costs	

Making office space more efficient

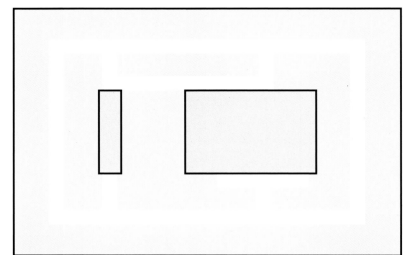

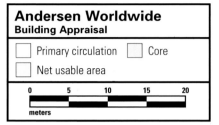

Andersen Worldwide
Building Appraisal

☐ Primary circulation   ☐ Core

☐ Net usable area

0   5   10   15   20

meters

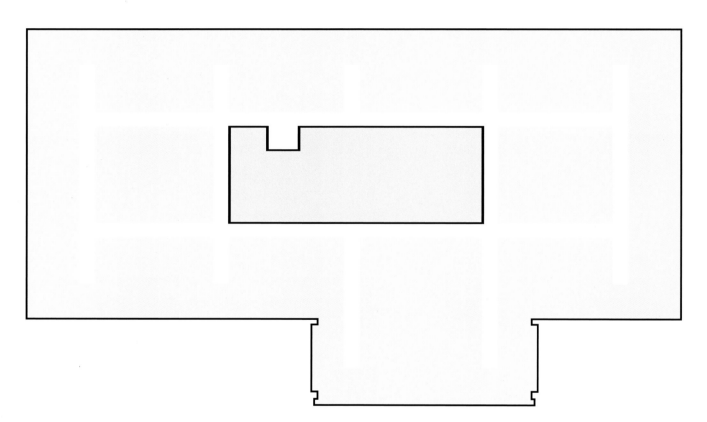

Above **Choosing the right building and putting the space to its best use is critical for achieving both efficiency and effectiveness. These two plans show the comparative landlord and tenant efficiencies of one floor in each of two buildings occupied by Andersen Worldwide in Chicago. The plans on page 235 examine the effectiveness of the buildings (see also pages 176–81). When the company moved from one address to another, their choice of new building was partly dictated by the tenant efficiency of the floor plan, i.e. the proportion of usable space that can be extracted from the total rentable area. The new space (lower plan) gave a 86 per cent tenant efficiency, which was one per cent more than that in their former building (top plan). This may seem a small saving, but on as large a scale as this, one per cent represents just under 400 sq .m/approx. 4,300 sq. ft of expensive office space that can now be put to productive use year after year.**

The efficiency of the planning within that space was even more critical. Formerly a total of 33,000 sq. m/353,000 sq. ft was occupied by 1,240 people (i.e. 27 sq. m/285 sq. ft per person). Now 1100 Andersen staff occupy 23,365 sq. m/250,000 sq. ft (i.e. 21 sq. m/227 sq. ft per person), an overall reduction of just under 30 per cent. This was made possible by space-use intensification and a major shift in the pattern of space use (discussed on page 235). The overall saving on annual rent and other occupancy costs will, in effect, have paid for the capital outlay on the project in less than four years. Modest annual savings can be more significant than swingeing capital cuts.

Making office space more efficient is relatively easy, perhaps rather more so in northern Europe, where efficiency has often been neglected – for the contextual social democratic reasons described earlier – than in Japan or North America, or even in the UK. There is often room for improvement in a number of areas: in the design of office shells; in space planning – by using less space to accommodate more people; in the design of fit-out and furniture – to drive down the cost of 'churn' i.e. to minimize the costs involved in work place moves; in increasing the productivity of space use – by sharing work-spaces and other resources, sometimes called space-use intensification; and in saving energy.

Better landlord and tenant efficiency

Avoiding waste in the design of office-building shells is critical. There are two very precise measures of the efficiency of space provision in any given office building. The first takes the landlord's view: 'How much rentable office space can I squeeze out of this building by getting the architect to design the smallest possible core?' The second takes the view more typical of tenants: 'How much of the space that I am paying for is taken up by corridors, and how much can I actually use to accommodate my people and their equipment?'

Landlord efficiency, defined in DEGW terms, is the percentage of the gross area of an office building floor that is available for renting after the building has been given an adequate infrastructure of services – ducts, elevator shafts, lavatories, escape stairs – to make it safe, habitable, and operational. Many office buildings only achieve a score of 80 per cent. Depending on how big the building is and how many floors it has, a reasonable target might be 84 per cent. But to achieve a higher percentage would not be better, because experience shows that very high figures indicate that such buildings are likely to be under-serviced. Hence, in practice, the margin for potential improvement between what is often tolerated, and what ought to be achieved by skilful office architects, is perhaps 4 or 5 per cent.

Tenant efficiency, again in DEGW terms, is the percentage of the rentable area of a given office-building floor that is available for use by tenants (or user departments) after the inevitable circulation required both for reasonable access to workstations and for means of escape has been identified and discounted. Here there is a wider discrepancy between what is often tolerated and what could be considered to be good practice – probably because tenants have been less well placed to assert their requirements than landlords and developers. Moreover, what suits the landlord's arithmetic may be against the tenant's space-planning interests. Some speculative office buildings are 'dogs', full of built-in inefficiencies from the users' point of view. Scores of 75 per cent, and even lower, are often tolerated. A target of 85 per cent is what a sensible architect with a good sense of the realities of space planning should be able to achieve – a margin of potential improvement in efficiency of 10 per cent.

Increasing density

Offices are not always occupied very efficiently, especially when space planning has been based largely upon grade and status, on what people think they are rather than on what they actually do. Such distinctions are notorious for adding layer upon layer of fat to space budgets. Other reasons for relative inefficiency include ungoverned storage

Below **Certain complex, highly interactive tasks can only be carried out amid the buzz and energy of high-density occupation. Dealing rooms and trading floors are well-known examples. This is the floor of the Tokyo Stock Exchange.**

schemes designed to ensure interchangeability of such components as partitions and furniture. Other solutions involve exploiting improvements in mobile and wireless telephony. Though not all these solutions are applicable in every type of office, it is not unreasonable to set more stringent targets for controlling the costs of churn. In fact, intelligent facilities managers, in the right circumstances, can often cut costs by half – a margin of saving of 100 per cent, enough to justify a significant capital outlay.

Intensifying space use

Time-sharing workstations first became a practical option about five years ago in organizations, such as sales offices in the electronics sector, in which information technology was taken for granted and a high proportion of staff encouraged to spend time outside the office. More general surveys of how people spend time in the office are becoming more common, and the results are tending to show a much lower level of occupancy than has usually been assumed, even in companies where most staff allegedly spend most of their

Above **A group space has been organized as a small combi-office, with individual workstations on the perimeters and a meeting area in the centre. Glazed partitions and ceiling-height sliding doors that face the top-lit atrium (see page 224) ensure good light and a high degree of visibility. CLM/BBDO, Paris. Architect: Jean Nouvel.**

and filing (which can easily take 10 to 15 per cent of rentable area), poorly designed furniture, and too much space given to secondary circulation. Often office densities in aggregate come to over 20 sq. m/ 200 sq. ft of rentable area per person. A reasonable target could be as low as 15 sq. m/150 sq. ft per person, a potential saving of 25 per cent.

Diminishing the cost of churn

Churn is the proportion of occupants in an office who have to move or exchange their work places in a given year. Organizations are becoming less and less stable. Since moving people, furniture, electronic, and, in some cases, the walls that surround them is often significantly expensive from a facilities management perspective; controlling the costs of churn has received a lot of attention recently. There are various strategies to reduce these, ranging from the unsatisfactory imposition of a draconian 'universal plan', in which all workstations are exactly the same and thus totally interchangeable, to fit-out

Right **Intensifying space use often means time-sharing individual desks. However, this is not always the best way to increase the productive use of office space. Often more can be achieved by zoning it. Here, special touch-down places, accessible to everyone, are set aside for concentrated computer work. Offices in an old factory converted for e-fact, an advertising agency, London. Architect: Architeam.**

time at their desks. Systematic observations are revealing not that individual workstations are usually half empty, as many people have thought, but that they are more likely to be two-thirds empty, even at peak times. For a great part of the day people are not at their workstations – they are engaged, perfectly legitimately, in the constant series of more or less informal meetings that constitute modern office life. As the infrastructure of information technology matures, so the opportunities to intensify space use will increase.

A modest assumption is that a decrease in the ratio of personal occupancy to individual workstations from 1:1 to 1:1.5 would be possible in some, if not all, departments of many organizations, large and small. This simple move would yield, were it successfully applied, a significant gain in space efficiency of 50 per cent.

Wasting less energy

Building by building, square metre by square metre, the significance of achieving greater efficiency in the use of energy through more sophisticated design is, at first sight, less

impressive than any of the figures on space use quoted above. The annual impact on occupancy costs of an efficient energy regime in a well-designed building compared to the standards that have been tolerated for far too long, is likely to be a reduction of 40 per cent.

There are, however, other strategic considerations to take into account that explain the tremendous spate of invention in designing buildings to perform better in every environmental respect. The cumulative impact on the economy of energy consumed in buildings is enormous – approximately 45 per cent of the UK energy load, for example, is expended in this way. Designing and improving the building stock to reduce this burden of unnecessary waste is a matter of the highest national and international importance. Not only is energy being wasted, but the production of energy to meet commercial demand is

one of the chief causes of the pollution that is perhaps the greatest threat to the quality of life in the next century. Contemporary architects and environmental engineers in the UK and in Europe generally have responded particularly well to this challenge. But still more needs to be done.

In addition, and perhaps most shocking of all, a huge amount of energy is expended – and pollution caused – by mass commuting. We have inherited entirely irrational locational patterns from previous generations, who could not conceive of any better solution to the problem of accommodating a rapidly growing office work force than by separating working and living. The combination of the enormous communicative potential of information technology and these powerful environmental policy issues are the two drives that are creating the new mixed-use urban landscapes and the emerging, dispersed, network-like geography of living and working that were referred to in Chapter 3.

Above **The best new office interiors are thriftily designed in every way. In this, for example, the best possible lighting for work and for effect is achieved with the minimum expenditure of energy. PowerGen offices, near Coventry, UK. Architect: Bennetts Associates.**

Making office space more effective

Improvements in the effectiveness of office space are less quantifiable than those in efficiency. They depend upon the ability of organizations to exploit the potential offered to them. The same qualification – and risks – apply when, for example, a further level of capacity is introduced in a company's telecommunications system. Making full use of this new potential depends, as every manager knows, not just on turning on the information technology tap, but upon more complex factors such as training, leadership, organization, and direction.

Below **The need for more, and varied, meeting space has been met in this conversion by a formal meeting room and an informal meeting place. Both are highly visible and adjacent to the main circulation routes, near the central escalators. Offices for Leo Burnett, London. Architects: Stanton Williams, YRM, and Fletcher Priest.**

The physical office environment is exactly the same: a management tool with lots of potential. The difference is that this potential is often unappreciated by many managers. It seems, however, that a growing and increasingly vocal minority of intelligent office users are frustrated because they have been given only restricted access to the full range of features that new ways of working demand. Offered here is an explanation of some of these features, with estimates of the power that they can add to conventional office space performance. This power is not in the form of the direct benefits that greater efficiency in space use can guarantee, but in the scope for potential improvement that the intelligent use of such features should give. Improvements cannot be taken for granted – each organization must judge for itself the appropriate balance between opportunity and costs, and recognize that successful implementation depends upon users who believe in what they have been promised.

More support space

Space for team and group activities is more often than not under-provided in conventional offices whose space budgets are based largely on the area required for elementary individual workstations. There is rarely much provision for the more elaborate kinds of support spaces, such as project rooms, libraries, and areas for display or video conference facilities that are increasingly required for collaboration, teamwork and project groups.

The new kinds of office illustrated in the case studies are much richer in extra facilities available to everyone to share than conventional offices. Whereas in a conventional office as little as 10 per cent of the available usable area would be given over to support, in an advanced kind of office in the category of den or club there could easily be as much as 30 per cent – giving, in effect, a 200 per cent increase in the potential to accommodate more complex forms of work.

A wider range of work settings

Similarly, conventional offices are very restricted in the range of work settings they provide for the increasingly varied activities that make up the work profiles of contemporary office staff. This is for two quite different reasons. The first is more understandable: originally most office jobs were very simple – it was only in the mid-1960s that the needs of new types

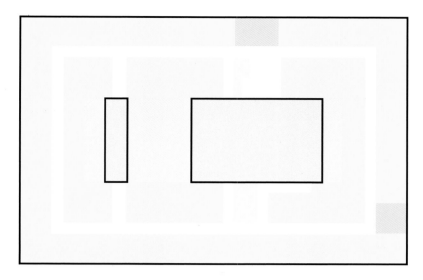

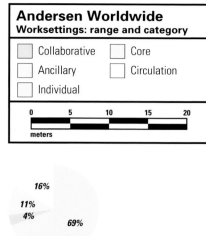

Andersen Worldwide
Worksettings: range and category

▢ Collaborative		▢ Core	
▢ Ancillary		▢ Circulation	
▢ Individual			

0   5   10   15   20
meters

16%
11%
4%
69%

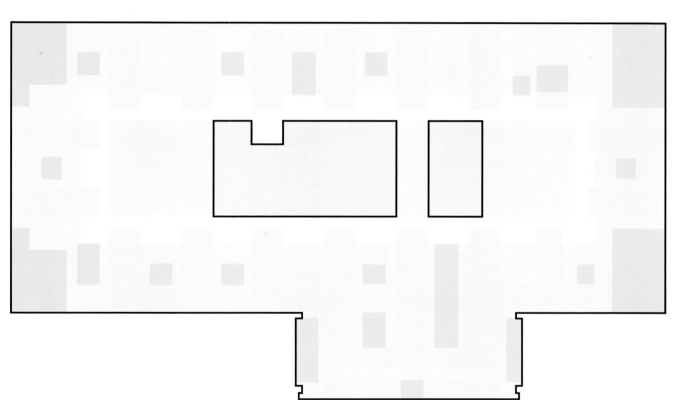

13%
31%
39%
17%

Above **These two floor plans show the striking difference between conventional office layouts and layouts based on an understanding of the potential for better and more productive work that is offered by more support space and a wider range of work settings. They are plans of the floors – of two buildings occupied by Andersen Worldwide – seen on page 230. The underlying statistics demonstrate the fundamental shift in the pattern of space use. In the old building (top plan) only 15 per cent of the available rentable space on a typical floor was given over to accommodating shared activities compared to 56 per cent of the floor in the new office (lower plan). Similarly, in the former situation only 4 per cent of the available space was given over to collaborative settings, such as project areas and meeting rooms, while in the new office the comparable figure is 30 per cent. In the old building, space was predominantly individually 'owned'; in the new one, a far greater proportion is shared. Despite this reorganization, the majority of Andersen Worldwide staff still have their own workstations, though these are generally smaller and far less status-oriented than they were in the old building. In other words, even within the framework of one-to-one allocation of work places to individuals, dramatic improvements are possible in the provision of support space, in the range of facilities offered, and in the use of zoning of activities to provide much better conditions for work.**

of office worker, analysts, and programmers who were neither clerks nor managers, began to be recognized in office planning. The second reason is more contemporary and more perverse: there is a movement, very much fostered by facilities managers looking for easy space-planning solutions, to deny the differences between various kinds of office work and to provide standard workplaces for all office workers. The overriding reason is to facilitate office moves and to cut the cost of churn. Sometimes this policy takes the form of the so-called 'universal plan', in which all work places, on every floor, in all departments, are deliberately made identical and thus interchangeable.

This solution ignores one of the oldest problems in office design. Because office work is, more often than not, simultaneously both interactive and concentrated, it is practically impossible to devise a workplace – or even layout – that provides equally well for both total accessibility and perfect quiet. To attempt to satisfy both requirements in one work place is to fail to do either properly. However, a solution to this ancient conundrum has now come within grasp. New ways of working, based on access to ubiquitous information technology, as can be seen in several of the case studies, is allowing layouts to be developed which are, in effect, zoned. It is possible for increasingly mobile office workers to choose the environment that best suits the kind of work they have do at that particular moment of the day – solitary or collaborative, requiring elaborate support or demanding practically no props at all, information-creating or judgmental. New offices are likely to become more diverse, offering more plural than single work places and a wider range of work settings.

Consequently the analysis of the range of work settings appropriate to diverse kinds of office task that an office layout has the capacity to offer is becoming a critical measure of potential office performance. Conventional offices might offer three such settings at most, while an advanced one might offer nine, an increase in potential of 200 per cent.

Buildings that stimulate interaction

A feature of office building design that deserves particular attention – partly because it has been so neglected in the North American tradition and has been so successfully addressed in many northern European office projects – is the use of architectural resources to generate interaction within

an organization – not just within a unit or division of a company, but across different departments.

North American office developers typically minimize circulation for economic reasons – to generate as much rentable area as possible. The result is that public spaces, except the ground floor entrance, are usually given little design attention. The most imaginative northern European offices – which are often custom-built – do exactly the opposite, creating relatively large amounts of circulation space, often in the form of internal streets. These not only make the organization visible to itself in all its varied and changing manifestations, but also considerably increase the chances of serendipitous contact. Circulation is deliberately used to ensure that face-to-face encounters are inevitable. In the best offices, these architectural means are reinforced by planning which ensures that spaces for inherently collaborative activities – such as training rooms, restaurants, major meeting rooms – are clustered together, so that

Left **The buiding for the SAS (Scandinavian airlines) headquarters in Stockholm is an example of an office deliberately designed round the idea of a highly visible and central street in order to maximize the possibility of chance encounters between staff in different divisions. The street is an inviting space – light, airy, and with attractive views out – and is furnished with informal meeting areas, cafés, restaurants, shops, and recreational facilities. The objective is that the whole organization should be open and aware of itself – even the board room is visible from the street. (See also page 38.) Architect: Neils Torp.**

the chances of intra-organizational interaction are further increased. In quantitative terms at least a doubling – a 100 per cent increase – in the potential for interaction can be generated by architectural means alone.

Creating the right image

One of the most underestimated functions of architecture is its capacity to express, powerfully and unambiguously, the values of those who commission and who use the buildings. Architecture is an expressive medium. Although many architects – through a long process of habituation – seem to have become desensitized to its full meaning, the language of conventional office design emphasizes two factors: sustaining barriers and reinforcing hierarchies. Analysis of most conventional office design – of architectural form, of interior layout, and, perhaps most of all, of office furniture – shows how powerfully strong is the emphasis on keeping office workers separate from each other and showing them exactly where they stand in the corporate pecking order. However, for an increasing number of forward-looking organizations –

including many featured in the case studies in this book – interaction and fluidity are the very different values that they wish to express through design and layout.

If office design contradicts organizational intentions, the business consequences are serious – exactly as they would be if an organization's public mission statement was being continually contradicted by managerial behaviour. Misleading, and especially untruthful, messages are quickly picked up by employees – leading to cynical and sub-optimal behaviour – and eventually by outsiders, customers, and suppliers, eroding trust, interest, and commitment. In other words, broadcasting the wrong message through design damages business. The margin between the effect of giving the right and the wrong message – easily measured, for example, by the Workplace Performance Survey – is at least 100 per cent. Saying what you mean to staff and customers, and also expressing it through design, doubles the positive impact of the message.

What this chapter, perhaps the most important one in the book, demonstrates is that office space is not a mystery nor something that can be delegated to technicians, but is instead a most valuable and plannable asset that can, and in fact must, be managed. Forward-looking managers who want to drive their businesses as hard as possible to survive and succeed must relate the use of office space to their overall business objectives; they must look at spatial resources in relation to human ones and information technology; they must solve accommodation problems in the context of change; they must compare their spatial performance, the productivity of building use, with what other businesses are doing. In other words, managers must treat office space not as something special nor remote, but in exactly the same business-like way as every other management resource.

Assessing the impact of introducing new working environments and new ways of working into the office is no more difficult than measuring the consequences of any other kind of managerial innovation. The measurement of performance is as important in designing as in managing the office. In the world of work, design and management coexist to achieve

Below **Architecture, even in its detailing, is capable of expressing powerful messages. The attention given to the design of this handrail – and staircase – says an enormous amount about the importance that the organization attaches to the quality of the day-to-day life of its staff. Channel 4 Television, London. Architect: Richard Rogers Partnership.**

Management, in fact, is much closer to the messy, creative, and open-ended process of design than many architects and designers realize.

Communication is what matters most. Performance measures that make equal sense to both managers and designers is the common language that has been missing in office design

What designers have to avoid is two traps: first, they must not convince themselves that design is so complex, mysterious, and unique that only their own individual intuition (or stubbornness) can be relied upon to determine what ought to be done; and, second, they must not allow themselves to be convinced by sceptical clients that an impossibly high standard of evidence and proof is needed – far beyond what is customary in other aspects of business – to justify any particular design intervention. Both lines of argument are sterile. Both limit the power of the design imagination.

The great benefit of the methodological advances described in this chapter is that, through them, the design of the office environment can now be seen as an integral part of a complex and open-ended system, that embraces rethinking work processes as well as skilfully using human resources to find the best and most profitable ways of managing change.

the same business purposes, the same organizational ends. Particularly in the new office, they are inextricably intertwined.

All management decisions are open ended and inherently complex. They are generally made under pressure, and they always depend upon observation and data as well as experience and judgment, but they are never made with complete information. And yet, just like designers, managers have to make such urgent but indeterminate decisions every day.

What managers must avoid is thinking that design doesn't matter. Like war and generals, design is too important to be left solely to designers. Improving business performance leads to the inevitable conclusion that clients and architects, if they want more productive offices, must work closely together.

Above **The image that this entrance projects to the outside world – clarity, lightness, elimination of fuss – is more than just stylishness. It is a critical and calculated component of a business programme. Jessica Square, London. Architect: Munkenbeck & Marshall.**

where to go for help

New offices give sophisticated networkers new choices in deciding where they work and live. That urban locations are no longer necessary for everyone all the time is vividly shown in this conversion of an old stone barn in rural Yorkshire, UK, into offices for a computer software company, Principal Ltd. Fitting a new office into an old building also demonstrates the changing balance between the long-term building shell and the short-term interior: converting the shell calls for sensitivity to the existing environment; fitting out the interior is an opportunity for individual expression – an opportunity seized upon here by the architect, Studio Baard.

Above **The open-plan offices for John Menzies, Edinburgh, UK, are spacious enough to offer opportunities both for informal interaction and quiet concentrated work. Architect: Bennetts Associates.**

What generates demand for the new office is fresh and continuing feedback – better expressed as 'feedforward' – connecting what office users want with what the office environment can provide. In a time of change, wise clients must tell architects, property developers, landlords, and furniture manufacturers exactly what they think they want. To do that with conviction, they must be as well informed as possible. Fortunately there are some straightforward ways, spelled out below, to catch up with this international, complex, and ever-changing field. These include reading the right journals and texts, visiting trade shows, and joining specialist organizations. For the real enthusiasts there are several stimulating networks offering an ongoing perspective on the links between design and business.

Anticipating developing user requirements is as important as keeping up with what is new, particularly when it comes to the preparation of that essential document – or series of documents – the brief.

INITIAL RECONNAISSANCE

There are three main ways to survey what is happening. First, regularly scan the magazines that deal seriously with office design issues. Second, read a few of the relevant books. Third – the quickest and most enjoyable way to discover the most up-to-date ideas – visit one of the major international office furniture, facilities management, and real estate shows.

Internationally read magazines

■ *alt.office.Journal.* This new supplement to *Contract Design* and *Facilities Design and Management* is bringing together excellent articles on many aspects of 'alternative officing'. 1 Penn Plaza, Floor 10, New York 10117–0053, USA.

■ *Architecture Intérieure Crée.* The best French interior design journal, frequently and intelligently dealing with the design of the working environment. SEP, Paris, France. (fax 33 1 46 22 98 79)

■ *Corporate Design.* Published by Itoki, the major Japanese furniture manufacturer, this offers excellent international coverage of projects, products, and ideas. Consistently well illustrated with photographs, plans, and diagrams. Predominantly Japanese text. New Office Age Co. Ltd, Tokyo, Japan. (fax 81 3 3664 5361)

■ *Eciffo.* Published by Kokuyo, a Japanese furniture manufacturer, this is arguably the most informed and most sophisticated of all magazines concerned with the design and management of the office. Text in English as well as Japanese. Kokuyo Institute of Office Systems, 2-1-1-Minato-mirai 2 chome, Nishu-ku, Yokohama, Japan. (fax 81 45 224 1760 e-mail ksmt@magical.egg or.jp)

■ *Facilities.* Founded by DEGW in 1984 to help build up the knowledge base of the emergent profession of facilities management, this UK facilities journal is now more academic than professional, but nevertheless contains occasional good material. MCB University Press, Bradford, UK. (URL http://www.mcb.co.uk)

■ *Facilities Premises and Management.* The best-established and most thorough of US journals in the field of facilities management, it now discusses the accommodation of new ways of working with increasing frequency. Gralla Publications, New York, USA. (fax 1 212 279 3955)

■ *Flexible Working.* The first of a family of publications dealing with the challenges of new ways of working. Though mostly written from a human resources point of view, this bi-monthly is strong on case studies, many of which have a locational and design dimension. Eclipse Publications, London, UK. (fax 44 171 354 8106)

■ *Mensch & Büro.* The principal German magazine dealing with design and business issues. MENSCH & BÜRO Verlags GmbH, Baden-Baden, Germany. (fax 43 72 21 266 84)

Key texts

The publications – books, research studies, and key articles – that have advanced the understanding of the new office are here grouped into four clusters: those written from a purely managerial and organizational point of view from which the impact on the physical environment has to be extrapolated by the reader; those that stem from a largely design and environmental position; the rare category that attempts to give environmental and organizational matters more or less equal weight in order to investigate the relationship between these two very different worlds; and, finally, those that have a historical perspective.

On organizational change

■ *Build a Better Life by Stealing Office Supplies, Dogbert's Big Book of Business*, illustrated by Scott Adams. Where it all begins and ends, unstoppable mockery directed at managerial gobbledygook and servile employee pretensions. Andrews and McMeel, Kansas City, USA, 1991.

■ *Delayering Organizations: How to Beat Bureaucracy and Create a Flexible and Responsive Organization* by D. Keuning and W. Opheij. A concerted attack on the bureaucratic structures that so much of conventional office architecture is dedicated to propping up. Pitman Publishing, London, 1994 (first published in Holland in 1993).

■ *Managing the Evolving Corporation* by Langdon Morris. Unique among management books in that its author not only takes the design process seriously enough to use it to illuminate business decision-making but is also interested enough in design itself to explore how office interior design can be used to enhance group performance. Van Nostrand Reinhold, New York, 1995.

■ *Organizational Architecture: Designs for Changing Organizations* by David A. Nadler, Marc S. Gerstein, Robert B. Shaw. A lively account of changes in organizational structure from bureaucracies to networks made accessible to architects by the comparison of business processes to architectural design. Designing high-performance work systems through reintegrating people, work, technology, and information is the big idea. Jossey-Bass Publishers, San Francisco, USA, 1992.

■ *Re-engineering the Corporation: A Manifesto for Business Revolution* by Michael Hammer and

James Champy. Perhaps the most important and ambitious argument for totally rethinking the design of the work processes in factories as well as offices. Hugely influential and not without critics who now question the book's more self-confident assertions, not all of which have been capable of being put into practice. HarperCollins, New York, and Nicholas Brearley, London, 1993.

■ *The Empty Raincoat* and *The Age of Unreason* by Charles Handy. Two key books, beautifully written, deceptively simple, describing trends and changes in the nature of work and society that seem likely to lead to new patterns of occupancy of office buildings, new timetables, new career paths, and new locational pressures on living, working, and leisure. Hutchinson, London, 1989, and Century Hutchinson, London,1994.

■ *The 5th Discipline: The Art and Practice of the Learning Organization* by Peter Senge. An important book emphasizing that organizations are intellectual entities that depend on collective learning: 'How can a team of committed managers with individual IQs above 120 have a collective IQ of 63?' Doubleday Currency, New York, 1990.

■ *The Virtual Corporation: Structuring and Revitalizing the Corporation for the Twentieth Century* by William H. Davidow and Michael S. Malone. Stresses the increasing importance for corporations to respond quickly to customer pressure, and hence the importance of the use of time in the workplace. Glimpses of the likely future as corporations learn how to produce 'virtual' products that are high in added value and instantly available. HarperCollins, New York, 1992.

■ *Thriving on Chaos: A Handbook for a Managerial Revolution* and *Liberation Management* by Tom Peters. The former includes rules for success in a rapidly changing world, including team-driven development and flatter organizations, organizing informal comunication networks, making innovation a way of life for everyone – all of which have a direct implication for the design of the workplace. Macmillan, London, 1988 and Alfred A. Knopf, New York, 1992.

■ *In The Age of the Smart Machine* by Shoshana Zuboff. An argument for 'informating not automating', i.e. how 'model companies' use smart machines in interaction with smart people. Butterworth-Heinemann, Oxford, UK, 1989.

On the environment of the new office

■ *City of Bits: Space Place and the Infobahn* by William J. Mitchell. A short but brilliantly written collection of insights into the ways in which information technology is certain to transform not just every aspect of the physical environment of our landscapes and cities but also the fundamental ways in which societies think and communicate. The MIT Press, Cambridge, MA, USA, 1995.

■ *CRE 2000* by Michael Joroff, Franklin Becker ,and others. A series of reports, written directly for the corporate client, describing the phases of the major research project on the future of corporate real estate conducted by the Industrial Development Research Corporation (IDRC). The more conceptual earlier parts of the study are eclipsed in usefulness by the very practical 'tool box' approach of later volumes. IDRC, Georgia, USA, 1995 and onwards.

■ *Designing the Office of the Future* by Volker Hartkopf and others. Reports on the development work on responsive building systems carried out in the School of Architecture, Carnegie Mellon University, Pittsburgh, PA, USA. Part of the studies involved international surveys of innovation in office design. John Wiley & Sons, New York, 1993.

■ *Edge City* by Joel Garreau. A fascinating account of how, at major intersections on the beltways that surround many North American cities, unplanned agglomerations of offices, housing, and retail and leisure facilities are springing up, creating a new kind of high-density, mixed-use settlement. Doubleday, New York, 1991.

■ *How Buildings Learn* by Stewart Brand. It hardly matters that this is mostly not about offices. Brand has such a novel and challenging attitude to how buildings should be designed to accommodate change that his latest book has become compulsory reading for anyone embarking on anything as open-ended and uncertain as commissioning a new office building. Viking Penguin, New York, 1993.

■ *Intelligent Building Studies*: a series of multiclient studies carried out by DEGW in association with Technibank, Northcrofts, Ove Arups and other consultants from 1993 and continuing today. The objective of the studies is to identify the performance, features, and specifications that distinguish 'intelligent' buildings, i.e. offices that anticipate and

satisfy business needs. The study has developed geographically: Europe, 1993/4; SE Asia, 1995/6; Latin America, current. Privately published by DEGW but an account of 'The Intelligent Building in Europe' has achieved wider circulation. British Council for Offices, The College of Estate Management, Reading, UK, 1992.

■ *Heritage and Technology* by Ron Harrison and Richard Oades. The first comprehensive examination of the potential that information technology, especially in its emerging wireless forms, offers for the non-intrusive adaptation and preservation of historic buildings. Contains an excellent account of IT infrastructure and applications, a summary of conservation issues and guidelines for planning conservation strategies that take IT into proper account. Lucent Technologies, London, 1996.

■ *Information Technology and Buildings* by Butler Cox. Following the ORBIT reports, this is the most useful and comprehensive guide to the physical accommodation of information technology in office buildings. Seriously technical but very easy to understand, it admirably meets the criterion of combining design and organizational information and making each relevant to the other. Butler Cox, London, 1989. Republished and brought up-to-date in 1992 by Butler Cox's successor, CSC Index, as *Intelligent Buildings – Designing and Managing the IT Infrastructure*.

Below **Glazing brings light and the opportunity for planting to an office 'street' for Oxford University Press, near Oxford, UK. Architect: Roger Stretton.**

Above **Large ceiling-height glazed doors provide flexible meeeting spaces in the offices for the French ministry of social affairs, Inspection Générale des Affaires Sociales, Paris. Architect: Alain Moatti and Jacques Moussafir.**

■ *Kombi-Büro* by Congena, the Munich based consultancy. A thorough, international, and technical survey of various manifestations of the 'combi-office', i.e. the combination of clusters of cellular office space and open-plan group resource space that has been the 'big idea' in German and Scandinavian office planning in the last decade. An interesting collection of cases. FBO-Fachverlag für Büro- und Organisationtechnik, Baden-Baden, Germany.

■ *ORBIT Studies*. The first ORBIT (Office Buildings and Information Technology) study was carried out by DEGW, Building Use Studies and Eosys in the UK in 1981/2 and published privately by DEGW in 1983 – at the same time that PCs and distributed intelligence were becoming a universal reality. It was the first thorough assessment of the likely impact on the office environment of the complex and converging series of phenomena then identified for the first time as information technology. ORBIT 2 was a follow-up study carried out in North America by DEGW, Harbinger (part of Xerox) and Facilities Research Associates (Franklin Becker and William Sims of Cornell University) in 1984/5, published by Harbinger in 1985. ORBIT 2 introduced a systematic way of appraising buildings in relation to different, and changing, profiles of user demand. This work was critical in developing the technique now known as Building Appraisal described in Chapter 5.

■ *Reinventing the Workplace* edited by John Worthington. A collection of 16 lively, well-informed papers from the 1995 University of York workshop that brought together office design experts and representatives from some of the most enterprising businesses in the UK and Scandinavia. Architectural Press, Oxford, UK, 1997.

■ *The Office* by Elisabeth Pelegrin-Genel. A book so handsome that it is in danger of being relegated to coffee table status. On closer reading, it is distinguished by a sharp, almost anthropological focus on what makes the individual office such a strong expression of power and personality. Flammarion, Paris and New York, 1996.

■ *The Office: A Facility Based on Change* by Robert Propst. A classic written by the designer of Herman Miller's 'Action Office', the most original and well worked-out office furniture concept of the century. Well worth reading, despite having been written a couple of decades before distributed intelligence changed the office for ever. The Business Press, Elmhurst, IL, USA, 1968; reprinted by Herman Miller in 1996.

■ *The Office, the Whole Office and Nothing but the Office* by P .G .J .C. Vos, J. J. van Meel, A. A. M. Dijcks. A product of the famous Delft University of Technology, Department of Real Estate & Project Management. This little book is a well-illustrated and extremely perceptive collection of definitions and key examples of the various terms used to describe the environment of new ways of working – from Telework and Satellite Offices to Combi and Non-territorial Offices. Very useful. The 'copyright' is worthy of note. Delft University of Technology, Delft, The Netherlands, 1997.

■ *The Responsible Workplace* by Francis Duffy, Andrew Laing, Victor Crisp. An account of one of DEGW's most important multi-client studies (carried out in collaboration with the British Government's Building Research Establishment) investigating the likely overall impact on office design of new ways of working. Expert papers on aspects of change in the office, international case studies of innovative office design, and recommendations on the design strategies to accommodate the consequences of change. Butterworth Architecture, Oxford, UK, 1993.

■ *Tomorrow's Office* by Roger Cunliffe and Santa Raymond. Covering a wide spectrum of practical, contemporary office design issues, this intelligently presented book is full of interesting case studies, many of which illustrate alternative ways of working. E. & F. N. Spon, London, 1997.

■ *Total Workplace Performance: Rethinking the Office Environment* by Stan Aronoff and Audrey Kaplan. An encyclopedic survey of the vast literature about the office environment which attempts to deal with productivity but without real commitment or conclusion. WDL Publications, Ottawa, Canada, 1995.

■ *Workplaces: The Psychology of the Physical Environment in Offices and Factories* by Eric Sundstrom. The best survey of all serious research on the relationship between people and organizations and such aspects of the working environment as light, ambient temperature, colour, privacy, and interaction. Unfortunately it was written five years before the interesting questions of how best to accommodate new ways of working were raised. Cambridge University Press, Cambridge, UK and New York, 1986.

On linking organization theory and design

■ *A Vision of the New Workplace* by Francis Duffy and Jack Tanis. Partly a polemic about the growing relevance of office design to business, the book is also an attempt to devise a model to explain the changing relationship between organizational structure and office layout. This model, derived from Duffy's earlier work, is also the basis of Steelcase's important innovation in workplace programming, known as Workplace Envisioning. Industrial Development (USA), April 1993.

■ *Kantoren bestaan niet meer – The Demise of the Office* by Erik Veldhoen and Bart Piepers. A cogently argued, well written and stylishly illustrated argument about how, from a Dutch point of view, the changing nature of office work is likely to affect office buildings and office interiors. 010 Publishers, Rotterdam, The Netherlands, 1995.

■ *New Environments for Working* by Francis Duffy, Andrew Laing, and Denise Jaunzens. A DEGW/BRE multi-client study addressing the issue of how environmental systems such as lighting and air-conditioning and must be redesigned and reprogrammed as space-use intensification becomes more common. E. & F. N. Spon, London, 1997.

■ *'Now' Offices, No Offices, New Offices – Wild Times in the World of Office Work* by Michael Brill. A tour around some new concepts, written in his inimitably challenging style, by one of the most inventive and experienced consultants in this field. The Buffalo Organization for Social and Technical Innovation, Buffalo, NY, USA, 1993.

■ *The Office is Where You Are* by Robert Luchetti and Philip Stone. In this now-famous article, as relevant to office design today as it was when first published in 1982, architect Luchetti and social scientist Stone proposed a radical revision of the office in order to provide a richer, more responsive, more subtle kind of environment consonant with what, even then, were perceived to be emerging organizational structures. In *Harvard Business Review,* March–April 1985, pp 102–117.

■ *Understanding Offices* by Alexi Marmot, Joanna Eley. A stimulating and informative text that addresses many of the issues that now face contemporary facilities managers, but a little short on facts and illustrations. Penguin, London, 1995.

■ *Workplace by Design – Mapping the High Performance Workscape* by Franklin Becker and Fritz Steele. The two leading authorities in the USA on new ways of working put a strong and practical emphasis on the enormous potential for change management through rethinking as well as replanning the office. Though well-written and highly accessible to non-specialist managers, it is weaker on what the new office should look and feel like. Jossey-Bass, San Francisco, USA, 1994.

■ *Workplace Strategies: Environment as a Tool for Work* by Jacqueline C. Vischer. A key text exploring how the relationship between organizations and accommodation can be systematically related. A strong theoretical base and interesting case material, but somewhat dowdy presentation of what are inherently design as well as organizational ideas. Chapman & Hall, New York, 1996.

■ *Workspace: Creating Environments in Organizations* by Franklin Becker. Possibly Beckers's most interesting book so far because it is discursive as well as wide and rich in reference. A good basis for understanding the changing relation of space and organizational preoccupations in order to make sense of subsequent developments. Praeger, New York, 1981.

On how the office came to be

■ *Form Follows Finance – Skyscrapers and Skylines in New York and Chicago* by Carol Willis.

A brilliant, scholarly account of the planning and financial background that determined the shape of seminal office buildings constructed in Chicago and New York during the critical half-century, 1890–1940. Cleverly illustrated with period postcards from the era. Princeton Architectural Press, New York, 1995.

■ *High Rise* by Jerry Adler. An account of 'how 1000 men and women worked around the clock for five years and lost $200 million building a skyscraper', the history of the building of 1540 Broadway. This is the story of the classic boom and bust economics of old-fashioned office development. HarperCollins, New York, 1993.

■ *Rise of the New York Skyscraper 1865–1913* by Sarah Bradford Landau and Carl W. Condit. The definitive account of the technological, engineering, and architectural advances that made the skyscraper possible. Lots of buildings are described, but little information is given about what they were built for, who financed them and how they were used. Nonetheless a beautiful and impressive book. Yale University Press, New Haven, CT, USA, and London, 1996.

■ *The Skyward Trend of Thought: The Metaphysics of the American Skyscraper* by Thomas A. P. van Leeuwen. An interesting, learned, and unusual account – written by an architect from a European point of view but with all the rich, comparative techniques of cultural anthropology – of the development of the skyscraper from 1870 to 1935. Quite the best book on the subject. MIT Press, Cambridge, MA, USA, 1988.

■ *White Collar: The American Middle Classes* by C. Wright Mills. A sociological classic describing the conditions that Taylorism created, which directly shaped the conventional office environment. Oxford University Press, New York, 1951.

The major international shows

■ **Neocon:** Held annually in Chicago in the second week of June, this is by far the most important North American show at which the widest range of new and existing office products, especially office furniture, can be seen. Contact: Merchandise Mart Properties, Inc., Suite 470 The Merchandise Mart, 200 World Trade Center, Chicago, IL 60654, USA. (tel 1 312 527 4141 fax 1 312 527 7782, www.neoconwtf.com)

■ **Orgatec:** Held every two years in October in Köln, this is the most important European furniture show. An enormous range of furniture and other office interior products is always on show. Contact: KölnMesse, Messe- und Ausstellungs-Ges.m.b.H, Postfach 21 07 60, D-50532 Köln, Germany. (tel 49 221 8 21 0 fax 49 221 8 21 25 74)

■ **EIMU:** Held in April in Milan, this international office furniture show is understandably dominated by the vigorous and stylish Italian office furniture manufacturing industry. It is beginning to lose a bit of its edge through being combined with a domestic furniture fair. Contact: COSMIT, Corso Magenta 96, 20100 Milan, Italy. (tel 39 2 485 921 fax 39 2 481 3580)

■ **IFMA:** Attached to the twice-yearly conferences for facilities managers organized by the International Facility Management Association, this show is less about office furniture – although a considerable amount is exhibited – than about the huge array of office products and electronic office systems now available for supporting the work of facilities managers. Contact: 1 East Greenway Plaza, Suite 1100, Houston, TX, USA. 77046-0194, USA. (tel 1 713 623 4362 fax 1 713 623 6124)

■ **EuroFM:** A smaller, but European equivalent to IFMA. It attracts good international speakers to the concomitant EuroFM conference. Contact: c/o IFMA European Bureau, 15 Boulevard St. Michel, B-1040 Brussels, Belgium (tel 32 2 743 1542 fax 32 2 743 1550)

■ **MIPIM:** Held in Cannes in March, this real estate and property convention is a good way to catch up with fast-moving projects, deals and gossip in property development, property law,

Below **Many of the workstations in the offices of British Telecom, Stockley Park, near London, are designed to be time-shared. Architect: DEGW.**

Above **When the offices for Glaxo, Greenford, UK, were updated, the entrance was transformed by an atrium that also provides an informal meeting space. Architect: Aukett Associates.**

DIGGING DEEPER

Starting a project makes necessary an entirely different level of practical knowledge about the latest and best practice. In a changing world the more global this knowledge is the better. Much information is very recent, being based upon current project experience, and exists only in the heads of corporate property managers. Consequently, one of the best ways of picking the managers' collective brains is to join one of the big organizations for facilities and real estate managers, and to attend the specialized conferences that are designed to bring such people into contact with each other. More focused contact with the best minds in the business can be maintained through membership of one of the networking groups mentioned below or, of course, from working directly with the principal consultants. Though their incomes are derived from selling advice, architects, property consultants, space planners, change-

architecture, city and regional promotions, as well as real estate brokering itself. Contact: Reed Midem Organization, 179 Avenue Victor-Hugo, Paris 75116, France. (tel 33 1 44 34 4418 fax 33 1 44 34 44 00)

management consultants, and others are often individually, and collectively through their professional bodies, surprisingly accessible, helpful, and articulate about problems and successes to serious enquirers.

Helpful client organizations

North America

■ **IDRC** *(Industrial Development Research Corporation):* One of the two leading bodies representing the interests of corporate real estate executives. Runs a very serious research programme – see CRE 2000 on page 243 – as well as organizing well-attended conferences. Publishes an excellent journal, *Site Selection.* Contact: 40 Technology Park/Atlanta, Suite 200, Norcross, GA 30042-9934, USA. (tel 1 770 446 8955 fax 1 770 662 8950)

■ **ULI** *(Urban Land Institute):* The main professional body representing mostly North American developers and investors in office and other property. It has international reach with regular international conferences. Excellent research and a good journal. Contact: 625 Indiana Avenue NW, Washington, DC 20004, USA. (tel 1 202 624 7000 fax 1 202 624 7140)

■ **IFMA** *(International Facility Management Association):* The oldest, largest, best-established organization in its field. Runs a big educational programme as well as conferences and a publishing programme. Contact: 1 East Greenway Plaza, Suite 1100, Houston, TX 77046-0194, USA. (tel 1 713 623 4362 fax 1 713 623 6124)

■ **NACORE** *(National Association of Corporate Real Estate Executives):* An organization for corporate real estate executives. Very similar to IDRC in many respects with equal ambitions and professionalism. Runs conferences, publications and research. Contact: 440 Columbia Drive, Suite 100, West Palm Beach, FL 33409, USA. (tel 1 561 683 8111 fax 1 561 697 4853)

■ **BOMA** *(Building Owners and Managers Association):* Represents many professionals in US real estate. An important function has been to collate statistics on rents and other aspects of occupancy costs throughout the USA. Sets standards for the industry. Contact: 1201 New York Avenue NW, Suite 3000, Washington DC 20005, USA. (tel 1 202 408 2662 fax 1 202 371 0181)

Europe

■ **BIFM** *(British Institute of Facility Management):* The British equivalent of IFMA, a smaller but well organized and rapidly growing institution representing many British facilities managers. Contact: 67 High Street, Saffron Walden, Essex CB10 1AA, UK. (tel 44 1799 508608 fax 44 1799 513237)

■ **BCO** *(British Council for Offices):* Represents a wide range of cross-disciplinary interests in aspects of the design, development, investment in, and management of offices. Runs an annual conference and has an influential research committee. Contact: The College of Estate Management, Whiteknights, Reading RG6 2AW, UK. (tel 44 1734 885505 fax 44 1734 885495)

■ **British Property Federation**: The main body representing UK developers. Acts as an interest group but not as big or as lively as ULI. Contact: 35 Catherine Place, London SW1E 6DY, UK. (tel 44 171 828 0111 fax 44 171 834 3442)

■ **RIBA** *(Royal Institute of British Architects):* By far the biggest British architectural institute with a considerable overseas membership. Has a useful Client Advisory Service, a Competitions Office and is setting up an architect/client group to study changing needs in the office. Contact: 66 Portland Place, London W1N 4AD, UK. (Tel 44 171 580 5533 fax 44 171 255 1511)

The Pacific Rim

■ **JFMA** *(The Japanese Facility Management Association):* Represents the growing Japanese Facilities community; conducts comparative research and organizes frequent study tours for its members. Contact: Landick Akasaka Mitsuke Building, 3-9-18 Akasaka, Minato-ku, Tokyo 107, Japan. (tel 81 3 5563 0241 fax 81 3 5563 0242)

■ **NOPA** *(National Office Promotion Association):* funded by the Japanese Ministry of Trade and Industry and the Ministry of Construction in order to promote better quality and more productive office working environments. Contact: 1-2-17 Noe Build 2F, Shiba Daimon, Minato-ku, Tokyo 105, Japan. (tel 81 3 5472 5921 fax 81 3 5472 5925)

■ **Property Council of Australia**: The vigorous body that brings together property and corporate real estate professionals in Australia. Excellent conferences. Contact: Level 26, Australia Square Tower, 264-278 George Street, Sydney NSW 2000, Australia. (tel 61 2 9252 3111 fax 61 2 9252 3103)

■ **FMA** (Facility Managers Association): the only body in Australia looking after facility managers. Contact: PO Box 397, Market Street, Melbourne VIC 8007. (tel 61 3 9229 2160 fax 61 3 9229 2162)

Study groups and networks

North America

■ **ISFE** (International Society of Facilities Executives): Founded by Kreon Cyros, the highly experienced Head of Facilities at MIT. ISFE membership is made up of senior corporate real estate executives who wish to share their experiences, problems and data in a supportive environment. Particular interest in Computerized Facility Management Techniques – CAFM. Information from: Kreon Cyros, c/o MIT, 336 Main Street, E28-100, Cambridge, MT 02141-1014, USA. (tel 1 617 253 7252 fax 1 617 258 8249 e-mail ISFE@MIT.edu)

■ **IWSP** (International Workplace Studies Program): Founded by Prof. Franklin Becker of Cornell University, one of the most respected leaders in the field who, time and again, has shown himself to be capable of consistently linking organizational, spatial, and facility planning issues. The Program is based at the university and has a considerable research program which provides the basis and rationale for workshops, conferences, study tours etc. Membership is international: the program has attracted members from many large corporations. Informative newsletter. Information from: Cornell University International Workplace Studies Programme, NYS College of Human Ecology, DEA Department/E123 MVR Hall, Ithaca, NY 14853-4401, USA. (tel 1 607 255 3145 fax 1 607 255 3542 e-mail iwsp@cornell.edu)

■ **TWN** (The Workplace Network): Established by Gerald Davis, for many years one of the greatest figures in research, programming, and procedures for the rational planning of space for organizational purposes. Much involved in developing standards for the whole industry. Information from: Director for the Central Office, c/o International Center for Facilities, 440 Laurier Avenue # 200, Ottawa, Ontario, K1R 7X6, Canada. (tel 1 613 727 1788 fax 1 613 723 9167)

Europe

■ **CBB-Rebus**: A real estate business strategy consultancy, based in London, which advises the boards of property development companies, major multinationals and banks on their business strategies in European real estate markets. Rebus is a founding member of the worldwide BFN (Business Futures Network) Partnership. Contact: Geoffrey Woodling, REBUS, 250M Bedford Chambers, The Piazza, London WC2E 8HA, UK. (tel 44 171 240 0983 fax 171 836 7690)

■ **Future Work Forum at Henley**. Based at the business school, this forum is less concerned with the physical environment of the new office than with helping members from the general business community as well as from government to explore the strategic and the technological and human resource implications of new ways of working. Information from: Henley Management College, Greenlands, Henley on Thames, Oxon RG9 3AU, UK. (tel 44 1491 571454 fax 44 1491 571574 e-mail michelem@henleymc.ac.uk)

■ **Office 21**: Joint Project On Visions And Solutions For The Office Of The Future. An ambitious research project on all aspects of the future office – technological, social and commercial – being conducted through a series of well-organized 'Delphi' studies involving experts from different industries and from various countries. Commenced late 1996 and led by the Fraunhofer Institut, the German think-tank is funded by both government and industry. Information from: Fraunhofer Institut, Arbeitswirtschaft und Organisation, Nobelstrasse 12, D-70569 Stuttgart, Germany. (tel 49 711 970 2123 fax 49 711 970 2299 e-mail Stephan.Zinser@iao.fhg.de)

■ **The Workplace Forum**: Designed to meet the informational and development needs of senior managers in corporate and governmental organizations who have property and facilities management responsibilities. Run by DEGW since 1991, The Workplace Forum provides corporate clients with structured access to developing ideas and data about how office design should relate to other aspects of business performance. The Forum consists of about 25 member organizations which meet regularly for four day-long sessions each year that incorporate a visit to a new facility. A two-day conference and study tour, always outside the UK, is held annually in June. Information from: DEGW, Porters North, 8 Crinan Street, London N1 9SQ, UK. (tel 44 171 239 7777 fax 44 171 278 4125 e-mail: sbradley @degw.co.uk)

Centres of research and advanced practice

Consultancies and university departments and other bodies that have developed the kind of programming and evaluative techniques described in Chapter 5, and who also have distinguished records in publishing and sharing information.

North America

■ **@Work Consulting Group**: Specialist consultancy. Programming for new ways of working, all scales from office interiors to regional planning, research, publications. Information from Prof. Franklin Becker (also at Cornell University, see IWSP left), 567 Armsley Square, Ontario, CA 91762 USA. (tel 1 909 460 1500 fax 1 909 390 8236)

■ **BOSTI**: Specialist consultancy. Programming for new ways of working, ongoing interest in developing measures of office productivity, research, publications. Information from: Michael Brill, 1479 Hertel Avenue, Buffalo, NY 14216, USA. (tel 1 716 837 7120 fax 1 716 837 7123)

■ **Bottom Duvivier**: Architectural Practice. Programming for new ways of working, space planning, and design. Information from: John Duvivier, 2603 Broadway, Redwood City CA 94063, USA. (tel 1 415 361 1209 fax 1 415 361 1229).

■ **Center for Building Performance and Diagnostics**: University-based research group. Concerned with the development of new building products and building services for the new ways

*Below **Ceiling-height sliding doors allow maximum choice in how the meeting rooms behind them are used in the offices for Herman Miller, New York. Architect: Fox & Fowle.***

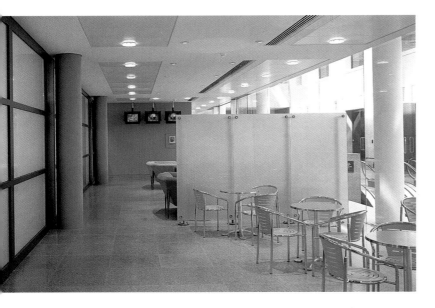

Above **When a former warehouse was converted into offices for Leo Burnett, London, provision was made for several different kinds of casual meeting spaces. Architects: Stanton Williams, YRM, and Fletcher Priest.**

of working. Information from: Volker Hartkopf, Department of Architecture, Carnegie Mellon University, Pittsburgh PA 15213-3890, USA. (tel 1 412 268 2350 fax 1 412 268 6129)

■ *Gensler & Associates*: Architectural practice, many centres. Programming, extensive knowledge of many sectors of office use, good data on comparative occupancy, space planning, and design. Information from: Art Gensler, 600 California Street, San Francisco CA 94108, USA. (tel 1 415 433 3700 fax 1 415 627 3737)

■ *Hellmuth Obata & Kassabaum Inc*: Architectural practice, many centres. Programming for new ways of working, space planning and design. Information from: Mary Breuer, Suite 2200, 71 Stevenson Street, San Francisco, CA 94105-2938, USA. (tel 1 415 243 0555 fax 1 415 882 7763)

■ *Robert Luchetti Associates Inc.*: Architectural practice. Programming for new ways of working, space planning, and design. Information from: Robert Luchetti, 14 Arrow Street, Cambridge, MA, 02138, USA. (tel 1 617 492 6611 fax 1 617 492 8441).

■ *MIT* (*Massachusetts Institute of Technology*): University-based research group. Research into office organizations and design. Information from Prof. Bill Porter, Leventhal Professor of Architecture, Graduate Program of the MIT School of Architecture, 10-461 M, 77 Massachusetts Avenue, Cambridge MA 02139-4307, USA. (tel 1 617 253 9415 fax 1 617 253 9407)

■ *Portsmouth Consulting Group*: Specialist consultancy. All aspects of organizational change

including the working environment. Information from: Fritz Steele, 1128 Beacon Street, Brookline, MA 02146, USA. (tel 1 617 738 0843 e-mail drplace@aol.com)

■ *Program Management International*: Consultants specializing in helping organizations to determine their space strategies. Programming and feasibility studies. Information from: Bill Adams, 119 One North Park, 8950 Central Expressway, Dallas TX 75231, USA. (tel 1 214 368 7747 fax 1 214 368 7749)

■ *Steelcase Inc*: Furniture Manufacturer, HQ in Grand Rapids. Programming for new ways of working using Workplace Envisioning, research, product design and development. Information from: Patrick Mohr, CD.42, PO Box 1967, Grand Rapids, MI 49501-1967, USA. (tel 1 616 698 4776)

Europe

■ *Congena*: Management consultancy. Programming for office and other projects, research and many publications. Contact: Richard Puell, Congena, Baumkirchner Straße 53, 8000 München 80, Germany. (tel 49 89 431 6017 fax 49 89 431 4825)

■ *DEGW*: Architectural practice, many centres. Programming and planning for new ways of working, development of techniques for measuring office and building use productivity, building appraisal, research, frequent publications. Contact: Stephen Bradley, DEGW, Porters North, 8 Crinan Street, London N1 9SQ, UK. (tel 44 171 239 7777 fax 44 171 278 4125 e-mail: sbradley @degw.co.uk)

■ *LET* (*Laboratoire Espaces – Travail*): Multidisciplinary university-based research centre for industrial and office work spaces. Contact: François Lautier, LET, Ecole d'Architecture de Paris – La Villette, 144 rue de Flandre, 75019 Paris, France. (tel 33 1 44 65 23 61 fax 33 1 44 65 23 62 e-mail LET@paris-lavillette.archi.fr)

■ *Quickborner Team*: Management consultancy. Programming and planning for offices, originators in the 1960s of office landscaping. Contact: Dieter Jaeger, Quickborner Team, Mittelweg 119, Hamburg D-20148, Germany. (tel 49 40 410 502527 fax 49 40 452644)

■ *Technical University at Delft*: Department of Real Estate and Project Management. A famous research institute. Contact: Hans de Jonge, Faculty of Architecture, Berlageweg 1, Postbus 5043,

26009A Delft, The Netherlands. (tel 31 14 278 4596 fax 31 15 278 3171)

■ *Twijnstra Gudde*: Management consultancy. Programming for new ways of working. Contact: Jan Griffioen, Twijnstra Gudde, Stationsplein 1, Postbus 907, 3800 AX Amersfoort, The Netherlands. (tel 31 33 4677777 fax 31 33 4677683 e-mail jgf@tg.nl)

■ *University of Reading*: Department of Construction Management. University-based research group, specializing in all aspects of the construction and procurement process. Contact: Prof. Ranko Bon, Whiteknights, PO Box 219, Reading RG6 6AW, UK. (tel 44 1734 318201 fax 44 1734 313856)

OFFICE FURNITURE MANUFACTURERS

The following is a selected list of manufacturers who have developed office furniture products that are relevant to the new office.

North America

■ *Haworth*: Work-setting products: Castelli 3D, Crossings; seating: Comforto. One Haworth Center, Holland, MI 49423-9576, USA. (tel 1 616 393 3000 fax 1 616 393 1570)

■ *Herman Miller Inc.*: Work-setting products: Ethospace, Relay, Abak; seating products: Aeron, Ambi, Equa; storage products: Meridian, Global. 855 East Main Avenue, P.O. Box 302, Zeeland, MI 49464-0302, USA. (tel 1 616 654 3537 fax 1 616 654 5279)

■ *The Knoll Group*: Work-setting products: Hannah, SoHo, Alessandri, Currents; seating: Bulldog. 105 Wooster Street, New York, NY 10012, USA. (tel 1 212 343 4132 fax 1 212 343 4185)

■ *Office Specialty*: Lateral cabinets. 67 Toll Road, Holland Landing, Ontario, Canada. (tel 1 905 836 7676)

■ *Steelcase*: Work-setting products: Context, TNT, Activity Products, Personal Harbour; seating: Criterion, Sensor, Swift. PO Box 1967, Grand Rapids, MI 49501-1967. (tel 1 616 698 4453)

Europe

■ *Ahrend*: Work-setting products: Mehes and Essa; cabinets and storage: Tambour. Postbus12390, 1100 AJ Amsterdam, The Netherlands. (tel 31 205641888)

■ *Bisley*: Storage: BLF. 155 Great Portland Street, London W1N 5FB, UK. (tel 44 171 436 7111)

- **Facit**: Work-setting products: lo range. Box 185, S-597 24 Åtvidaberg, Sweden. (tel 46 120-815 00)

- **Martela**: Various work settings. Strömbergintie 5, 00380 Helsinki, Finland. (tel 358 0 560 31 fax 358 0 553 264)

- **President**: Kyo worksettings. The Arenson Centre, Arenson Way, Dunstable, Beds LU5 5UL, UK. (tel 44 1582 678200)

- **Steelcase Strafor**: Work-setting products: Context, TNT, Personal Harbour; seating: Criterion, Sensor, Swift. 56 rue Jean Giraudoux, BP 6K-67035, Strasbourg Cedex, France. (tel 33 88 288888)

- **Unifor**: Work setting products: Misura, Mood, Satelliti, Move, Flipper; interesting storage as well. Via Isonzo 1, 22078 Turate (Como), Italy. (tel 39 31 2 967191)

- **Vitra**: Work-setting products: Adhoc, Metropol; AC1+2, Axion and VisaVis, T-Chair, Figura and Persona chairs. Klunenfeldstrasse 22, CH-4127 Birsfelden, Switzerland. (tel 41 61 3151515)

- **Wilkhahn**: Work setting products: Confair; seating: FS and Modus. Postfach 2070, D-3252 Bad Munder 2, Germany. (tel 49 50 428010)

The Pacific Rim

- **Itoki**: 7-3 Ginza 3-chome, Chuo-ku, Tokyo 104 Japan. (tel 81 3 3566 5315)

- **Kokuyo**: 1-1 Oimazato Minami, 6-chome, Higashinari-ku, Osaka, Japan. (tel 81 6 972 9505)

WRITING THE BRIEF

Skilful programming or, as the British say, brief-writing, is essential if clients and users are to get the office buildings that they need to make businesses flourish and to enjoy lives worth living. Programming for any project should be an interactive, highly communicative, and open-ended process, and this is particularly true in the highly populated and political field of office design. Good programming involves regular feedback throughout the construction of a project between clients, advisers, and the design or project team. Consequently, because all office projects involve and integrate so many people and interests, even the simplest requires a whole series of documents, each taking the preceding one to a greater level of detail.

In order to get the maximum benefit from a project, a client must regularly and systematically: ensure that relevant options for design solutions are being evaluated and that appropriate decisions are being made; ensure that there are sufficient resources of the right kind for programming throughout the project; manage, and take ownership of the series of programming documents that will be developed.

Although effective programming is essential all the way through any office project, the most valuable time is spent at the outset, working out what is really wanted and how what is wanted will affect business performance. The golden rule for clients to remember is that, broadly speaking, the later changes are made, the heavier the price to be paid for them. Early investment in thinking hard about the brief and about design will pay for itself many times over. (More detailed guidance is given in the Construction Industry Board document 'Briefing the Team', available in the UK from Thomas Telford Publishing, tel 44 171 987 6999.)

There are four initial stages:

1 *Statement of Need*: a document prepared for Board approval at the outset of a project, which defines the objectives and needs of the client organization in relation to a specific property or constructional opportunity.

2 *Options Appraisal*: a formal review of the relative value to the business of the chief options open to the client – including possible use of existing resources rather than constructing, or moving to a new building or acquiring more space – and the calculation of the benefits and drawbacks of, and the risks associated with, any such option.

3 *Strategic Program*: the setting out of the broad scope and purpose of the project and its key parameters including the overall budget and timetable; it should include an outline specification which explains in clear terms what is expected of the project.

4 *Project Execution Plan*: an explanation of how the project should be implemented, including details of the procurement system that will be applied and the appointments to be made by the project team.

The design and construction phase of a project should develop in three further steps:

5 *Project Program*: this involves converting the Strategic Brief into construction terms, putting initial sizes and quantities to each element of the project and giving each of them an outline budget.

6 *Concept Design*: once the Project Program has been agreed by the project sponsor, the project team can begin to test the design options which will contribute towards the eventual Concept Design. The tests should not just be about the cost and speed of the construction programme but should also examine whether the concept design is likely to meet the criteria expressed in the client's business case for the project. Beware, in other words, of the bias towards supply-side criteria characteristic of the thinking of most of the construction and property industries.

7 *Detailed Design*: the Concept Design having been agreed and signed off, the project team can begin the development of detailed design, specifying the performance requirements for all the elements of the new office. The detailed design should freeze as much of the design as possible, defining and detailing every component of the construction work.

Evaluation throughout the constuction process and after completion is also very important. *Post-Occupancy Evaluation* should be continuous, and compare the finished office against the objectives agreed in the Statement of Need and the Strategic Program. When used by clients who build serially, such evaluations can help to shape the management, procedures, and content of future construction projects and cumulatively improve performance. But even for clients with smaller, one-off projects, the benefits are enormous.

Below **The Freedom Wheels range of office furniture, designed by Pekka Toivola for Martela, is lightweight and easily adjustable.**

Acknowledgments

Author's acknowledgments

A book as complex as this could not have been prepared without a great deal of help, collaboration, and occasional downright exploitation.

First on the list of people to be thanked is the architectural writer and critic, Kenneth Powell, who was responsible for researching and writing the twenty case studies and who was an intelligent and active support throughout. Rosalind Long, with help from Agatha Taylor, was responsible for preparing the plans and statistics on the case studies. Dr Andrew Laing of DEGW provided, particularly through his pioneering work on the *New Environments for Working* multiclient study, much of the intellectual underpinning of this book. Yas Hirai, Shoji Ekuan, and David Height provided invaluable help on recent developments in the Japanese office.

The following people were particularly helpful in providing the information, the plans, and the photographs for the case studies at the unreasonable times and in the inconvenient ways we asked for them: *British Airways:* Robert Ayling, Denis Taylor and Steve Embley; *Sharp:* Tetsuo Kusasabe; *Kajima:* David Height; *Edding:* Mr Schliewiensky and Hans Struhk & Partners; *Gruner + Jahr:* Dr Groffy and Steidle + Kiessler; *Sun Micro:* Ann Bamesberger and John Duvivier; *Michaelides & Bednash:* George Michaelides and Simon Henley; *Vitra:* Dr Rolf Fehlbaum and Frank Gehry; *Imagination:* Gary Withers and Alex Ritchie; *Channel 4 Television:* Frank McGettigan, Jill Monk and John Young; *Nickelodeon:* Geraldine Laybourne, Richard Fernau, and David Lau; *Steelcase:* Jim Hackett, Jim Lawler, and Jack Tanis; *Andersen Worldwide:* John Lewis, Bill Johnson, Bethany Davis, Jim Nixon, and Neil Frankel; *Lend Lease Interiors:* John McBeath, Sue Wittenoom, and Katherine McPherson; *IBM (UK):* Mike Brooks, Peter Wingrave, Lady Hopkins, and Peter Romaniuk; *Chiat/Day:* Laurie Coots and Gaetano Pesce; *Digital Equipment:* Bertil Arnius; *Rijksgebouwendienst:* Marcel Maasen; *British Telecom:* Alan White, Neil McLocklin, and David Sadeghi; *Benevia:* Nancy Nevin, Rod Vickroy, and Sarah Busch. We are indebted to them.

The editorial team at Conran Octopus has been incomparably skilful and helpful throughout – better than any in my experience as a writer. Rachel Davies has proved to be a prolific and inventive picture researcher. Tony Seddon's graphic ability is evident on every page. A brilliant and supportive team: my very warm thanks are due to them all.

As always DEGW has been a very great support to me. The influence of Mick Bedford, James Calder, Stephen Greenberg, Andrew Harrison, David Jenkin, Despina Katsikakis, Dr Andrew Laing, Graham Parsey, Jonathan Reed-Lethbridge, David Sadeghi, Tony Thomson, and John Worthington is particularly evident throughout. Without the continuous, assiduous, and intelligent help of Debra Lewis, my PA, very little would have been achieved.   **FD**

Publishers' acknowledgments

The publishers would like to thank Martin Hargreaves for the index, and Tessa Clark for her proof-reading skills.

Photographic acknowledgments

The publisher thanks the following photographers, architects and organizations for their kind permission to reproduce the photographs in this book:

1 Chris Gascoigne (ORMS)/View; *2-3* Richard Bryant (Foster & Partners)/Arcaid; *4* Francesco Radino/Eciffo; *5 above* Lars Hallen (Love Arben & Claesson, Koivisto, Rune); *5 centre* Dennis Gilbert (Foster & Partners)/View; *5 below* Archipress (Jean Nouvel); *6* Katsuhisa Hasegawa/Eciffo; *6-7* Peter Paulides/Tony Stone Images; *8-9* Richard Bryant (DEGW)/Arcaid; *9* Chris Gascoigne (DEGW)/ View; *10-11* Roberto Carra/Eciffo; *11* Martine Hamilton-Knight (Boots)/Arcaid; *12* Lars Hallen; *12-13* Courtesy of SC Johnson Wax; *15 above* The Kobal Collection; *15 below* Edward Hopper/ Metropolitan Museum of Art; *16* Hulton Getty; *17* The Kobal Collection; *18* Francesco Radino/Eciffo; *19* Peter Mauss/Esto; *20-21* Buffalo & Erie County Historical Society, Larkin Collection; *21 below* Frank Lloyd Wright Foundation, Scottsdale, AZ; *23* Peter Mauss/Esto; *24* Ezra Stoller/Esto/Arcaid; *24-5* Yukio Shimizu/Eciffo; *25* Frank Lloyd Wright Foundation, Scottsdale, AZ; *26-7* Ezra Stoller/Esto; *28-9* Peter Mauss (SOM)/Esto; *30-1* Wayne Andrews (Roche Dinkerloo)/Esto; *31 below* Michael Moran; *32-3* Richard Bryant (Richard Rogers Partnership)/Arcaid; *34* David W Hamilton/ The Image Bank; *35* Ulf E Wallin/The Image Bank; *36-7* Richard Bryant (Herman Hertzberger)/Arcaid; *38-9* Lars Hallen (Neils Torp); *40-1* Jan Derwig (Alberts & Van Huut); *42* Peter Cook/View; *44* Jon Riley/Tony Stone Images; *45* Lars Hallen (Love Arben & Claesson, Koivisto, Rune); *46* Chris Gascoigne (Pringle Brandon)/View; *47* Francesco Radino/Eciffo; *48-9* Jim Holmes/Axiom; *48 above* Beucker Maschlanka + Partner; *48 below* Peter Cook (Bennetts Associates)/View; *49* Grant V. Faint/The Image Bank; *50* Elizabeth Handy; *52* Cornell Capa/Magnum; *53* Steven Ahlgren; *54 above* Dennis Gilbert (Sevil Peach Gence)/View; *54 below* Wynn Miller/Tony Stone Images; *55 above* Eciffo; *55 below* Katsuhisa Hasegawa/ Eciffo; *56* Hulton Getty; *57* Nacasa & Partners; *59 above* Francesco Radino/Eciffo; *59 below* David Roberts of The Big Picture (Orange); *62 above* Bridgeman Art Library (Frederick Cayley Robinson); *62 below* Katsuhisa Hasegawa/Eciffo; *63 above* Bridgeman Art Library (Antonello da Messina); *63 below* Tim Goffe (Baker Nevile Design); *64 above* Bridgeman Art Library (Giovanni Stradano); *64 below* Dennis Gilbert (Foster & Partners)/View; *65 above* AKG, London; *65 below* Francesco Radino/Eciffo; *68-9* Courturier (Jean Nouvel)/ Archipress; *68* Eduard Hueber (Res 4 McCann Erikson); *70-1* KL. Ng (TR Hamzah & Yeang SDN BHD); *72 above* Ian Lambot (Foster & Partners)/ Arcaid; *72 below* Ian Lambot (Foster & Partners); *73* Richard Bryant (Foster & Partners)/Arcaid; *74* Peter Cook/View; *76 left* Richard Bryant (Harper Mackay, Zumbtobel Lighting)/Arcaid; *76* James Morris (Gollifer Associates)/Axiom; *76-7* Chris Gascoigne (ORMS)/View; *79* Peter Cook (Terry Farrell)/View; *80 & 81 above* Peter Cook (Bennetts Associates)/ View; *81 below* Dennis Gilbert (Sevil Peach Gence)/ View; *82* Chris Gascoigne (Ralph Erskine/Marshal Cummings Marsh)/View; *82-3 below* Kyo-President Office Furniture; *82-3 above* Courtesy of Steelcase Inc.; *84 above* Ahrend Ltd.; *84 below* Miro Zagnoli/Vitra; *85 above* Kokuyo; *85 below* Wilkhahn; *86 above* Kyo-President Office Furniture; *86 below & 86-7* Ian Lambot (Foster & Partners); *87* Kokuyo; *88* Niall Clutton/Arcaid; *88-9* John E. Linden (Michael Hopkins & Partners)/ Arcaid; *89 below* Martin Charles (Edward Cullinan); *90 above* Richard Bryant (DEGW)/Arcaid; *90 below* Nicolas Kane(DEGW)/Arcaid *90-1 & 91 above* James Morris (Foster & Partners)/Axiom; *91 below* Johnson Controls; *92-3* Peter Cook (Bennetts Associates)/ View; *92* Chris Gascoigne (Ralph Erskine/Marshal Cummings Marsh)/View; *93* Martine Hamilton-Knight/Arcaid; *94 left & right* Ian Lambot (Foster & Partners); *95* Grant Faint/The Image Bank; *95 left* Struhk & Partner/Martela; *96* Wolfram Janzer (DEGW)/Contur; *96-7* Peter Cook/View; *97* Katsuhisa Hasegawa/Eciffo; *98* Paul Warchol; *98-9* Katsuhisa Hasegawa/Eciffo; *100* Francesco Radino/Eciffo; *100-1* Elliott Kaufman (American Design Company); *101* Eduard Hueber (Katherine Huber & Mary Buttrick); *102* Steve Dunwell/The Image Bank; *103* Marcus Harpur; *104* Richard Bryant (Richard Rogers Partnership)/Arcaid; *105* Francesco Radino/Eciffo; *106-7* Peter Mauss (Pentagram)/Esto; *111 right* Chris Gascoigne (Aukett Associates)/ View; *111-4* Chris Gascoigne (Aukett Associates)/ View; *115* Jo Reid & John Peck; *117-9* Corporate Design Magazine; *121-2* Shinkenchiku-Sha/The Japan Architect; *125-9* Struhk & Partner/Martela; *131-134* Gruner + Jahr; *137-40* Sun Micro (Bottom Duvivier); *143-6 left* Peter Cook (Buschow Henley)/Conran Octopus; *149-53* Richard Bryant (Frank•O Gehry)/Arcaid; *155 left* Peter Cook/View; *155 right* Imagination; *156* Martin Charles; *157* Peter Cook/View; *158-9* Imagination; *161 left* David Churchill (Richard Rogers Partnership)/Arcaid; *161 right-164* Peter Cook (Richard Rogers Partnership)/ View; *167 left & right* Jeff Goldberg (Fernau & Hartman)/Esto; *168 above & below* Scott Frances (Fernau & Hartman)/Esto; *171 above* Jeff Goldberg (Fernau & Hartman)/Esto; *173-5* Marco Lorenzetti (Steelcase)/Hedrich Blessing; *177-81* Marco Lorenzetti (SOM)/Hedrich Blessing; *183-6* Bligh Voller; *189 left* Paul Harmer (Hopkins & Partners)/ Building Magazine; *189 right-190* Tim Soar (Hopkins & Partners); *193 above* Donatella Brun; *193 below-196* Francesco Radino/Eciffo; *197* Donatella Brun; *199-201* Digital; *203-4* Jan Vonk; *207-11* Chris Gascoigne (DEGW)/View; *213-7* Steve Hall (Environments Group)/Hedrich Blessing; *218* Peter Cook/View; *219* Nacasa & Partners (Tetsuro Kurokawa + Design League); *220-1* Chris Gascoigne (Ralph Erskine/Marshal Cummings Marsh)/View; *222-3* Richard Bryant (Richard Rogers Partnership)/Arcaid; *224-5* Philippe Ruault (Jean Nouvel); *225* Nicholas Kane (DEGW)/Arcaid; *228* Peter Cook/View; *231* Jim Holmes/Axiom; *232 below* Tim Goffe (Architeam/e-fact); *232 above* Philippe Ruault (Jean Nouvel); *233* Peter Cook (Bennetts Associates)/View; *234* Chris Gascoigne (Stanton Willliams/YRM/Fletcher Priest)/View; *236-7* Lars Hallen; *238-9* Dennis Gilbert (Munkenbeck & Marshall)/View; *238* Peter Cook (Richard Rogers Partnership)/View; *240-1* Jeremy Cockayne (Studio Baad)/Arcaid; *242* Peter Cook (Bennetts Associates)/View; *243* Harold Metcalf (Roger Stretton)/Oxford University Press; *244* Nicolas Borel (Alain Moatti & Jacques Moussafir); *245* Chris Gascoigne (DEGW)/View; *246* Peter Cook (Aukett)/View; *247* Paul Warchol (Fox & Fowle); *248* Peter Cook (Stanton Williams/YRM/ Fletcher Priest)/View; *249* Martela (Pekka Toivola); *254* Francesco Radino/Eciffo.

Every effort has been made to trace the copyright holders, architects and designers and we apologise in advance for any unintentional ommission and would be pleased to insert the appropriate acknowledgement in any subsequent edition.